FIERCE & TENDER

HEALING THE DEEP MASCULINE

A Memoir Of
An Urban Medicine Man

By

Dene Maria Sebastiana

D1572404

LUNA MADRE PUBLISHING

I

FIERCE & TENDER

HEALING THE DEEP MASCULINE

A Memoir Of An Urban Medicine Man

Author: Dene Maria Sebastiana

Cover Design: Cecilia Martini Muth, CC Design
Book Design: Priscilla Mead, PM Design LLC

Paperback ISBN: 979-8-9854869-0-2
eBook ISBN: 978-0-9962065-9-4
Library of Congress (pending):
Copyright © 2022 Dene Maria Sebastiana
All rights reserved.

Luna Madre Publishing
3463 State Street, Suite 225
Santa Barbara CA 93105
Info@LunaMadre.com

"I have come into this world to see this:
the swords drop from men's hands,
even at the height of their arc of anger,
because we have finally realized
there is just one flesh to wound,
our Beloved's."

Hafiz

Dedicated to:

M3DMS

Forever My Inspiration

Acknowledgments

While this book is my personal journey since boyhood, and the people and experiences that contributed and shaped this book are too numerous to mention, I am deeply indebted to several who have inspired and supported me along this path.

I want to thank my beloved Mignon Mead-Shikaly and our sons Dakota and Dylan Mead-Shikaly for their undying faith in me and my work. Their love has provided the inspiration, and much of the context that appears here.

Special thanks to my writing coach Linda Newlin, for seeing my creative potential, for encouraging and guiding me through my many moments of fear and self-doubt. She always helped me remember the 'why' … my need to further my own integration, my need to awaken men into the importance of opening their hearts, and my commitment to transform the world, beginning with me.

A thanks to my mom and dad, Mary and Al Shikaly, for the fertile ground they provided, and for delivering both the gifts and the soul wounds that gave rise to my mission.

I am thankful for my work partner George Daranyi, who graciously received me back into the Tucson men's circles, and the group work for men that we continue to do.

Thank you, Michael Greenwald, my mentor, and his brilliant insights into the true plight of men and the masculine alive on the planet today. Over the years, through our spirited talks about the masculine and the feminine, we found our common ground, and the necessity for men to turn their attention to the great healing work that stands before us.

And finally, a deep loving thank you to Ann Levin, my first true mentor, who saw my deep pain and heartache, who guided me toward my healing, and ultimately who gave me my heart back. For this, I am eternally grateful.

Testimonials

"Dene Maria Sebastiana offers many lessons for us: Authentic power lies at the intersection of vulnerability and truth. A man's emotional and spiritual truth is embedded unconsciously in his cells. The connection to the Soul, and to the mystical center of all faith practices are embodied in man and woman, awaiting mindful awareness. Dene brilliantly integrates vast insights into men and Masculinity with ongoing personal transformation at the deepest level of his soul. This is the memoir of a man who has made a living through initiating and coaching men and creating communities around that work. It is tempting to allow the radical significance of Dene's contributions to MensWork and WomensWork to overshadow the profound intimacy and authenticity of this memoir. It is the memoir of a man who, with courage, ego-sacrifice, and brutal authenticity, confesses his everlasting struggle with his own demons and addictions. He candidly takes account for the damage he has done (and then some) in his work, his relationships and his parenthood. He brilliantly integrates vast insights into men and the deep masculine with ongoing personal transformation at the deepest level of his soul.

Michael P. Greenwald
Co-Founder of the New Warrior Network Chicago, Attorney, and
Leader Emeritus – Chicago, IL

"Dene's personal inquiry combined with real life evolutionary experience with thousands of men is the fertile ground you can plant yourself in and become your longed-for self. He reveals the evolutionary fire that has fueled his role as leader, husband and father. He is not shy about describing the fruitful darkness he has emerged from, and how it gave him strength to love unabashedly. The book will call to your heart. It will remind you of what you long for as a way to know love, and not just think about it. This is a book that will work its way into your heart and mind as a sacred ally."

David MacKenzie
Medical Intuitive, Artist, Photographer, Wisdom-Keeper –
San Miguel de Allende, MX

"*Last weekend, I witnessed the work of Dene Maria Sebastiana, a man filled with unconditional love for women. I marveled at his passion, conviction, and willingness to fully offer himself up to a group of women who needed his wisdom, tenderness, and ultimately his strength. I was sustained in a way I could not have anticipated by the way he guided us, and then walked with us into the fire of truth. He is a man magnificently balanced in his masculine and feminine energies, full of grace, willing to put himself on the razor's edge. I am lifted up and humbled by the knowledge that my path to authentic womanhood was to be revealed to me by a man. Men and women healing and evolving together – hope is alive.*"

Krista Karter
Participant "Leaving My Father's House" workshop -
Account Exec., Silicon Valley, CA

"*In this book, Dene shares his journey as a man into the depths of his soul. He relays how his continued diligence in doing his own work heals, while creating an opportunity for us the reader to look within and do our own healing work. Dene facilitates healing using his fierce yet tender approach to life. I have witnessed his skills in many circles, supporting both men and women, bringing forth clarity and growth. Through his writing, Dene expands the perimeter and deepens the context for both men and women. His reflections are captivating, vulnerable, fierce, intense, loving, thoughtful, and mystical. He invites us to question our own feelings and beliefs, and how we carry our past woundedness into our present lives.*"

Francis Borchers
ManKind Project Certified Leader - Landscape Designer and Contractor, Santa Cruz, CA

"I have known Dene Maria Sebastiana for over twenty-five years. Through his remarkable journey, wisdom, and passion for his work, he has helped thousands of people heal and thrive. This book gives Dene the opportunity to share his story and his wisdom with a much broader audience as he continues his work as a healer and leader to many."

Diana Mead
CEO – DL Acquisitions, Denver, CO

"Dene's book reflects a man who has done the inner work to know himself, rendering him open to the full range of human experience, and thus capable of deep compassion. Both as teacher and healer and now as a writer, Dene is gifted and exceedingly capable. Unafraid, but not without the cautions born of wisdom, Dene sees what is needed and moves into the fire in search of healing solutions."

John Fisher-Smith
Architect – Ashland, OR

"Dene is a world class facilitator and brilliant coordinator of group dynamics. And now, a writer of this important book. His ability to go deep with the individual and similarly invite the collective ... a rare combination of talents ... arises from his own depth. Dene's strongest gift is his compassion: a poignant ability to see with deep feeling and to feel with great vision. This book is a must for both men and women."

Don Miller
CEO – New York, NY

Foreword

There is a moment in every waking man's life when he knows not only that he has a story to tell, but that it must be told – his story.

Some, because they remain asleep, do nothing. Others, who cannot convince themselves that they have a story worth telling, simply will not do it. Other men have an important story to tell, but remain silent. Most men never really take the chance. And a rare few, like Dene Maria Sebastiana, who has been telling parts of his story for decades, knows it is now the time and place to tell his whole story.

Dene's story must now be told to a much larger audience – loudly, proudly, without defensiveness or apology. Dene understands that his story is not just his own, it is the archetypal story of "every man"… at least every man who came out of a working-class immigrant family, regardless of color or creed, that arrived in America in the early 20th century. The story of those who assimilated, worked, struggled, and ultimately endured in that New World. It is the story of the son of one of those families. It is, essentially, my story too.

I met Dene at a meeting in early 1992 in Tucson, AZ. I heard him speak near the end of the meeting. Something happened to me while I listened to him. It was not his words that had the greatest impact – it was his presence: fierce, clear, tender, open, vulnerable, available. And, importantly, deeply and authentically Masculine. All of that struck me, like a sword had penetrated the membrane of my chest. I knew I had to learn more, so I approached him after the meeting and asked him: "Who are you? And what do you do?" He told me his name and said: "I do men's work."

Ironically, I had been sitting in a men's recovery circle for nearly three years at that point. I told him I had no real idea what that was. I was 34 years old, married, sober, a new father, a successful lawyer. I knew some things, but knew nothing about what it meant to be a man. A real man. A conscious man. He handed me a crumpled business card from his back pocket and told me to call his office and make an appointment to meet with him. I saw him the next week, and we met weekly for a whole year. That chance meeting and what followed these past 30 years transformed my life and all my relations.

Dene helped me to understand early on that I had the emotional and psychic maturity of an adolescent boy, living in a grown-up man's body and grown-up man's life. I was completely disconnected from my feelings and from myself. I was hanging on by my finger-nails and fear had me by the throat. He convinced me to participate in a rite of passage into the mature masculine which I completed later in 1992. It was then that I landed in my body. My body finally became congruent with my mind, and my emotional landscape. From there, Dene and I were off to the adventure of our lives.

I helped him build a men's community in Arizona and stew-arded it for 20 years. He mentored me in becoming a master facili-tator in deep men's processes. He confronted my entitlement, arro-gance, grandiosity, and my need to be "safe" and "comfortable". As I integrated that, Dene then became my peer. At times, I even became his teacher. Dene told me recently that, other than his wife, I probably know him better than any other person in his life. I think he is right about that. It has been my privilege to have known him in this most intimate way.

For the past five years, we have reconnected and are now actively engaged in helping heal the hearts of men – wherever we find them. We have discovered, once again, that those broken-hearted men are everywhere. So, while this book is about Dene, and for Dene to com-plete his journey into the elder, sacred, masculine, it is also for every one of those men who, at their core, still suffer from the deep wounds imposed on them by the circumstances of their lives. It is a book about healing, transformation, forgiveness, and ultimately, grace for all of us. That is why this book is also my book. Let it be yours, too.

George H. Daranyi – Attorney, Former Chairman of The ManKind Project, Leader Emeritus – Mescal, AZ

Table of Contents

Introduction

We stand at a crossroad, the Hopis called this *'the end of days.'* In the middle of the road stand the angels and demons. Not literally, but maybe. The intersections are many … red vs blue, white vs color, men vs women, haves vs have-nots, religion vs religion. Each claims the light for itself, each projects the darkness onto the other. The hard-to-see truth is that we are one, each is other, each is both. This very blindness to our oneness is the greatest danger of all. In 1968, the photos from space of this swirling blue and white ball without barriers transform human consciousness … we can no longer deny that we are one. Yet we consistently choose to. And now, for the first time in the history of mankind, we have the technology and weaponry to bring human civilization to a fiery end. And this is precisely why *this* crossroad is like no other.

Within the great cycle of time, we are currently in a *'liminal space,'* a threshold, the space *'in between'* the end of the current time and the beginning of the time that follows. Like the space beneath the door frame … no longer in the room leaving, and not yet in the room entering. The 60's marked both the beginning of the Age of Aquarius and the ending of the Age of Pisces. Each age lasts about two thousand years. Pisces began with the birth of Christ, it is the last of the Zodiac's twelve ages within the Great Cosmic Year of 24,000 years.

In its decline, the Piscean values of faith, suffering, power, control, materialism, sacrifice, redemption, religion begin to diminish. Simultaneously, the values of the coming age arise. Many believe, including this writer, that Aquarius began with the psychedelic awakening, with values of freedom, unity, human rights, brother/sisterhood, integrity, spirituality, science. In the current overlapping of these ages, competing archetypal values give rise to global conflict and misunderstandings. As there is no exact time measurement to this concurrence, discord may be around for awhile.

If indeed this is a planetary *'end of days'*, it will require us to think and feel about our lives, individually and collectively, from a much larger scale. Covid has already initiated that task upon all of us.

Current identity politics has us at war everywhere, it's hard to know what is right, true, and trustworthy. Men at many levels are under attack, many believe that all men are toxic. The *#metoo* movement opened women's voices, and opened many eyes to see the dark underbelly of our collective gender and sexual behaviors, and the long-time global mistreatment of women. That voice is long overdue, and we all need to listen. However, the great danger in demonizing men is that it misses two essential elements of the modern masculine. First, that men have been culturally programmed over thousands of years with qualities of toughness, strength, success, tenacity, fierceness, control, protection, provision … along with no pain, no weakness, no emotions, no tears … just get the job done. Second, we are also builders, creators, tenders of gardens, producers of food, inventors, risk-takers, poets, writers, scientists, entrepreneurs, athletes, and lovers. Just look at the magnificence of our post-modern world. Without creative masculine energy, we would still be living in caves. The dark side of the first is that we lose touch with our connective qualities … with our tenderness, with our life-affirming side, with our caring hearts, with the emotional side of our nature. The dark side of the second is in the horrific efficiency of *'weapons of destruction'*, and the arrogant disregard for our planet's resources. Men love war and battle and competition, bumping up against each other, sharpening and crossing swords, jousting to see who's got the biggest dick. We stand at this current crossroad simply because the dark side of the masculine has dominated for too long a time, bringing us to the edge of our own destruction. The *'old warrior'* way of doing things is over. The toll on everyone … men, women, children, entire species, institutions, cultures, the Earth … is no longer sustainable. Quite simply, we change or we die.

INTRODUCTION

MensWork is my passion, my whetstone, my soulwork, my right livelihood … it is my life's calling. It is tempting to write about 21st century gender issues, and the danger that we are in. Instead, I have followed my son Dakota's sage advice: *"Dad, this is not a manifesto, it is a memoir. Write about **your** journey."* MensWork and Marriage are the vehicles through which I have traveled this medicine journey. My tools, insights, sufferings, lessons, healing, and transformation have been forged in the interplay between the two. Like the caduceus, it is the exquisite dance between the masculine and the feminine.

I write this book for both men and women, equal in our responsibility to find a true healing. It is a roadmap depicting the degree of difficulty in our collective quest for love, the price we pay, and the reward we reap for opening our hearts. We have gotten to this dark place together. We are all voracious consumers upon a planet with diminishing resources. I cast no blame, we are each responsible for this cosmic moment, and it will take a heroic joint effort to transcend our collective predicament. It is essential that we find our way together through the darkness to transformation.

Through menswork, I have learned to truly love men, and to love my own masculinity. I emotionally *'fall in love'* with men all the time. I love all of our wonderful qualities, and I understand and sometimes relish in the darker sides of our nature. I am no saint, I have done my fair share of damage. At midlife, my soul's mission awakened in me … to place a stake in the ground for the awakening of the *'sacred masculine'* … in myself, in other men, and in service to the collective good. Masculine energy is beautiful … contained, grounded, protective, purposeful action, structured, direct, problem solving. However:

> *The truly sacred in a man arises when he opens to his 'feeling side.' The 'feminine' in a man is not female, not sex, not gender … it is simply the awakening of his emotional body.*

Our feeling nature is open-hearted, receptive, intuitive, connective, sensitive, tender, caring ... the part in us too long ignored, too long denied, too long given a bad rap. The current *"manbox"* definitions of masculine and feminine are Piscean constructs, steeped in binary thinking. Men are typically depicted as strong, tough, angry, successful, in control. Underneath, men are confused, scared, ashamed, emotionally shutdown, isolated. As long as we stay within this box, we are dead men walking. And from that inner numbness, we are capable of great damage. I know both the sacred and profane in myself, I have witnessed this beauty and horror in other men.

> *I do not believe that all men are toxic, nor I do believe that the masculine is intrinsically toxic. I do believe that men who do not attend to their own emotional wounds are more likely to inflict wounds upon others. I do believe that unconscious wounded men do unconscious wounding things.*

I also believe that women are not innocent. While their victimization is deeply legitimate, merits a compassionate, heart-opening response, and deserves men's accountability and commitment to change, I do not believe that women can long hide in the safety and judgments of victimhood, while projecting the perpetrator onto all men. While it is true that men commit the majority of the violence across the planet, I do not believe it is anchored in our hardware, we are not born violent. Rather, it is deep in our software, in the six-thousand-year-old program imprinted upon boys from the crib. I believe this software must be upgraded if we are to survive and thrive.

Thankfully, there is a global awakening, where men and women are resurrecting the sacred masculine and feminine once modeled by our indigenous ancestors. Their wisdom reminds us of our connection to the earth and to each other, offering us a more balanced way to live. Jung insists that: *"One does not become enlightened by imagining figures of light, but by making the darkness conscious."* When we pay attention to our own patterns of separation, when we look to heal our individual and collective wounds and broken-heartedness, there we shall find the sacred. Rumi says: *"You have to keep breaking your heart until it opens."* Each heart is embedded with a calling, a purpose for being here now. Gurdjieff, the Russian mystic and medicine man, called it a magnetic center … we are drawn to a life.

I had my first awakening at nine years old. Unknowingly I said yes that day to a whispering tender voice in my ear, I say yes still. A life is determined by what we say yes and no to. In each moment, the simple choice is between love and fear, consciously or otherwise. Living a called life is terrifying, the lessons painful, the heartache shattering, the suffering often unbearable. But for me, the love and transformation have been worth the price.

Many years ago, my dear friend Nonine told me about her dream: *"I saw you with a book in your chest, as the golden pages flew open."* She looked at me and said: *"Dene, you are the book!"* This book has been inside me since I was a young man, and honestly, I have been afraid to write it. In Sep '19, I posted my first blog, and was delightfully surprised with the response. A year later, I hired a woman writing coach, and started this book. In the beginning, it felt like a burden, like wrestling a bear. I had so much material collected over the years, finding the arc took a long while. Today, it has morphed into a privilege, maybe even a responsibility. A man speaking about the feeling side of men is not popular. A man being willing to stand accountable for the shit he has done to women, the earth, and the feminine is not popular. A man revealing his fears, failures, and vulnerabilities is not popular. In these pages, I share with you my very personal journey, a journey of transformation, a lifelong call to awaken and heal. To say yes to this soulwork, to walk this not-well-lit path requires saying yes to my own shadows and darkness and self-doubt. The calling takes me down to the scary places where my unresolved pain hides. A *'medicine man'* is someone who chooses to penetrate his own darkness, wrestle with his own demons, and hopefully … if his heart is true … he may be blessed and burdened to bring back a healing medicine for the individual and the community. It is through initiation and rites of passage where we find our true medicine.

My first initiation was at nine years old into the *Halos*, a New York dead end street gang. Throughout my life, I have followed my magnetic center and that whispering voice into the initiatory places. At nineteen psychedelics, at twenty-two on the road, at twenty-four therapy, at thirty psychodrama and primal scream, at forty menswork, shortly thereafter, marriage and fatherhood. At midlife, I confronted my darkest demons ... as my life unraveled, my past screamed in my face, as I lost my beloved, as I lost my health. Within this darkness is where I found my calling.

> *"In the middle of the journey of this life,*
> *I found myself again in a dark forest,*
> *for I had lost the pathway straight and right."*
>
> Dante Alighieri
> The Divine Comedy

To know that one is lost is the beginning of finding oneself. There comes a time in the middle of a man's life, when he must answer two essential questions: *"Who am I as a man? and What am I called to do with this life?"* In the absence of these questions, a man's life typically revolves around doing chores, solving problems, working a job, getting laid, providing and protecting, thinking, and living a life of quiet or not so quiet desperation. In some men, this breeds a need to cause trouble. Other men die slowly and silently.

These existential questions are always within us. Some ask early, some ask at middle age, some ask on their deathbed, some don't ask at all. Usually, a man tries to answer these questions by himself. Maybe he joins a club or fraternity, the military, a church or business organization, maybe he reads self-help books. He rarely finds answers there, and the questions linger, unanswered ... for years, decades, lifetimes. The more he avoids the questions, the more insistent and annoying they become. Yet the soul is relentless, it has all the time in the world.

*"Sometimes a man stands up during supper, and walks
outdoors, and keeps on walking,
because of a church that stands
somewhere in the East.
And his children say blessings on him
as if he were dead.*

*And another man, who remains
inside his own house, dies there,
inside the dishes and in the glasses,
so that his children have to go
far out into the world,
toward that same church, which he forgot."*

Rainer Maria Rilke

One day, the man arrives at a personal crossroad: a place where circumstances force him to consider these questions from a deeper place ... a drug addiction, a personal illness, a midlife crisis, a gnawing pain in the heart or gut, a marital break, growing impotence, a car accident, a kid on drugs, a pregnant teenage daughter, repeating dark dreams, the death of someone close. This is his magnetic center calling ... *his soul inviting him down.* Usually, he avoids this call, distracts himself, has an affair, works harder, buys a new car, drinks more, takes more drugs, crawls into pornography. Frighteningly, some elusive part of him knows he must answer this call, if his life is to have any meaning. Within some men, this magnetic center is attracted to magic, mystery, or poetry. Sometimes to motorcycles, tattoos, rock'n'roll, the blues. Maybe to psychedelics or plant medicines. Some to violence, trouble, crime. Some just stay numb and stuck inside their self-prescribed box. All have a deep yearning, an emptiness, a longing ... perhaps an unreachable or unexplainable ache in the center of their being.

*If a man says yes to this call, his life will never be the same.
If he says no, his life will always be the same. The way we
do anything is the way we do everything.*

Whatever it is that awakens you, follow it. Pain that lingers is pain worth looking into. The old wounds can be healed, we have the emotional and spiritual technology to rewrite our original software code. But only if we turn our gaze courageously inward, and back to the beginning, the genesis of the original imprint … layered deep in the cells of the body, disturbingly and unrelentingly waiting for you.

The heart is the center, the place of greatest pain, the place many men avoid. The path from the head to the heart is the longest and toughest journey of a man's life. Likewise from the cock to the heart. We have been programmed from the crib, our operating system telling us to deny feeling, weakness, vulnerability, anything feminine. The media constantly bombards us with images of violence, sex, toughness, power. This keeps us firmly in the box where the fear and shame of our not-enoughness stubbornly frame our real powerlessness. The multi-generational definitions of masculinity remain very much in effect. Our ability to feel is dysfunctionally limited, we stay silent to our pain, we refuse to be vulnerable, we pretend that we are powerful and capable. Soon the heart closes.

With the heart closed, we are capable of anything, and from here we do our greatest damage. Fortunately these days, more men are turning their eyes and ears to the soul's call … desperate for something different, tired of drugs and porn and pretending, looking for something to take away the heart's pain and its inevitable numbness. This is when they knock on the doors of our men's circles.

The *'men's movement'* is still very much alive, as more men awaken to the sacred masculine that lives within our hearts and souls and bones and balls. We confront ourselves, we begin to tell the hard truths, we rediscover our long-lost feeling side as buried anger and grief arise … for all that we have lost, for the damage done to us, for the damage we have done to others. The world can no longer tolerate the *'old warrior masculine'*. He has taken us to this *'end of days'* crossroad, and if we stay blind, he will push us all into the abyss. It is time for a new masculine to step upon the world stage … a man balanced in the paradox of fierce and tender, steadfast yet flexible, clear yet okay with not-knowing, focused yet intuitive, logical yet with deep feeling, tough yet compassionate. And with women who are equally balanced, we collaboratively weave a new reality. My calling is to *'midwife'* men, as *'a rigorous space of awakening inquiry,'* as an entry point into this work. Offering a context to understand the soul and its accompanying wound, a reframe of masculine and feminine, and most importantly, presenting the scary choice to open to the feeling body, especially the heart. Where there is a willingness to change, courage to shed the armor, strength to be vulnerable, we discover a new way of being a man … unarmored, open-hearted, honest, compassionate, courageous … where the true self accrues true power. There is a growing sense of urgency inside me, as the world hurls headlong into growing darkness. Instead of being pulled into its seductive allure, and lose valuable energy, I turn toward the simplicity of what is right in front of me … my self-care, my writing, coaching, teaching, workshops, and my most intimate relationships. For this is all that I can control.

In this book, I share what has come through me over the years … stories, dreams, poems, insights, commentaries, bursts of light, holes of darkness … the good, the bad, and the ugly of my deeply soulful human experience. My prayer is that this book inspires you to reclaim your life, your fierceness and your tenderness, your deep true self. This is not easy, nothing good ever is. In opening the heart, rage and grief precede the healing and love, only then will anything change. Over the years, so many men have said to me: *"Dene, I'm afraid if I start to cry, I will never stop!"* or *"If I let my anger out, I'm afraid I'll kill somebody."* And I say to them something that few men in their lives have ever heard from another man: *"Brother, your rage and your tears are welcome, they are safe here."*

Today, I invite you to open to your own journey … to seek out the buried places deep in your body, to challenge the old beliefs that keep you stuck, to work to heal your past, and to rediscover how to be a good man. This healing path says: *"The only way out is through."* Joseph Campbell calls it *'the hero's journey'* ... each man's unique battle to find a soulful life. Your willingness to say yes is the first step. You do this alone and you do this with others. If you are already on this road, I say: *"Hey brother."* If not, I say: *"Welcome brother."*

> *"We have not even to risk the adventure alone*
> *For the heroes of all time have gone before us.*
> *The labyrinth is thoroughly known ...*
> *we have only to follow the thread of the hero path.*
> *And where we had thought to find an abomination, we*
> *shall find a God.*
>
> *And where we had thought to slay another,*
> *We shall slay ourselves.*
> *Where we had thought to travel outwards,*
> *We shall come to the center of our own existence.*
> *And where we had thought to be alone,*
> *We shall be with all the world."*
>
> Joseph Campbell

Part I: Family of Origin

Chapter 1: Poppy

I call my grandfather Poppy, his real name is Latchin, everyone calls him Latch. Still a handsome man at seventy, with a full head of wavy white hair, he wears wire-rimmed glasses, smokes Chesterfields with a cigarette holder, and shaves every morning with a straight razor sharpened on the black leather strap that hangs in the bathroom. He dresses daily in a 3-piece suit, starched white shirt and tie. A scar adorns his left cheek, incurred in some sword fight in the old country, I imagine.

When I am little, on cold winter mornings, I crawl into bed with Poppy. Our apartment is like ice, we have to bang on the walls to get the coals stoked for heat. He wears long-johns, I nuzzle my back into his soft belly. He wraps his arms around me, holds me close. I smell his body, his cologne, his morning breath. He tells me stories of the old country, of his adventures leaving home. He is Persian, descended from the ancient Assyrians. Around 1900, he and his younger brother and their two cousins came up through Turkey and Greece, and boarded a ship bound for New York.

Back in the old country, Latch's parents had come from a small village in the northwest part of Persia. His father had been a musician, a drummer, his band traveling around the towns, playing at weddings and celebrations. He was also quite the lady's man, and many a time when his band would spend the night away from home, some woman would find her way into a musician's bed. Rumor was that he had produced a number of children out of wed-lock.

Latch's mother was a fiery red-headed woman, prone to temperamental explosions of jealousy and anger, especially when she suspected that her husband was fucking around. She would accuse, he would deny. She would yell and scream, he would still deny. Finally, she would get so furious, she would attack him with claws bared, scratching and screaming, biting and kicking. He would defend himself by kicking the shit out of her, giving her welts, bruises, broken bones, and many a black eye.

In turn, she started to take in other men when her husband was away. Latch and his brother would see all of this ... the drunken orgies on the road, then the fights back home, and the hot sex that followed. Their father would go away again, their mother's lovers would come, and so it continued. Soon Latch began to drink, and he came to enjoy the times when he and his brother went on the road. Latch was a handsome teenage boy who the women found attractive. His brother went the other way, shy, introverted, afraid of women, passive and timid.

Latch's father found his son's emulation quite amusing. Increasingly, he would bring his son into the bedchambers with another woman, even a man sometimes. He would encourage the boy to have his way with the woman, then make fun of him that he wasn't as good as he was. They would laugh, Latch would slink away in shame, pain, anger, rage.

My uncles tell stories about Latch's misdeeds, my father tells about his violent boyhood household. My father was the youngest of three and watched his two sisters and mother get beaten countless times. My uncle tells that Latch kicked his wife in her belly when she was pregnant with my father. Both girls fled early ... multiple marriages, alcoholism, no children, their childhood trauma lasting their entire lives. Finally, at sixteen, my father intervened, grabbing his father's raised hand, and says: *"You ever lay your hands on my mother again, I'll kill you."* Too little, too late, the damage was already done.

Sometime after my brother was born, poppy's hands begin to creep further down my body. This feels familiar, as he has done this before. I can't remember, but my body remembers. I feel an odd mixture of emotions and sensations, as I love him, and cherish his affection. The only other place I am getting any love is from Nona, my mother's mother. Unfortunately, we don't see her that much. My mother and father are too busy, too tired, too impatient, too worried to pay any attention to me, unless I'm getting in the way.

As I get older, I feel sorry for Poppy. I see that twistedness in his eyes, his sick and paranoid side. I sense the jagged edges inside his fucked up psyche … dark, violent, cruel, sadistic. Perhaps his only redeeming quality was his kindness to me. Or maybe it's just his own dark distorted need for love, I'm too young to tell the difference. We cuddled when I was little, I'm not so little now. While I had tolerated the old man's wandering hands, recently they got down too low. I leave the bed, it doesn't feel right, it feels dangerous, I stop going to him. I don't yet understand why love has to hurt so much. It seems like the head and the heart and the body have altogether different agendas. So I stay away, and it breaks my heart.

Chapter 2: **My Father**

My father comes back from the war in December, '45. His mother, whom he adores, is in the hospital, riddled with bone cancer. She is 58, looks 85. He has plans to go to college on the GI Bill. Not in the cards.

One evening, as my father is walking down the hallway in the hospital, he sees a young woman sashaying in front of him. When a man sees a woman, from the front or the back, and has a knowing in that deep down low place, there is no force in nature that can stop him from pursuing her. Success or failure matter not, the impulse drives him forward. Such is it for him when he sees her. They marry nine months later, I am born eleven months after that. They are married for sixty-three years.

My grandmother dies before I am born, but she knows that my mother is already pregnant. My father has his hands full … a sick mother, a hostile useless father, a new bride, his mustering out pay long gone on hospital bills, working day and night to support this dysfunctional configuration. The last thing he needs is a kid on the way, and that must have scared the shit out of him. He has no knowledge of the secret pact that the women have made. Grandmother wants a grandchild before dying, mother desperately needs to fill the emptiness inside her. Within my mother's secrecy, without my father's knowledge, in the absence of any spoken agreement, I am conceived.

One night, sitting with his mother in the hospital, holding her fragile hands, she makes him promise to care for his father. Why she gives a shit about the man who beat her without mercy, who could ever know. Saint, sacrificial lamb, helpless victim … some women love, and stay beyond what is rational. My father believes his mother is a saint, maybe she is. She dies on New Year's Eve '46. I imagine she is one of my guardian angels. A testimony to my father's good character, he never lays a hand on my mother, hits me a few times, mostly with just cause. But inside him, something is deeply broken. A boy cannot witness all that violence without a fracturing in his core. Yet his loyalty, his commitment to his mother and to his family, his often blind stubbornness, his fear, pain, anger, they all drive him. I am like my father in many ways, and by grace, I am luckier than he, my wounds are different.

I remember the arguments and fights, usually at the dinner table, spoken in their native tongue, my father and grandfather wage their domestic war. Too young to comprehend the context of their hostility, my body internalizes the content of their poison. If the wound is the birthplace of the mission, mine is born and nursed at this table. At six, I hit the streets … baseball and stickball, punch-ball and whiz-ball, alleyways and dank cellars, concrete school-yard, girls and deadend street kids. Irish, Italians, Greeks, Germans, Arabs, Negroes … working class families, 6-flat apartments, kids born in the 40's. What is happening in my house is happening in all the other ones up and down my block. Truck drivers, factory work-ers, laborers, WWII vets … wounded in body and soul with the unfulfilled promise of post-war America. The fathers drink, knock up their wives, kick the shit out of their sons. As shit ultimately rolls downhill, so do the fights that spill onto our mean streets. My body is small, slight, mercurial. I make my way through quick feet and wits, as I have no brawn to speak of. Being smart, a good athlete, and just edgy enough, I pay my dues into the company of the neigh-borhood toughs.

We have a dozen guys in the club, age nine to sixteen. School is done for the summer, we have just finished a game of stickball, all the *Halos* street gang are there. It is getting dark, the street lights have just come on. Charlie walks over to me and puts his arm around my shoulder. He tells me there will be some tough tests coming up if I am to become a member of the gang. Yeah, I say, acting cocky on the outside, scared and excited on the inside. All the guys line up in front of me, and my first welcoming into their keep is a hard punch from each of them. No head, no balls, every place else fair game.

I can see the struggle inside those guys who like me, and don't want to hit me too hard. Yet the unflinching hardness of the macho code wins out over the tenderness of caring for somebody. A three-quarter punch from a fourteen-year-old in the gut of a nine-year old still hurts. The ones who don't like me just let it rip. I hold my tears, the most important price of initiation. I run home, up the stairs, eyes beginning to flood.

My father is sitting in his easy chair, grandfather in the other one, mother in the kitchen. When my father sees my tears, he asks me what happened, I tell him the story. With a disgusted look on his face, he stands up and slaps me, tells me if I can't take it, don't play with the big boys, and walks away. Hurt by the guys in the club, betrayed by my father and the macho code of American men, I swallow my tears and pain, again.

In the summer of 1956, I have my first spiritual epiphany ... Elvis Presley singing "*Hound Dog.*" The way he dresses, the way he wears his hair, the snarl on his lips, the twitch of his hips, the loud and insistent drum beat up my ass, and the raucous twang of guitars ... oh, my fucking god, I can't sit still. While I love baseball, music is the missing ingredient. I have this big box of a radio that I carry everywhere, I even strap it to my bike so I can listen to Elvis, Conway Twitty, Chuck Berry, Johnny Cash, Little Richard, Fats Domino, Jerry Lee Lewis. I grease up my hair, get a pair of white bucks, practice snarling in the mirror ... I am a real diddy bopper.

There is a space in the school yard, down the steps and hidden in an alcove, where the guys gather. When the music plays, these once tough kids show a different side. Singing the new rock'n'roll music, imitating Elvis, slicking back their hair, laughing and dancing and hand jiving, the light in their eyes sparkling, this is a good time to be alive.

My father doesn't give me much, but he does give me baseball and music. He and my mom grew up in the 30's and 40's on big band music, and we have a record player in the house. Benny Goodman, Glen Miller, Duke Ellington, Count Basie, Ella Fitzgerald, Frank Sinatra, Ray Charles, all the jazz greats. Every once in a while, he and my mom pull back the carpet and dance in the living room. Of course, I am embarrassed watching them move and eye ball each other, but they are actually good dancers. Doing the Lindy hop, she spinning and twirling, he cool as fuck, very little movement, always in the right place to keep her in motion. Sometimes, my mom takes out the broom and tries to teach me to dance, he never bothers.

One Sunday night, Elvis comes on the Ed Sullivan Show, we gather around the TV. I am so excited, twitchy in my pants. My dad sits in his chair, stoic and unmoved. After the performance, he says: *"That shit is not real music, it will never last."* Like a knife in my heart, the pain goes in deep. Once again, I swallow, suck it up, and leave the room.

Chapter 3: **My Mother**

My brother is four and a half years younger than me. Where I was born in the sweltering heat of August all fiery and intense, he is born in the rain of early spring, fluid and easy. I remember that day, they name him Al, after my father.

It is early March '52, with my expecting mother in the hospital ready to give birth, I am staying at my grandparents' house. I always love being here. Nona and Pappy came over separately from Italy during the first World War, settling into a little Italian neighborhood called Park Hill. She through New York, he through New Orleans, they met in Brooklyn and got married in Mt. Carmel Catholic Church in Yonkers, NY. The church is the center of the community at the top of the Hill, with Caffé Puglie just down the street. The men sit outside, drink anisette, strega, thick Italian coffee with lots of sugar, nibble on cookies and pastries. They jabber away, laughing, arguing, playing cards, boccie, and watching the women.

People come from all over Westchester County to the Caffé, even up from New York City. It has the reputation as being one of the best Italian bakeries in all of metro New York. Their cakes and cookies are exquisite. On the weekends when we're with our grandparents, Pappy walks my brother and me down to the Caffé on a Saturday morning to buy assorted sweets. Sometimes, if he runs into some friends, we sit awhile. My parents never let us drink coffee at home, but Pappy, bless his heart, always indulges us. I get a big cup of Italian coffee, fill it with milk and sugar. He buys ladyfingers or biscotti and we dip into the coffee. We always take some home to Nona.

Pappy is like a banty rooster. He dresses impeccably, trousers sharply creased, shoes spit-shined, sharp as a tack. He struts with his chest sticking out, always looking to bump up against someone. Sometimes I imitate his walk, my brother and I like to make fun of him. Across the street from the Caffé is the American Legion Post, and Pappy likes to hang out there, drink and play poker with his cronies. Once in a while, he leaves us at the Caffé, and steals over to the post to hoist a few. On a couple of occasions, I have to steady him as we walk home. Nona gets pissed off when he comes home shit-faced, and he yells back at her in his sharp-tongued way. I know he has a good heart and means her no harm, but it always bothers me when he barks at her. She has this wonderful capacity to slough off his harshness. She loves that man deeply … they were married for sixty-two years.

My Nona is the saving grace of my childhood. I am her special one, I can do no wrong, never a cross word between us. Born in 1900, at seventeen she came over from Sicily, on a boat across the Atlantic swarming with war ships. Her father was called *'The Sparrow'* because he had business adventures across the entire Mediterranean. No one ever quite knew what those businesses were, but I fantasize that he ran guns, or was some Mafia chieftain. Who knows? Whenever I ask about him, they are silent or change the subject. I vaguely remember him, he died when I was five. He had thick white hair, a big bushy white mustache, a twinkle in his eye. He seemed sweet, yet mischievous. His wife was crotchety, so I understood why he would seek all adventures away from home. She was a great cook, and he mostly ate at home. But I imagine that he dined elsewhere.

When my mother and father were courting, they would go to the Sparrow's house in Brooklyn. He grew grapes in his backyard, in the basement he had casks of wine. He'd take my father down to the cellar, pull out two glasses, and pour each of them a bit of wine from each of the barrels. He'd speak in Italian, my father didn't understand a word. But after the first glass, it didn't much matter. They'd be giggling and laughing and carrying on like best buddies. He liked my father, and that mattered to my mother.

My Nona inherited her mother's culinary talents, but my mother inherits neither. Nona makes the best spaghetti sauce and meatballs ever. I know there are many Italian kids who would make that claim, but I swear her meatballs are *'touched by the puti.'* Years later I ask her for the recipe. She tells me: "*... a little garlic, some onions, some olive oil, a little of this and that, and a lot of Romano cheese.*" When I ask her how much is a little, she shrugs, wrinkles her nose and smiles. I know she isn't going to tell me, she knows I will figure it out. Some unspoken things are sacred. I have been cooking her recipe for years.

Of course, my mother does not trust Poppy at all. With his negative attitude toward women, she does not escape his twisted judgments. He thinks she's a whore, imagines she's fucking every guy in the neighborhood. Yet I can see his eyes roam up and down her lithe body when she gets dressed up. My mother is attractive, a curvy sexiness about her. I sometimes wonder if he ever puts his hands on her, especially when my father is working the night shift. Those times the sexual tension in the house silently screams.

My mother is high strung by nature. She is not warm or affectionate, always barks at me or my brother about cleaning up toys, clothes, some shit. Although my father is scary in looks, my mother is the one who cracks the whip. Her patience with me is constantly stretched thin, her sharp tongue issues one warning, then a swat across my ass.

One time we're in a department store, my eyes on a pair of cowboy six-shooters with a picture of Hoppalong Cassidy on the box. They're gleaming silver, fake white pearl handles with a fake black leather tooled holster. I am about six. She's up the aisle, calling me, I just can't pull myself away from those guns. I hear her call me a number of times, and suddenly she's standing over me. It's summertime, I have on a pair of shorts and t-shirt. She has taken off her belt and slashes me across the legs with it. I let out a blood-curdling scream, as she grabs my hand and high tails it out of that store. The other people stare at the commotion. She drags me by the hand all the way home.

Our apartment is like a string of railroad cars. My parents' bedroom is at the front end of the house. Next is my bedroom, then Poppy's. The living room is in the middle, with the front door opening to the downstairs. Then from the living room, a hallway with the bathroom, followed by the kitchen and an enclosed back porch. No doorway between my parents' room and mine, just a set of heavy dark green satin drapes. I hear everything.

One night I awake from a dream, I am four or five years old. I am being chased by a dark shadowy man, a dream that repeats across my childhood. Trembling, I call out: *"Mommy, please come and lay with me."* It is a pleading more than a call. I hear her mumble something, it's her angry tone. I call her again, and her voice is sharper, telling me to go back to sleep. Yet my need calls her a third time, and in a flash she is up and out of bed, heads right past my bedroom toward the kitchen. She comes back to my room, yanks the bed covers down, and starts wailing on my little body with a big wooden spoon. Over and over she whacks me, on my legs, arms, ass, with a rhythm driven and relentless. I cry, and the more I cry, the harder she hits me, until all that's left is a whimper. From some imagined voice deep inside my body, I hear myself say: *"I'll be good Mommy, I won't need you, no more never."*

It's strange how a kid learns about the world … what is safe, what isn't, where to go, where to stay away from. We do it on our own, we watch the models around us. Nurturance is at such a premium, and a kid is lucky to have even a bit. Working class fathers hardly home, babies flooding in to repopulate from the war. Mothers stretched thin on resources … at home the boys are mostly in her keep. On the streets, we just have each other.

While fathers are violent, mothers are no walk in the park. A smile on the outside, impatient, punishing, angry, and numb on the inside. That day I learn that asking my mother for anything is pointless, she has nothing for me. Every once in a great while, she allows me to play with her long auburn hair. But I can tell from her exasperated breathing that she is just tolerating me. Mothering is something I simply come to ignore. I bury that need deep inside my small body, that need for nurturance, comfort, for tender caring. Denied on the outside, the unmet need layers on the inside. And thus, I bury my own capacity to nurture and care. I learn to believe that having needs will be punished, and later I punish women for needing me, or I feel shame for being needy. The message is clear: *Do not be needy, do not ask for anything.* The wooden spoon is at the center of my mother's kitchen. She rarely bakes cookies, but often that spoon finds my body.

My earliest experience of my mother is not cognitive, it is cellular. I am conceived deep within her body, created and held in the unfathomable mystery of that empty sacred womb space. How she carries me is her first teaching ... with fear and resistance, or with love and welcoming. Likewise, from birth to six, I am predominantly in her keep. Her moods and feelings, her hopes, dreams, and desires, her fears and doubts, her attitudes and beliefs, her horrors, her every experience ... they all infuse themselves into my developing body. She is my primary conduit to the world. **Safety, nurturance, care, danger, neglect, abuse ... whatever she gives me becomes imprinted. This is what I learn to call "love."** As she carries me, I also carry her, as the unconscious feminine energy encoded in my cells. She is my first woman, and pleasing her is not an option, it is a survival necessity. And I see every woman in my life through this lens.

Chapter 4: My First Initiation

Charlie stands on the street corner, tall and lanky, tight blue dungarees, black garrison belt, white socks, black Keds. His dark wavy hair is slicked back in a duck's ass, the pompadour drooping strategically over his forehead. His white t-shirt is tight to his skinny torso, arms sinewy, muscular, street tough. He carries a short black satin jacket, with pink piping, the word *"Halos"* written across the back. Too hot to wear, too cool to leave at home, it is summertime 1956, dead-end New York street kids, and we are the coolest motherfuckers in town. I am nine years old.

I like hanging out with the older guys on the corner, they smoke Luckys, some weed when they can get it from the colored boys, they pass the bottle … singing the new rock'n'roll music, hustling girls, talking shit. But being with them has its cost. The entry fee for my initiation into the *Halos* is the willingness to fight. They match me with a kid named Billy. He is a year older than me, he's a bully, and he likes to pick on me. I am small, wiry, fast feet, faster mouth. I usually talk my way out of shit with Billy, and when I can't, I can outrun him. So the next time we meet, he has forgotten any prior shit. Billy is not too smart.

It is Saturday, the match is set for 7 pm. After dinner, I make my way out of the apartment, across the street, and down the stone steps of the schoolyard to the large alcove alongside the building. It is covered and hidden, out of the rain, a perfect place for *Halos'* business. I get to the den, Charlie is standing at the entrance. Charlie the Greek is the captain of the *Halos*, and the toughest cat in the neighborhood. One time, I saw Fat Jimmy give Charlie some shit about the Greeks, and Charlie kicked his ass up and down the block. He even bit Jimmy in the cheek, drew blood. Jimmy ran down the street screaming. No one fucks with Charlie.

He silently motions for me to take a seat on the bench. I sit down, take a deep breath, I have butterflies in my belly. Truth is, I don't like to get my pretty face messed up. Besides, if I get my dungarees too dirty, my mother will give me all kinds of shit. She doesn't like me hanging out with these guys, somehow she thinks I'm better than them. My father doesn't say much, he knows that a boy needs toughening up.

In a few minutes, the guys roll in … singing, hand jiving, talking shit. Billy walks into the circle with his older brother Butch, they take a seat opposite me. He doesn't look at me, I know he's a chicken-shit at heart and I can take him. I think of Prince Valiant, Crazy Horse, The Lone Ranger … battle stories, I feel courageous.

Charlie strides to the center of the circle, everyone gets quiet. He slowly walks around, looking at each guy, then says: *"Everybody knows why we're here tonight. Little Denny wants to become a member of the Halos. We all know he can play ball, he sings the new harmonies good, and can even take a punch. But is he tough enough to fight? Can he kick ass, or get his ass kicked, and not run home crying to his mommy? Tonight, we'll see if he belongs."*

Charlie motions me and Billy into the center of the circle. The guys move the benches and chairs back toward the walls, the ring of battle made ready. My heart is pounding, my breath shallow, I feel all my blood rushing through my body. All I can see is Billy's ugly fucking face. Charlie barely steps back, and I am all over Billy's shit. I grab his dirty blond hair, wrestle him to the ground. We fall on the concrete, I bang my knee going down. Billy falls underneath me. He lets out a gasp, I can smell his stinky breath. He swings wildly, hits me in the head, I feel no pain. I push him down onto his back. I strain hard, get one knee up on his legs, inch my way up onto his body. I pin his arm underneath my leg, push my forearm into his throat. I have access to his face and I start slamming away. Bam, bam, bam … I keep hitting him, over and over, I can't stop hitting him. I land one on his nose, blood trickles down his nostril.

In that moment, I remember the last fight at home, my grandfather sprawled on the floor, his nose bloodied from my father's punch. I hide in the shadows, trembling. I want to put my arms around Poppy, wipe his face, comfort his pain. I look down at Billy, and suddenly these big tears come welling up from deep in my gut, traveling up through my heart, up toward my eyes. I choke them back, hard. Tonight, I know that I have won his fight, and probably gained entry into the *Halos*. But I have come face to face with my own demon … that I can feel another guy's pain. And my own weakness … that I actually care, even about Billy.

I hear the guys screaming, they are hungry for blood. Billy has his hands up over his face, his body limp, I cannot hit him anymore. I get up off him and go sit next to Charlie. He pats my back, I am indifferent to his acknowledgment. The other guys are all looking at me, the circle is silent. All I can feel is fear and shame.

Tonight, I have learned a hard lesson. If you're a guy on these streets, and you want to belong, there are some things you have to watch out for: always hide what is soft inside, never let them see that you give a shit, and above all, never ever, let them see you cry. I swallow hard, I swallow again, and I swallow for a very long time. Years later, these tears will arise from my body, like a hurricane exploding out of me, first as rage, then as wave after wave of grief.

At a very early age, my tender heart is already broken and betrayed. At nine, it clanks shut, and stays that way for many years. There are so many times in my childhood when I feel so angry, I want to hurt someone. But meanness is not one of my traits, nor is body size. My gift and my curse are the ability to see and feel another's pain. My grandfather abuses me, I want to hold him and make him feel better. My parents abuse and abandon me, I want to tell them that everything is okay. The tough boys in the neighborhood push me around, and I still want to play ball with them. The little girls in school come to me when the boys bully them, I hold their hands. The natural instinct is to shut down the hurt, or hurt the one who hurts, or run away from the hurt. My nature is always to turn towards the hurt.

A week later, I am standing on the front porch of our apartment building, watching the guys play stickball in the schoolyard across the street. Someone unseen taps me on my left shoulder, she whispers: *"Welcome back."* In that moment, the light looks different, my nose twitches with street smells, I hear the far-off conversations in the schoolyard, everything slows down. I am in my first twilight zone, this is my first calling.

Chapter 5: **The Final Shattering**

It is October 10, 1958, a night I remember forever. Curious how a singular event can leave such a permanent mark on a life. Actually, it's a series of experiences, shaped into a pattern that imprints into the neural pathways ... a belief, an attitude, a way of being. Often, one circumstance stands out as the pivotal event, the breaking point, layered shadowy in deep memory.

That night, we are watching TV in the living room. My father is reclining on the couch, his tired feet propped up on a pillow. Poppy sits in his big armchair, smoking Chesterfields in his cigarette holder. My mother is in the kitchen, finishing up the dishes. My brother and me are playing on the living room floor with our toy soldiers, watching Science Fiction Theatre.

Poppy says something in Assyrian to my father. I see my father's body stiffen, like an electric shock passing through it. Oh shit, I think. My father blurts out a quick: *"Pa, don't start."* My mother must have heard the first short salvo, quickly comes in and scoops up me and my brother, takes us into the back bedroom.

Even from down the long passageway, we can hear their voices go from zero to ten in no time flat. They are hurling Assyrian hand grenades, the space between the living room and the back bedroom becomes a no man's land. The shelling continues, the blasts more shrill, landing with deadly accuracy, the blood spurting out of severed veins, dirty and full of ugly shit. I have no idea what they are saying, but my body knows this is the Gettysburg of our domestic civil war.

Within 10 minutes, it is out of control. For some reason, they have moved into the kitchen, and my mother instinctively scurries in to defend her turf. My brother and I look at each other, peek through the open doorway down into the battle zone, stealthily creep down the hallway to watch, taking cover in the shadows. When my mother enters the kitchen, my father quickly gives her the gist of the argument. Her body stiffens like a board, and she barks some shit in Poppy's general direction. He slowly turns his mean eyes on her, and through snarled lips, lets flow a torrent of slime and filth that nature keeps safely contained only in snake's venom. As my mother speaks no Assyrian, he hurls his accusations in English, and my brother and I hear every word.

"You fucking cunt, you slimy whore bitch, you temptress of men, you slut of the devil." I cannot believe I am hearing this. Poppy's face is twisted and distorted, eyes bulging with an unearthly hatred. I had seen the alien monsters on Science Fiction Theatre, they have nothing on this guy. My mother stands there, silent for a moment, the short-lived eye of the tornado. A look slowly creeps over her face, and she turns her body directly facing him. Her hands move up and cup her breasts, as she smiles lasciviously at him, licking her lips, her hands moving up and down her lithe body, slowly finding a rhythm. The words slide from her lips: *"I bet you would like to fuck me, wouldn't you? I see you looking at me, at my tits and ass. You probably lie in your bed and jerk off thinking about me, you hypocritical prick."*

I cannot believe what I am hearing, the whole scene playing out in slow motion. My mother's hands find a groove, and her body begins twitching and quivering. My father's mouth drops open. Many a time, behind the dark green satin drapes, I hear them going at it hot and heavy. As much as they try to stifle the sounds of sex, once they find their rhythm, her moans grow in volume and intensity, met in kind by his deep guttural grunts and thrusts. Yet as my father watches my mother unashamedly stroking herself, his face registers first shock, then confusion, then outrage, until finally he laughs right out loud. Here is his sweet little wife, the mother of his children, working herself into a lather. I look at my brother, we don't know what to think.

Poppy's eyes bug out of his head, his face turns red with shock. *"No, no, you are a good woman. I go to church every Sunday and give thanks to God that my son married a woman who cares for me like a daughter."* I almost piss in my pants, what a crock of shit. The old bastard never goes to church, I never once hear him say thank you to my mother. She washes and irons his clothes, changes the sheets on his bed, cooks him three squares a day and he stuffs himself good, she even buys his Chesterfields. Not one fucking thank you and here he is backpedaling from his own twistedness into some phony holier than thou, praise be to Jesus bullshit. Who the fuck is he trying to kid?

My mother's ministrations slowly come to a stop. She turns away from Poppy and looks down towards where me and my brother are hiding. The look on her face is one that I have never seen before. Her mouth resembles a smile, a smirk, I can't tell. But her eyes, her eyes are haunting. She has this faraway look, like she either isn't home inside herself, or something has taken over her body. I have seen *'Invasion of the Body Snatchers'*, and I wonder if they have stolen my mother. She looks at me, but her eyes don't see me.

My mother takes two steps back and opens the drawer near the sink. She slowly brings forth the big kitchen knife, raises it up overhead, takes a step towards Poppy. My father, who has been standing still, watching this insanity play out in front of him, is suddenly a man in motion. He grabs my mother from the back, and wraps his arms around her waist. My mother starts screaming at the top of her lungs. *"I'll kill you, I'll kill you, you fucking bastard."* My father lifts my mother off the floor, and carries her through the door out onto the back porch. As they exit the kitchen, something instinctive comes alive in me. I get up from where I am crouched, and run out into the kitchen towards the porch. Poppy stands frozen in the middle of he room. I grab the kitchen door and pull it shut. Just then, my mother lets the knife fly from her hand, along with her continuing curses, in the direction of Poppy. The knife point is headed straight toward his chest. All in slow motion, Poppy's eyes widen in shock, my father's face twisted with helpless horror, as the point of the knife crashes through the window of the door that I have just pushed closed. Glass shatters, the knife falls harmlessly to the floor.

Through the shattered windowpane, I can see my mother collapsed on the porch. She alternates between hysterical laughter and screams of outrage. In between, the grief wracks her body, tears gushing up out of her once-frozen heart. My father sits on the floor, holding her, helpless, not knowing what to do. Something inside her fragile psyche has slivered like the glass on the floor. Some inner demons, trapped since childhood are suddenly out of their prison. Her angry father, her distant mother, her abusive grandmother, the shaming imprint of the Roman Catholic Church, the hot lava that flows up between her legs, the incessant demands of an over-worked husband and two wild and needy kids, the unrelenting lasciviousness of Poppy's twisted sexual thoughts. My mother breaks that night ... and she is never the same.

Finally, my mother struggles to get up, and with my father's support, manages to come back into the kitchen. She stands there, quiet for a moment. My father put his arms around her, and in the screaming silence, I can hear her whimper again, as she falls crumbling into the chair. I make my way through the carnage, scampering back down the hallway toward my brother. Inside the safety of our dark bedroom, we look at each other, and just hold on tight.

My father calls my name, I look at my brother. I sure as shit don't want to go back into that battle zone. Poppy sits in the corner, moaning and groaning and talking to himself. My father calls me again. I pat my brother on the head, tell him I'll be right back. I scoot down the hall into the kitchen, carefully stepping through the minefield. My mom sits at the table, still dazed but physically okay. My father is kneeling next to her, wiping her tears with his handkerchief. I kneel down next to them, my mother grabs my head, cradles it into her chest, and begins to sob again. I barely contain my own tears, and say *"It's okay ma, it'll be alright."*

Poppy's mumblings stop, then he looks directly at my father and says something in Assyrian. My father's body stiffens, my mother asks what. My father repeats what Poppy said, words that are the final shattering that night, words that will echo for years down the hallways of our family: *"You fucked your mother and your sisters, just like I did. You are a motherfucker, just like me."*

My father's face is ashen, the blood completely gone, having flooded into his upper torso. His eyes pop out in utter shock at the poisonous words. He slowly stands up and moves over toward Poppy. With his left hand, he grabs him by the shirt collar, lifts him out of his chair, and with right arm cocked like the hammer of a pistol, from the depths of his rage, uncoils his fist straight into the old man's face. The sound of bone on bone is gut-wrenching, my father's fist shattering Poppy's nose, sending him crashing to the floor. An old red radio rests on the shelf in the corner, and as Poppy falls, it comes crashing down on his head. Blood spurting out of his nose, blood oozing out of the top of his head, blood and snot all over his face and down his white shirt ... it is a knockout.

My father stands very still, looking at the carnage. Perhaps, in that one brief moment, he clearly understands what has happened. As the adrenaline in his body begins to subside, the soldier in him assesses the situation: body count taken, wounded identified, calibration of gain and loss made. My father knows all too well what has been lost here, his father lying right in front of his eyes, his promise to his mother broken. For now, his only win is the immediate sense of relief. What he does not see, and what he never factors into his inner equations, is the damage done inside him, and inside the rest of us. He is always blind to the inner terrain, self-absorbed to the end. And most importantly, he is unable and/or unwilling to be accountable for the wounds to the soul, especially those wounds on his wife and children. Perhaps the drivenness of his ambition, some unconscious ego need salves a deep wound. Perhaps his guilt and shame bind his eyes shut. Perhaps his horrific model of fatherhood. Or maybe the weight of responsibility is just too painful to bear. All I know is that the fist that crushed Poppy's face is also the blow that breaks my young heart ... split down the middle between the two men I love the most. A soul wound like this either shatters a life, or drives it into who knows where.

My father comes over to me and my mother. My mother quivers in her own pain, I am doing my best to tough it out. My father is

31

surprisingly calm and cool. He pats me on the head, tells me to go next door, and ask the neighbors to call Nona and Pappy. John and Adele are the owners of our apartment building. We are not close to them, thinking they are cheap in giving heat to our place. Adele is the biggest gossip on the block, spreading shit all over the neighborhood. But they have heard enough fights over the years, and often have taken my brother and me in. My father repeats: *"Go tell John to call Pappy."* I walk out the front door into the hallway, there is only a dimly lit bulb, I am afraid of the shadows. I also remember that my brother is still down the hallway, so I scurry back into the bedroom, take him by the hand, and we walk out the door.

I knock on the door, surprised when it opens so quickly. Adele stands there in her bathrobe, a worried but tender look on her face. As she pulls us into her arms, my brother cries, and I do my best to swallow it down. She holds us close, his small body quivering, mine a bit stiff. I tell them what I can remember, recalling the fear, pain, and horror of the night. After a few minutes, I remember the task my father had charged me with. I ask Adele to call my grandparents, she yells down to John to make the call. I hear him dial the phone, he quickly tells Pappy the short story. He hangs up, comes back down the hall and sits down with us. Adele is wiping my brother's tears, helping him blow his nose. John tells us that our grandparents are on the way.

The Park Hill section is only about a fifteen minute drive from where we live. Adele gets us some milk and cookies. I feel a bit torn, like I should go back in and help my father. But I am afraid, I have seen enough horror tonight. Besides, the milk and cookies taste good, and I can actually feel myself breathe again. I bend over and put my arms around my brother, he holds on tight. A short while later, there is a knock on the front door, and in walks Nona and Pappy. Nona comes over to the couch and wraps her arms around both of us. She holds us as John asks me to tell them what happened. I tell them about the argument, the knife and broken glass, my father breaking Poppy's face, my mother crying on the back porch. I can feel Pappy's body stiffen, his rooster anger rising. Often I hear Pappy pleading with my father: *"Son, why do you stay? Don't you know you got a family to take care of? I would either leave or kill that son of a bitch. If he ever lays a hand on my daughter ..."* If he only knew.

Pappy's fists are clenched, his face red, the fighting cock in him has come alive. As I hear him mutter some obscenities under his breath, readying himself to charge into the ring, I grab his hand and say: *"I wanna go with you."* I'm surprised to hear those words come out of my mouth. While the idea of revisiting the battle field scares the shit out of me, my sense of duty speaks louder. Yet I am also aware that I am deeply divided. I love my mom and dad, but I also love Poppy.

I instinctively know that me and my brother, my mother and father will be leaving that night. The big explosion has finally come, with damage beyond repair. My heart aches in my chest ... afraid for my mother, confused with my father, angry at Poppy. Part of me hates him, I hate his filth and distortion, I hate his paranoid fucked-up mind, I hate his whining and carrying on. Another part is already missing him, missing the closeness, the warmth and affection, the care that I am not getting any place else. My heart is cleaved, breaking in two, as it quietly goes numb.

Loyalty is a word I hear on the streets all the time. Loyalty to our team, to our block, to our gang. Mostly it is the *Giants* and not the fucking *Dodgers*, the *Halos* and not the *Clinton Street Gang* or the *Bebops*, the colored gang. The south end kids and not the north side rich pricks. You are in or you are out. Here it is not so black and white. In between, where the shadows live, choices are harder. Most times, my gut or heart clearly tell me what is true. But tonight, I just don't know. I begin to feel a wave of nausea come up the pipes. The milk and cookies are shushing around in my belly, making a rumbling noise. I know I can puke if I let myself.

Pappy knows I am not asking, so he takes my hand, pats me on the head, and we both march straight back into the battle zone. My father has somehow gotten my mom into the living room, they are both sitting on the couch. When we walk in, Pappy takes one look at his daughter, as the rage rises up out of his body. *"You son of a bitch"* he yells down the hallway. Poppy has somehow managed to get his ass up into a kitchen chair, clearly in Pappy's field of vision. Dad, my father says, he calls Pappy dad. *"Dad, please don't dirty your hands."* Pappy hesitates for a moment, but he has already worked up a lather, and his rage needs a release. My father repeats his wise plea, Pappy steps back, pounding his fist into the back of Poppy's armchair ... one, two, three, four times he punches that chair, in rhythm like he is hitting a punching bag. The last blow is so hard that the wooden shoulder on the back of the chair pushes a hole right into the wall.

Soon Pappy quiets down, as Nona and my brother come through the front door. *"You're coming home with us."* Pappy barks, more an order than invitation. My father takes my hand and we walk into the back rooms. He pulls down a couple of suitcases from the top shelf of their closet. My father takes some of his clothes out of the closet, some of my mother's stuff from her dresser. He gives me the smaller suitcase, tells me to pack some stuff for my brother and me. We both have our pajamas on, so I grab our sneakers from the bottom of our closet, put mine on. The weather is cool, I throw our dungarees, sweatshirts, baseball hats, underwear and socks into the suitcase, grab our fringed cowboy jackets. We walk back into the living room.

My father gently puts my mother's coat around her shoulders, and eases her onto her feet. She can barely stand up. I put my brother's sneakers on his feet, tie them up. Nona and Pappy walk my mother and brother out the door, and down the stairs. I linger a moment at the door, watching as my father walks back into the kitchen. Poppy sits at the table, trying to clean himself up. I quietly steal down to the shadows of the hallway. I watch my father grab a clean dish towel and wet it. Poppy's face is caked with blood and snot. My father gently wipes his father's face, dabbing the gash on top of his head. He pours a glass of water, and holds Poppy's head as he drinks.

I am confused, watching my father tend to his father's wounds with such tender strokes. Just an hour ago, the fury between them had created a bloodbath of epic proportions, at least in our small world. Now, to see my father so loving, in a way that I have never seen him before, never with me or my brother, surely never with Poppy ... I don't understand. Why aren't they that way all the time, I think? Why do they have to hurt each other so bad before they can be tender? Tenderness between guys seems always short-lived. Seems like we're afraid to be gentle, like it's unmanly or something. Instead, we carve out our turf, piss along the perimeters, strut like cocks across our defined territory, defending when another guy comes around. I see it on the streets, too, always looking for trouble. Sometimes it scares me, but I see this stupid game of cocksmanship.

True to form, Poppy says something to my father in Assyrian, my father bolts up straight. He throws the dish towel into the sink, turns on his heels, and walks out of the kitchen. He sees me standing there, reaches down for my hand, and walks us out the front door. I hear Poppy's voice from the kitchen: *"You won't leave, you'll be back."* My father takes one last look, and gently closes the door behind us. We never go back.

Part II: Awakening

Chapter 6: The Lights Go On

In the fall of '64, I enter my senior year in high school, I am seventeen. Thoughts of college are my dominant preoccupation, as I am the first in my family to have the privilege. Too much information, confusion, pressure … I find myself drinking bourbon on the weekends, smoking cigarettes on the sly. My anger leads me into many a fight on the sports field, and arguments everywhere else.

Other than sports, this is the first real fissure up from the volcano buried inside me. One day at lunchtime in the cafeteria, I get up from my apple pie to get some milk. When I get back, the guy across from me, a friend I thought, has taken a bite of my pie. Without a moment's hesitation, I jump across the table with my fist in his face. Ending up in the principal's office, once again, the old man asks me why such a smart kid, a national honor student, a varsity athlete, would be fighting so much. I have no answer. I just feel this edginess, like a ticking time bomb.

I give some thought to applying to West Point, maybe a good place to express the rage that is burning inside. With the news coming out of Cambodia and Vietnam and the Congo, and Mississippi and the civil rights shit in the south, thoughts of joining the army do not seem like such a good idea. I get into Georgetown and visit the campus, pictures of Jesus everywhere. The last thing I need are his soulful eyes looking at me, I have way too much to hide.

In the fall of '65, I enter Harpur College, a small, liberal arts left-leaning university situated in upstate New York with a full ride scholarship. I'm a freshman, and it's my first real time away from home. Everybody sounds so fucking smart, and the shift to being a little fish in a big pond deeply disturbs my fragile and insecure psyche. On probation after my first semester, I retreat deeper into bourbon, beer, pizza, sloth. Thoughts of medical or dental school go out the window. I gain thirty pounds, lost, confused, scared, I have no fucking idea how to cope. In the summer of '66, I find my elixir.

The first time I smoke marijuana, a light turns on in my head, as the space between my brain and my body increases exponentially. I can finally breathe without feeling pain in my chest. Wow, how cool. Soon, I can't get high enough. From '66 to '69, college is the inconvenient backdrop to drugs and radical politics. Marijuana, hashish, acid, speed, cough medicine, psilocybin, mescaline, cocaine, and weekly SDS meetings. Medicating myself as often as possible, my anger and twitchiness are still close to the surface.

In late summer '66, just before going back to college, I am at the basketball courts. We have some brutal encounters on this concrete, we always seem to be playing for blood. An angry and turbulent time, every one of us is either drunk, stoned, or on the edge in some way. My brother comes over and tells me that some kid has taken his basketball and kicked him off the court. I look over and see a kid who lives around the block from us. He and I do not like each other, never did. I walk over to him and thrust my fist right into his face. It became the last punch I throw. He whips me good, leaving two black eyes and a very injured ego. Filled with shame, I walk into our apartment, my mother asks what happened, but my father looks at me with disgust. No surprise.

I return to college battered, bruised, ashamed, scared, confused, and I cannot get stoned enough. During these years, the west coast draws my attention. Hippies, the Beatles and Stones, acid rock, the Blues, Jimi and Janis and the Lizard King … the music soothes my soul and speaks to the insane fire within. It speaks to my growing social conscience and offers a whole new set of personal choices in the face of the politics of the time. I find myself increasingly disenfranchised from the status quo of the Establishment. From potential West Point cadet to West Coast acid-head longhair within a short time, this sure isn't what I had planned.

My father easily embodies to perfection the projected *'dark father'* in our culture. Our arguments over politics and social issues are violent in tone, as we replay his childhood, my childhood, America's post-WWII childhood. America has never seen a generation like this. The great drama of the 60's is the first time where the sons overtly challenge the power of the cultural and personal fathers. Like the Civil War a hundred years earlier, families blow apart, a country divides, a world awakens to the shadow politics of colonialism and racism. The war in Vietnam reflects the social and economic war in the heart and soul of America.

I remember being in Oakland in '68, seeing six Black Panthers marching down the street in lockstep. I grew up with Negroes in my neighborhood, these are no Negroes. This is a whole new breed of American men, black and proud, beautiful men who clearly take no shit. I wonder why I am so angry all the time. These guys have something to be angry about, I sometimes wish I am black. I see Fred Hampton and Huey Newton and Bobby Seale in the news, I read Eldridge Cleaver's Soul on Ice, vote for him in my first presidential election that year. I watch the returns on TV, stoned on acid, not knowing whether to laugh or cry. I realize it doesn't much matter.

On the day I graduate college, I tell my father to his face to go fuck himself. The poor guy looks so shocked and hurt. While our household has always been a war zone, my father and I are in a new war, as is so many fathers and sons across America. They do not realize that Vietnam is only the tip of a much bigger war. It is the first time that the true nature of the United States shadows gets revealed. The death of John Kennedy is the first real shock. The civil rights war in the south, the deaths of Martin Luther King, Bobby Kennedy, the Black Panthers follow. Rock'n'roll defines my generation, it sings the anthem to the truth. The overt war claims the lives of its young men, the covert war claims the lives of its truth tellers. A philosophical split that once again tears America open down the middle: father vs son, brother vs brother, group vs group. A country born from war, steeped in violence and racism, and here we are again … same shit, different day.

Every American war claims the soul of its people, especially its deep and beautiful young men. We have been trained to be soldiers since the crib. Desensitized, programmed into a hard masculine, locked up early in the tight confines of masculinity, it takes a bloody toll on men, and upon those who love us.

Lives in the Balance

"They sell us the President the same way
They sell us our clothes and our cars
They sell us everything from youth to religion
The same time they sell our wars.

I want to know who the men in the shadows are
I want to hear somebody asking them why
They can be counted on to tell us who our enemies are
But they're never the ones to fight or to die.

And there are lives in the balance
There are people under fire
There are children at the cannons
And there is blood on the wire."

Jackson Browne

PART II: *Awakening*

Chapter 7: **The Draft or My Life**

June '69, a degree in Political Science, draft number thirty six, officer candidate school, a second lieutenant in Vietnam ... too soon sent home in a box. This is my future, sure as shit. I can see the whole picture laid out in front of me, and it does not include my living very long. Am I afraid to die in a war? You bet your ass I am. But once awakened to the true nature of the American Military Industrial Complex, I cannot unring that bell.

However, I am not yet ready to face the draft board. I need a break from school, and I do not have many options for work that do not include becoming part of the military and corporate machinery. So I rationalize that I can make a difference working with little kids, teaching them to read, write, think for themselves, and get along with each other. Besides, teachers are given a draft deferment. A great short-term option.

I interview for the job at PS #77, an elementary school in the East Bronx. I am hired to teach 1st grade in the fall, working under the Head Start program. I take education classes at City College, they're easy and fun, I am ready for this gig. It's summertime, and I hear rumors about this concert in upstate New York near Woodstock. It's not that far, me and a couple of buddies are intending to go. A friend and I have been looking at apartments in Greenwich Village, as living with my folks is hardly bearable. We live in two different worlds, my brother and I get high together, but we hang with different crowds. Music is alive in me, and virtually every week, I attend a concert at the Fillmore East in the village. Since, '67, I see Jimi, Janis, Santana, Buffalo Springfield, The Who, Van Morrison, The Doors, Jefferson Airplane, Grateful Dead, Cream, Crosby, Stills, Nash, and Young. I go to other clubs to see the Blues Project, Paul Butterfield, James Cotton, Frank Zappa, The Fugs, Miles Davis, and the Electric Flag.

The first time I see Santana, Carlos comes onto the stage in black leather pants and tank top, jewelry all over his body, his long black hair wild like Medusa, stoned as fuck. Big drum set placed high on the center platform, double congas on both sides of the stage, big pounding base in the back, and Carlos' screaming guitar up front. Something new comes alive in me, almost like Elvis in '56. This time, I have my whole body moving to the Latin rhythms, my ass can't sit still.

My best friend from high school drives up to Woodstock mid-week in August, intending to buy a handful of tickets. I get out of class Friday mid-morning, it's only a couple of hours, I will drive up right after school. He calls me Wednesday night, says *"It's such a fucking mess here, it's raining, mud everywhere, roads closed, a zillion people ... don't bother coming, you'll never get in."* A bit disappointed, little do I know that this is the place that the music of my generation defines itself. Over the years, I see many concerts and films and documentaries on the Woodstock Festival. A bit of twinge in my heart for having missed that seminal experience, and so much gratitude and pride for what *'my generation'* brought to the world.

> *"We are the awakening of global consciousness, we are the truth tellers who named the king without clothes and laughed. We are the intrepid psychic travelers, the bringers of change. We are the exponential leap in vertical awareness, the ones who shouted from the rooftops ... 'We Are One.' All brought to you by the Beatles, the Stones, and the entire band of Psychedelic Choirboys of the 60's."*

PS #77 is in a ghetto neighborhood, my kids are all Black and Puerto Rican. The program gives me ample support inside the classroom: one full time assistant, and two volunteers, usually mothers whose kids are in the program. Each volunteer comes in for six weeks. After three weeks, the second volunteer comes, with rotation every three weeks. Being Persian and Sicilian, growing up in a multi-ethnic neighborhood, having played ball throughout school with black and brown kids, I am very comfortable in this environment. A rock'n'roller since nine, music is in my blood.

PART II: Awakening

I bring an old record player and two albums into the classroom. Every afternoon, we move the tables, I put on Santana and the Jackson 5, and everybody dances. Then we all lay on the floor, they run their hands through my long hair, place their little heads in my lap, and they take a nap. It is sweet to love them all, it is sweet that they love me right back. I sit at my desk, looking at them, appreciating the quiet, and I smile. For the first time in a long while, my heart is quiet.

The New York City Board of Education is an ugly bureaucracy, and even though our Head Start program is somewhat shielded from the bullshit, the crap still rolls into our laps. One of the assistant principals is a woman, five feet tall, very tight and controlling, and she does not like my hippie ways. Always reinforcing the rules, demanding perfect paperwork, visiting my classroom at inopportune times, she is a pain in my ass. Actually, she is harmless, I have departmental protection, I laugh at her sometimes, still I have to deliver paperwork to her as well. One afternoon, I am returning from lunch into the schoolyard. All the kindergarten, first, and second grade classes are lined up to go inside. The little commandant walks up and down the lines, like a military machine, helplessly trying to get a hundred little kids' fidgety bodies into some kind of order. I can tell she is losing it. As soon as my kids see me walk through the gate, they all run out of line and grab me, hug me, jump up into my arms. The commandant's head gets so red it looks like it could explode off the top of her body. I cannot help but laugh at the absurdity of the moment.

I last one year here, the wanderlust in me is too strong. I want to get out of New York, on the road in America, and let my freak flag fly. The only thing that stands between me and that imagined freedom is the US Army draft board. I hear that there is a group of Quakers sympathetic to the draft called the Society of Friends. I know that I am not committed enough to be a conscientious objector, but I sure do not want to go to war. I go to a few meetings, lovely people, kind and compassionate, helpful with lots of information.

They give me the names of a couple of doctors who are writing letters on behalf of young men like me. I make an appointment with one. The doc is a sweet man, not much older than me. He asks me if I have any physical conditions, I tell him no, other than a twitchy stomach. He writes a letter that says I am unfit to serve. With that flimsy letter, I make an appointment at the draft board for a physical. Not convinced that the letter will be enough, I figure my best option would be to show them firsthand that I am unfit to serve. I get on the bus at 8 am, and promptly drop a tab of acid. The one thing I vividly recall about that lengthy experience is when they ask me to bend over and spread my cheeks. I fall over laughing my naked ass off. They look in my eyes, read the letter, and send me packing. A couple of weeks later, I get a letter in the mail with my 1Y status: *psychologically unfit for service*. I recall reading a book written by one the guys from The Fugs called *"1001 Ways to Beat the Draft"*. My favorite is: *"Bend over, crawl up your own asshole, and disappear."* Psychologically unfit, fucking 'eh !!!

Chapter 8: **On The Road**

The feeling of freedom is exhilarating, heady, light, spacious. I walk out of that draft board still tripping, the sun warm on my face. No school, no job, no draft. I am a happy man.

Over the next month, I sell my car, buy some on-the-road gear, say goodbye to family and friends, and head south to Philly. I have a cousin there, our plan is to motorcycle cross country. My cousin's friend is a pharmacist, he provides my first exposure to really good cocaine. In the month that I am there, plans change. My cousin flakes out, I meet a hippie couple who have a 3-year old kid, a van with a Harley hitched to the back, heading to the west coast. One more guy joins us, and we are the merry pranksters. In a rigged up Ford Econoline, a ton of coke, weed, and assorted other brain food, we hit the highway.

I love being on the road, cannot get enough sex, drugs, and rock'n'roll. When it gets boring or fucked up, we hit the road again, not looking back. It is easy to run away from shit, not so easy to run away from myself. We are on the road for a few months, and our troupe finally makes it to the west coast. We separate outside of LA, I hitchhike up to San Francisco, but by late '70, the Haight -Ashbury district is riddled with junkies, hustlers, street kids, acid heads with tombstones in their eyes. The summer of love is long gone.

The next bed, the next trip, the next joint, the next place to flop, the next woman to lay, always looking for the next … my own here and now is mostly unbearable. I walk around with a big black hole in my heart. About once a month I call home, and after two minutes, wonder what I want from them. Something, but I have no clue what it is. I feel a nagging sense of guilt, waves of anger, deep sadness, and no desire to see them. Home has nothing for me, the road lonely, I am twenty-three, and lost in America. The only consolation is plenty of drugs and plenty of company.

My dreams are dark, alienated, helplessly looking for a place to rest, unable to stay anywhere long enough, shadows chasing and catching me, often I wake up screaming. The pain throbs in the middle of my chest, it never goes away. One cold morning in March, I am hitchhiking from Las Cruces to Santa Fe to visit friends from college. Standing there with my thumb out and long hair flapping, freezing my fucking ass off, cars passing by, looking at me like I was a freak. Shit, I am a freak, and I have never felt so fucked up and alone. Suddenly, she whispers to me as clear as a bell: *"Go home, start again, at the beginning."*

"Go home, start again, at the beginning"... I have no idea what those words mean. The East Coast is the last place I want to go, let alone home, I can never go home. Yet within two weeks, I am back in San Francisco, I gather my gear, say goodbye to friends ... it takes less than five days to hitchhike to New York. A few days living with my folks tells me all I need to know. I find an apartment, get a job working at some crappy gas station, and start to run with a nasty drug crowd ... lots of heroin. One of the guys is an old classmate from junior high, and we start hanging out on our own. One day Larry says to me: *"My old man owns a fashion company, and he wants me to build it. You're a pretty smart guy, you and me get along good, come and work with me, we can make a lot of money."* What the fuck, why not, I have nothing else.

Chapter 9: Annie

When I start work with Larry in September '71, I am twenty-four years old. A handful of young attractive women work here, and I start running my game right away. But my eyes keep looking down the line at this older woman. She is the owner's sister Annie, forty-four years old, married with three sons, one almost my age. She has long silver streaked hair pulled back into a ponytail, torn jeans, sneakers, an old hippie woman. She does not say much, but there is something about her that intrigues me and scares me. I know she sees right through my bullshit, as if she understands me in my core.

One day soon after I start, we're sitting in the back lunch room, and I'm giving her some line of shit, trying to hustle her too. She raises her head, looks directly into my eyes and says: *"The only eyes I have ever seen that have more pain in them than yours, were my own eyes when I was your age."* Holy shit, I feel my chest start to pound. Never have I felt so exposed, so transparent. I feel those familiar deep tears start to well up in my chest, headed north to my eyes, so I mumble a few bullshit words, and run out of the room. It takes me two weeks before I talk to her again. I am not really afraid of her, I can feel her incredible kindness and wisdom. I am afraid of her power in seeing through me. I am in a world of hurt, and my cocky hustling ways are just a cover-up. When I finally do talk to her again, she doesn't say much, just gives me a piece of paper with a man's name and phone number, tells me that he'd be a good man to talk to. I call him the next day, start therapy with Carl the following week.

Am I ready for this? I ask this question over and over throughout the whole week. I sense the work it will take, the pain I will feel, I so want to run away. I have been on the road for a long time, I have done all the drugs that I could cram into my body, I have fucked myself silly ... none of it takes the pain away. I am self-absorbed, every effort designed to shove some kind of medicine into the dark hole in the middle of my chest. Nothing works. Fuck, I have nowhere to run or hide, nowhere to get away from myself. I finally admit … I am desperate, my shit has finally caught up to me. And I fucking dread that I will finally have to face my past.

Men don't go into therapy easily, I went in kicking and screaming. I do not want to admit that I am broken, I do not want to confirm the bad reflections that my life is giving me everywhere. Arrogance, denial, defensive deflections, drugs, sex, and the anger that protects those vulnerable places deep inside … they ease the pain, but not for long. This feels very true for me now that my *'medicine'* has stopped working. I quiver at what this means. Then I recall that voice on the road in New Mexico: *"Go home, start again, at the beginning."* Does *'the beginning'* actually mean my whole past? Is this what she meant? In that moment's recollection, I take a deep breath, and think: *"Could this actually be good for me?"* I shiver at the thought.

I like Carl, he smokes Luckys, I toke Camel non-filters. We smoke and talk and drink coffee for the hour. He is a Bronx guy, maybe forty, been around, knows bullshit when he sees it. And I throw him every line and curve I know, every rationale and excuse that my running scared brain can conjure. He just smiles at me, keeps asking me: *'What's the real truth, and how does it feel.'* He waits patiently, never judges me. It takes me awhile, but I actually begin to trust him. The anger comes first, I feel angry at everything … been angry forever.

Proudly, I tell Annie that I am now in therapy, she just looks at me. When she was in her 20's, she was in Freudian analysis with an older woman for a couple of years. *"Saved my life,"* she says, *"I woulda committed suicide."* She understands the *'work'* … realizing the great longing deep in the heart, the imprint from family and culture, the bullshit self-loathing lies that we carry, and the infinite array of 'medicines' we take to ease the pain. She looks at me with that no nonsense look and says: *"If you're just here to jerk off, do a quick fix till you feel a little better, then you can do this on your own, I am not interested. However, if you are serious, if you truly want to heal and know yourself, if you are ready to do the hardest work you will ever do, then I will be your friend. Think carefully before you answer me."*

I am at a crossroad. I think back on my childhood ... the *Halos* and street kids, a sexualized household, the constant domestic violence, the cops, the never-ending anger and fear and tension. I remember the dangerous times ... the insanity of the 60's, the darkness of my college years, the countless acid trips, the empty sex, the ongoing war and protests, the hard whack of a policeman's billy club. And the ever present need to be stoned all the time, as the loneliness and isolation and horror are unbearable. I have traveled the highways and byways of America, I have slept under bridges, fucked another man's wife, cheated and stolen to get a meal, and to feed the endless pharmaceutical hunger in my body. I have dark thoughts of suicide and death. I feel old, weary, lost ... way before my time. I look around at guys my age, they all look fine, except the ones who don't. Maybe they hide their shit better than me. Fuck, I feel naked, like my inside is on the outside.

Yet how many times, with my life on the edge of a razor, have I felt *'her'* close by, some energy guiding me through troubled waters to safe harbor. Invisible and unknowable, forgetting her more than remembering, still undeniably, she is there at my times of greatest need and terror. Could Annie be *'her'* in the flesh, here to guide me through this next passage? I ask her if she is my guardian angel, she says, *"... or maybe your worst fucking nightmare."* She grins.

My mother and father live nearby. I obligingly visit them, I have nothing to say. Yet I feel a pull, I just don't know what it is. When I'm with them, they piss me off, they are so out of touch. Even though my brother and I tried to teach them what rock'n'roll and the 60's was all about, they refused, they still refuse. I realize their stuckness, their small mindedness, they are not very smart people. They are no longer the imposing power that is imprinted in my little boy brain. I have my own agency, and some distance from them. I know they will be in the crosshairs of my work, and I am ready for this. This may be the first time that I actually begin to feel some real inner power. And all from saying: *"Yes, I am willing to look deeply at myself."* I know that this will take everything I've got. What I do not know, is how much more it will take, and how much it will give back.

Larry teaches me everything about his company's work. We are an importer and distributor of women's costume jewelry. He works downtown with his father, I love working on the inside. I bring my organizational and mathematical skills, and I don't have to cut my hair. They like my work, they like me. How strange that in my commitment to do my family of origin depth work, another *'family'* shows up to keep me grounded and supported. Little by little, the pieces to this huge jigsaw puzzle of my life begin to make sense. I become part of Annie's family, part of Larry's family, and increasingly distance myself from my blood family. I think about what *'family'* means: more than the blood one, maybe it doesn't even include the blood one, maybe it's who we feel *'kin'* with … who we *choose* to call family.

My therapy deepens. I start remembering things I have long forgotten. I am uncomfortable often, but I have stability. My outer life is solid, I'm making money, I have a car, a new puppy, an apartment, I'm OK. I have Carl and Annie, I can handle this. One thing troubles me … the guy who's apartment I share is part of the dirty crowd. While I have done my share of drugs, heroin is something that feels a little too dangerous. I like dabbling with it, I know its ecstasy. But I do not want its agony … and I like it way too much. These guys are constantly around the apartment, my roommate is deep in, I know I have to get out. Larry and I talk about finding a place together. It takes us awhile, but soon we find a little house in northern Westchester, about a forty-five minute drive to the shop. In early '72, Larry and I and my new pup Nina move to the country.

Larry and I have a friend from high school, Jeff is a year younger. His father owns a film company, lives in London. Jeff is married to an Argentinian gal, they live in Buenos Aires. Once quarterly, Jeff travels from BA to NY to London to Hong Kong on business. Long before Colombia and the cartels reveal themselves, Jeff carries some really nice blow on his trips to NY … Larry and I always have way more than enough. While I am in therapy, I still use. These days my daily routine includes coke, reefer, Courvoisier, camel non-filers.

I know that my inner work will not grow beyond my self-imposed limitations. I see clearly how my drug use defines those limits.

Nina is eight days old when I get her. She is a German shepherd, smallest one in the abandoned brood in the cardboard box, third one from the left. I bottle feed her for a month, I train her on the streets, she loves riding in the car, she finds a safe place inside my healing heart. When we get to the country, I mate her with a friend's black lab, Nina gives birth in the fall. Jeff is in town, staying with us. We invite Annie to come up, all of us together to midwife Nina and her babies. After many hours, Nina is exhausted, all the babies feeding at her breasts. At that point, Larry and Jeff and I are so stoned, we pass out, leaving Annie to handle the afterbirth. She is pissed at us, as she tends to the brood throughout the night. She tries to wake us … we snore right through it. Beautiful Nina, she delivers seven pups, three all black, four with mixed markings, all with down ears. We find homes for all of them, we decide to keep one. He's a little bruiser, mixed colors, a lovable mug, and he loves nestling snug in my lap. No name yet.

One night, I am watching the NY Knicks on cable. Dave Debusschere is having one of those nights, everything he throws up goes in. He rebounds, blocks shots, a triple double. With each sparkling play, I yell *"Debusschere!"* And with each yell, the pup turns his head up toward me. After a few times, I look down at the pup and ask him: *"Do I really have the balls to name you Debusschere?"* He looks up at me, licks his chops, and puts his head back down. Now it's Nina and Debusschere, both delicious beauties find their way into my home and heart.

The business is doing well, Larry spends more time at the showroom in the Empire State Building. He travels to France often, our vendors live outside of Paris, they send cases of brandy every Christmas. I anchor the distribution center in Yonkers, the drive is challenging for both of us. In late '73, we decide to move into Manhattan, find an apartment on W. 68th St, just off Central Park West. The dogs love the park, the city is a gas, we got money, drugs, women. Annie watches this, in her own way she understands, yet still wonders when I will finally grow up and face my sober self.

Coke attracts women, and there is no shortage. Darlene is tall and sexy, long black hair, loves the powder. One weekend we take off to a concert up along the Hudson. After three days of play, on the Sunday night drive home, my body is intensely feverish. We barely get home, I go right to the hospital. I have a hundred and five fever, I'm convulsing, they keep me on intravenous liquids for three days. I get home, grab my big coke stash, give it all to my brother. He thinks it's Christmas, I breathe a long-needed sigh of relief. Annie says to me: *"One down."*

Annie gives me books to read ... Freud, Jung, Nietzsche, Alice Miller, Arthur Janov. James Clavell, Kurt Vonnegut, JRR Tolkien, Toni Morrison, Tom Wolfe. Carlos Castaneda, Rajneesh, Gurdjieff, Ouspensky ... I devour everything I can get my hands on. I return to school to study psychology. During my college years, I majored in drugs and radical politics, a miracle that I got a degree. My grades were not good. Still, now that I'm in the city, I decide to take the LSAT exam anyway. I do surprisingly well, and apply to only one school, the Brooklyn College of Law. I know it's a long shot, I don't hear back for awhile, I wonder if they are seriously considering me. One day, a letter arrives in the mail ... *"After careful consideration, we are unable to ... blah, blah, blah."* Not surprised, a little disappointed, yet somehow trusting where my life is headed. And by this time, I cannot imagine actually being a lawyer ... I am way more into the psychological and mystical side of my life.

Annie and I go to see Arthur Janov speak. His book: *"Primal Scream"* moves through me like a hurricane. Having unplugged the dike, the raging river has been let loose. Annie holds the space for my fiery rage, then for my seemingly endless river of tears. I see how the two go hand in hand, how my anger has always protected me from feeling the pain and loss and shame and grief underneath. Since early childhood, maybe since conception, who knows before that … this pattern has finally revealed itself. Underneath my anger is always the terrifying pain below. With Annie, I unravel into the depths of my darkness, with Carl, slowly I put my pieces back together.

One Saturday afternoon, Annie and I are downtown, and we come upon an advertisement for a psycho-drama performance that evening. We head over to the west village, grab a bite to eat, then find this funky little out-of-the-way theater. We are shocked and moved by the material. There are about a dozen young women and men in the troupe, the director an older man named Alexander. He's been in theatre forever, teaches classes in psycho-drama, knew Fritz Perls. The changing vignettes depict varying combinations of individuals, couples, groups … exposing, revealing, challenging, confronting the darker textures of the psyche and its relational impact. Most of it is improvised role play, with awareness focused on seeing what issues we carry from the past that project into our present-day conflicts. The language is raw, the material so relevant to where I'm at right now. We stay after the performance, hang out with the cast. The folks are cool, open, funny, they tell us about the classes, the performances, their whole schedule. We tell them about us, where we are at and what we are doing. We smoke a little weed, drink some wine, they like us, we like them. They invite us to join them, Annie and I look at each other, we say: *"Great!"*

In my personal catharses, in therapy, in psychodramas … little by little, I unravel my past, it feels never ending. All of this material, buried underneath years of avoidance, pretending, covering up. Years of rage and grief, seething and unacknowledged, lying in the bottom of my belly. Years of projecting it at every turn, and here it is, in full living color ... my whole fucking shadow life. In our psychodramas, each of us speaks for the personal, each speaks into the collective. We release the dark energies, praying that there is something good underneath. Surprisingly, what arises from the ashes is relaxation in the body, peaceful, almost tender. Emotionally, my heart is alive. Having felt that black hole in my heart for so long, it is such a relief to breathe again, to feel love and tenderness.

In '77, I read my first book by Rajneesh. I listen to his tapes, his voice goes deep into my heart. His softness, his musicality, his intensity, his wisdom ... he brings a spiritual awakening in me that is altogether new. In college, I read a book on Zen, take a bunch of philosophy courses including one on religion, imagine I'd *'seen God'* in lots of places while tripping on acid and assorted psychedelics. But this is different. Maybe because there is more space within me, more room to land. I fall deeply in love with Rajneesh, and I contemplate going to Poona, India, where he lives. This feeling is new, I have never chased a guru before. His American followers have an ashram in northern New Jersey. I go to visit, see them all dressed in orange and burgundy robes with wooden beads. I roam through their bookstore, ask the folks some questions ... about Rajneesh, about the available books and courses, has anyone traveled and been with him? They are cold, standoffish, arrogant, like they have something to hide or protect. I think to myself: *"If this is how his students are, maybe this is not such a good idea. And while India is probably a fascinating place to visit, it's also fucking dirty. I don't think so."* Still, I love Rajneesh's books and tapes, and I continue reading and listening.

Living in New York City is taxing for the hardiest of people, it is a constant bombarding of the senses. Add to that, unrelentingly, it has its hands in everyone's pockets. Living right near Central Park is exciting and convenient ... for the dogs, for our access to art, theatre, music, architecture, museums, and a zillion great restaurants. To be sure, New Yorkers are wonderful when there is a crisis, disasters, strikes, protests. Otherwise, they are a hostile, obnoxious pain in the ass. Increasingly, I find this city life taking its toll on my body, and my sensibilities. I contemplate giving up drugs, and I can't imagine coping without them. Still, I cling to my camels, and I keep returning to the more creative places.

One day, quite by *'accident'*, I am cleaning the apartment, and on my bookshelf there are two of my unread books thick with dust ... Gurdjieff's *"Meetings With Remarkable Men"* and Ouspensky's *"The Fourth Way."* I sense a new readiness in me, I devour them both, their concepts about life and consciousness strike a deep chord. I see myself awakening, and importantly, more often than not *I see how asleep I am.* They both talk about mystery schools, secret places dedicated to the teachings of the masters, what Ouspensky's terms: *"the psychology of man's possible evolution,"* and what Gurdjieff calls *'The Work'.* I investigate, it's hard to find *'secret mystery schools'* in the yellow pages. Shortly thereafter, in one of my psychodrama classes, a woman mentions Gurdjieff. Excitedly, I ask her a bunch of questions. She tells me there's a *'Fourth Way'* school somewhere in Westchester called the *'Renaissance Group'.*

In early '79, I move out of the city, taking residence in an apartment complex in Tarrytown, middle Westchester. I take Nina. Larry keeps DeBusschere and stays in the city. Out of the hustle and bustle of New York, I find some peace up north. The complex has a pool and tennis court, the space is quiet with abundant foliage, I'm out of the city's traffic, it is a closer drive to the shop, and one of my first tasks is to investigate this Renaissance group. Turns out that they have a large *'teaching house'* in White Plains, not too far from where I reside.

The following week, I go to my first meeting at the house. There are eight people living together in this beautiful house, elegant but not ostentatious, and they are all friendly without being familiar. There are two couples, with two single men and two single women. They have a detached way of speaking and engaging, it is unusual, different than my street mouth, but not off-putting. They dress well, no one wears jeans or sneakers. They ask me many questions, I openly tell them about my past. They invite me to a musical recital at the house the following weekend, ask me to wear a coat and tie. They also invite me to come early for dinner. Strange though they are, I like their cordial formality, I like their attention to finer things, I like them. And they seem to like me.

In '80, Annie and her family decide to move back to southern California. Her husband, a musician, composer, and arranger, has a large musical project in LA. She is excited that I have found the Gurdjieff group, she believes it will be very good for me. And as she knows how much I will miss her, she is glad that I have found some friends. They move in the Spring, we tearfully depart after more than eight years in the work together. Once again, I feel that space in my chest, dark and cavernous, almost like it was before we met. This time, I weep and grieve the loss of this incredible human being, someone who has changed my life more than I could ever imagine. Someone who looked into my soul and saw my deep pain. And in spite of my *shuck'n'jive* bullshit, saw right through to the beauty and potential in my being. My time with her is special, my healing monumental. I am a different human being for having been in her teaching and in her company. She saved my heart, she saved my life, I am forever grateful. I know we will be friends for life, I know we can talk on the phone and visit periodically, I know I will miss her like crazy. And I know that I will be okay, because finally, I am okay.

The teaching house is a haven, I am fully and deeply connected to a group of people who are on this earth to awaken. I read all of Gurdjieff and Ouspensky's books, plus other related material. There are teaching houses all over the world, including a center in northern California, where the teacher of the US group lives on a private vineyard. Students travel globally to visit the various centers, teaching houses, and teachers. Two hundred students live and work at the vineyard, practicing the work in a communal setting.

I drop out of the psychodrama classes, I am grateful for the experience. Larry has found the love of his life, they stay in the city, our lives have taken different paths. On my own, living more simply, less sex and drugs, healthier lifestyle, I spend more time with the students and teachers. I am like a sponge … going to museums and learning about art, going to concerts and learning about classical music, learning about the friction inherent in all conflicts, precisely the friction that births awakening. Gurdjieff put all of his students through rigorous interpersonal exercises, to increase the conflict and friction potential, to practice the hard work of staying present, to learn to stay centered and non-identified with outside distractions, to build an internal discipline. The harder I work, the more I see my mechanical unconsciousness. I understand when Gurdjieff says that we are sleeping machines, programmable and highly predictable.

In late '80, Larry's brother joins the company at the executive level, accelerating their father's retirement. All in the family is wonderful in concept, excruciating in practice. Old family issues, the usual power and control, money, wives, competition, jealousy … plenty of unresolved material that inevitably finds its way into the workplace relationships. What was once a fun and funky place to work, has now become a drudgery. Watching the constant ego battles, I slowly withdraw. While I once imagined that there would be room for me at the executive level, I now see the writing on the wall.

In the spring of '82, at the teaching house in White Plains, the woman in charge asks if anyone is interested in building a garden on the property. Being a city kid, I have no idea how to do that. I never remember plants in our apartment, but I do recollect the greenery of my Nona's house. She had a green thumb, herbs and flowers everywhere, I recall the sweet smell of basil on her kitchen windowsill. So I raise my hand and say: *"Sure, I will."* Over the next few weeks, I do some research, get a couple of books, talk to some of the women at the house, and lo and behold, I build a garden. I create six or eight raised beds, mulch the pathways, plants seeds and small sprouting plants, fence it in, cover everything in plastic when the nights get cold. Thankfully, I live close by and enjoy being at the house. I love the physical and creative work.

My life in New York has become stable, my therapy is complete, I feel healthy. I sip a little brandy or sake when it's cold, I smoke a little reefer when inclined, I have a woman friend in the city with benefits … none of this feels out of control. I have purchased a condo in Tarrytown, have a good job, drive a nice sports car. I travel, got some nice threads, some money in the bank, have good friends at the teaching house.

One day in early '83, word circulates that the Renaissance vineyard in California is looking for help in their organic garden. Surprisingly, I find myself thinking about this option. I ask myself why I would even consider something like this. My life is good, stable … really, move to California? I think I might have lost my fucking mind. Still, I can't get it out of my head. I think how insane this is, yet the idea persists. Since the *'flower power movement'* in '64, California has always held an allure for me. Even though I have been there, it still pulls at my old hippie heartstrings. I'm a New Yorker by birth, but my heart is in San Francisco.

I talk this out with the folks at the house, they are encouraging me to take the risk. They remind me to trust my intuition, follow the invisible call, follow where the work is taking me. And it feels like the wind is blowing west. In April, I say goodbye to New York. My folks are a bit sad, but no real loss on either side. My brother has long departed with his wife to Florida. Larry is not surprised when I give notice. Annie is happy for me, knowing what a hard decision this is. I sell my condo, liquidate everything, ship a bunch of boxes to Annie's house, pack the car, and Nina and I head west.

At Renaissance, I take the job as an assistant gardener. The vineyard is not organic, but the garden is run by a local fellow, an old California stoner turned organic farmer, who knows a ton about large scale gardening. There is three and a half acres under tillage, *'Farmer John'* wants to expand to five acres this year … and my job is to weed and pull rocks. The community is eclectic, several women come to the garden daily to harvest and gather flowers. The work in the vineyard is rigorous, we work ten-hour days, six days a week, I put on some much needed muscle.

The evenings are transformative. There is a large Victorian house at the top the hill, parking lot down below. It houses a large commercial kitchen with an elegant dining room. It has rooms for study and quiet reflection, a library and film room, a small concert hall with a dance floor, paintings and sculptures all around, and vases filled with flowers. And a beautiful wine bar ... after all, it is a vineyard. The teacher lives in an alabaster house called the *'Academy'* ... Italian marble, European style formal dining room, French kitchen, a three-story library, climate-controlled wine bar with a million-dollar selection, a dozen bedroom suites for global visitors. There are rumors that he is gay, beautiful young men wait on the teacher's every wish. I have yet to meet him. The important vineyard personnel live on the property, others have RV's and Airstreams scattered about. Some folks have houses in town, a little nothing place called Oregon House. I rent a room in a small house owned by a couple, he Arabic, she French, they have a six-year-old daughter. They welcome me and Nina, I have landed, none the worse for wear.

The level of commitment to conscious learning is impressive. Still, the unconsciousness that births the everyday human drama is everywhere ... the intellectual snobbery, the *'perfect student'* act, the competition for the teacher's favor and affection, the creative disguise of the ego's power and control games. It is comical, and terribly seductive. I become more aware of the depth of shadows behind all human interaction, especially mine. I start to verify that Gurdjieff and Ouspensky are right on target ... humans are stimulus response sleeping machines. And I am one of them.

The summers are scorching, the melons heavenly. I crawl through tomato vines, they have end-rot and grasshoppers ... I cannot eat tomatoes for a year. I learn to drink wine, and eventually tend the wine bar. In the winter, I spend the workdays cutting manzanita in the pouring rain, freezing my ass off. The dining room has a huge roaring fireplace, lunch and dinner tables always have a bottle of red and a bottle of white. There is constant talk of the art and architecture of Europe, I am thinking of doing a pilgrimage.

In January '84, I buy a round trip ticket to Frankfurt, Germany, open-ended for one year. There is a couple who live nearby who fall in love with Nina, they offer to take care of her. I fly from Sacramento to New York to Frankfurt, landing in Europe in the chill of winter. While it is quite cold, there are also many less tourists. Germany is beautiful, cold and clinical, the language off-putting, I try to ignore my historical judgments.

A few weeks later, I take an overnight train from Munich to Vienna, arriving early Sunday morning. I'm cold, tired, couldn't sleep on the train, and it's raining. I store my luggage in a locker, and walk into town. San Stefan's cathedral stands in the center of Vienna. I walk in, it's empty well before mass. I sit in the back, just a few people scattered around the pews. I look up at the structure, the stained glass, the paintings and sculptures, the incredible Catholic iconography. I put my head back and just breathe in the ancientness of Europe, and the exquisiteness of this cathedral. The altar is beautifully decorated with layers of adornment. From the far side, I see men and women emerge onto the altar. I hear the organ warming up, looks like the choir is preparing to sing. And for the next full hour, they sing Bach hymnals in four part harmony. I feel like I have died and gone to heaven. After they depart, a priest in black robes ascends the altar and starts barking in German. I smile to myself, thinking: *"This is where I came in, it's time to go."* I recall Jeff telling me about the cafes in Vienna, and the very unique Sacher-Torte Cafe. I find it close by, it's Sunday morning, crowded, I order a double cappuccino and a Sacher-Torte pastry. Pretty soon, I am wired on caffeine, teeth-chattering chocolate, God, and Bach hymnals. I fall in love with Vienna.

For ten months, I travel by train across Europe … Germany, Austria, Belgium, Switzerland, Italy, France, England. Museums, churches, opera houses, historical monuments, walking the streets of the great cities, dining on the incredible food, meeting the people, traveling through the beautiful countryside.

One morning in Florence in early spring, I sit in the Uffizi, alone in a room filled with paintings by Leonardo DaVinci, Michelangelo, Botticelli, Rafael ... the greatest of high Renaissance Italian art. And I pinch myself, amazed and grateful that a kid like me, from the streets of Yonkers, New York, could be here doing this. I look around at all the angels in the paintings. They are looking at me, smiling with delight. I chuckle to myself ... thank you for reminding me, and thank you for getting me here.

There are Ouspensky's Fourth Way mystery schools' students scattered across Europe, living in teaching houses, accommodating to US students as we are to them. I take refuge in several of them ... their kindness and commitment to '*the work*', their generous hospitality ... I am grateful. For the first time, I sense the global impact of this work, and the great many people working on themselves trying to awaken. They give me a feeling of stability, a slight sense of home in a foreign land. Still, I am thirty-seven years old, I am alone, I know I must return to the US, I have no idea what awaits me. I write to Annie often, we talk as I am able. That dark feeling in the chest still haunts me, and as hard as I do my inner work, I know that something is missing. Often I imagine it is a life partner. As hard as I try to fill my own emptiness, I fail miserably. All I have is my writing, and my ache fills many journals.

Money starts to run thin, I think about returning to work in the US. I have experience in the business world, excellent organizational, management, and leadership skills. But the growing and evolving technology in the work place changes everything. I ran our computer systems back in New York, I consider going to computer school. I return back home in the fall, and go back to LA, visiting Annie, to start anew. Then I drive up to Renaissance to pick up Nina. The couple who were supposedly caring for Nina had let her go a month before, she was sleeping under a car when a nearby friend took her in. She has cataracts in both eyes, serious hip dysplasia, my heart breaks with sadness, guilt, and shame. She is so happy to see me, I hold her close, I cannot let her go. We drive back to LA, I find a teaching house, and Nina and I move in. I attend computer school for six months. Happily, I am successful at learning this important skill. I see Annie regularly. After graduation, I apply for jobs. I have several interviews, nothing feels right yet. In the meantime, Nina declines daily. I bring her over to Annie's house as often as I can, we sit outside, loving on her, remembering the old times … I dread what is right in front of me. I look at Annie, and through my tears say to her: *"It's time, isn't it? Time to put her down?"* Annie puts her hand on my shoulder: *"Yes, it is."*

It is May '85, Annie and I bring Nina to the vet. He gives her a sedative, giving us time to say goodbye. When we're ready, he gives her the injection … in seconds she is gone. The boy who shut off his tears at nine years old and rediscovered them at twenty-four, is now a man who weeps freely for almost everything tender. I weep for having left her behind, for the times I treated her badly. I weep for my own selfishness to move on with my life. I weep for the loss of my best friend. I weep for all the love that she has brought to my heart. And I weep in my final goodbye to Nina.

I cry for three straight days. Annie cries right along with me. A week later, I get a job interview with Electronic Data Systems. EDS is run by Ross Perot, the Texas billionaire. It has large government and military contracts, EDS is run military style. And it is supposed to be a great place to work, learn, and grow. Naively, I look at the upsides, don't stop to consider the culture. I get hired, my first assignment is in Portland, OR with the Bonneville Power Administration. In two weeks, I'm in Portland. I rent a small furnished suite in a downtown hotel, once again, I am on my own … less damaged, more centered, more focused. The job is easy, learning my way around the technology is challenging. Everyone on the project is busy, I have no real mentorship, and a lot of downtime.

There is a woman who has an office down the hall. She has a PhD in something to do with water conservation, and she is one of the top people on this project. I stop in to say hello, introduce myself, we talk for an hour. Over the next few weeks, we get to know each other. Even though we're from very different backgrounds, we find some common ground ... literature, art, music, food, motorcycles ... she has a Honda 750. She lets me take her bike around town, I like riding in front of and behind her. We cook a couple of meals together, go to the movies, she drives me around Portland, showing me the parts hidden from the tourists. It is magnificently beautiful, and the summer weather is exquisite.

She is about my age, never been married, her clock is ticking. It's easy to charm her, she is vulnerable; we lay together for the first time. I like her, I like being with her. And I am not ready for a relationship, and knowing I am here only for a short while makes this safe. At some point, I will go to school in Dallas, EDS headquarters, it's part of the program to train systems engineers. But I am here till at least the Fall. In this exchange with her, I get a glimpse of my desire, maybe even need, to be in a constellation with a woman. I also see how I fear entrapment, commitment, getting too close. I know the issues with my mother are driving this pattern. Being friends with Annie was safe, it was vertical, she as teacher, I as student. Going horizontal is different, something powerful is at play here that I do not understand. Given my history with women, I wonder how many I will love and leave before I learn this lesson. I have never asked myself that question before this.

In mid-September, I drive to Dallas. I take classes in Computer Theory, Assembler, and Cobol. Most of the students already have degrees in computer science, many of them have programming experience. I am in new territory, as programming was not the area I took in computer school, I was in operations. The class starts with thirty students. The instructor is right up front when she says that less than ten will continue on. I do not recall in my interview the seriousness of Phase 2 of this program. Yet it makes sense. Phase 3 is a full-time job assignment at a client site, and EDS wants to ensure that only the best get to work with clients. I try to imagine what I will do if I wash out … not a pretty picture. Instead, I buckle down to work, I commit to giving this everything I have. My lack of experience shows up in class, as I ask rudimentary questions that everyone else seems to know. I can tell from their faces that they think I'll be gone at the first cut.

Ha!, I say to myself; they have no idea how tough I am at crunch time. So I keep on asking questions, sometimes the teacher even gets annoyed. Yet she answers my questions nonetheless. To everyone's surprise, I make the first cut, and the second. For the final third, three months later, we have to deliver data on a multi-layered, complex set of programs. I am one of eight who make the final cut. Everyone, especially the teacher is surprised. Even *I* am, and so fucking happy.

The last week of class is when jobs are assigned. I have strongly petitioned for a California assignment, anywhere but the East Coast. Mid-week, there is an envelope on my desk with my assignment … I am headed to Ft. Sheridan, IL, an army base just north of Chicago. Fuck … *Chicago in the winter*, I know no one there … fuck. That weekend, I am packed, loaded, and take off for Chicago. It is mid-December, I start in ten days.

I make it up to Chicago in two days. Thankfully, EDS has been paying me weekly since my first assignment in Portland, so I have some money saved. In my last paycheck, they also include some money for moving expenses. I check into a little motel in Highland Park, and look for a place to live. A young man is offering a basement apartment in his house in Highwood, not far from the army base. I meet the guy, he's a young smart ass, but nice enough. I tell him my short story, I rent the apartment on a month-to-month basis. It is furnished, comfy, cozy enough, good heat, with a little kitchen. I buy some basics, I know this is short-term. I check out the base, it's just an ugly shit-colored bunch of wooden buildings, ugh. I think: *"Man, I coulda been living in one of these fifteen years ago as a soldier. Better this way than that!"*

PART II: *Awakening*

In '85, Chicago is alive with *"Da Bears."* I remember when I was a rabid Knicks or Mets or Giants fan, the fever is magical and contagious. The Giants come to Chicago in the playoffs, the Bears kick their ass. I watch the game with a bunch of young guys in the house, they bust my balls big time. I grin, eat crow, I've done a lot of this same shit in NY. Still, I am no Bears fan, no fan of the second city at all. It isn't called the Second City for nothing, Chicago fans don't seem to get that.

The folks at work are eclectic. The project bosses are all men, ex-military, the crew is run with lots of rules and regs. There is a small local software company who has a portion of this contract, their programmers, all ex-military guys, working alongside the EDS crew. The rest of the staff are all kids, maybe a dozen twenty-two to twenty-eight year olds, many just out of college with a computer science degree. They are all cheery, some with their first job, bright as hell, innocent, naive, and anxious to get to work.

Boy, am I in the wrong place. From the get-go, I am the round peg not quite fit for the square hole. Still, I have a blue collar work ethic, so I roll up my sleeves and dig in. It is my first gig like this, I have lots of technical questions. The kids are helpful, but the older guys from the other company are more experienced. They like to work the night shift, so when I roll in early in the morning, they are still hanging around, talking shop, a great time to shoot the shit and get my questions answered. I am assigned some projects with these guys, so my early learning curve is deep and steady. I have always been a whiz in math, and I quickly come to understand that programming is not about math, but rather the ability to hold complex relationships mentally in abstract space.

As soon as I get the basic rules down, I am off to the races, finishing my projects on time, quietly going about my business, and not getting involved in the chit-chatty bullshit of office politics. I am up early, into the shop by six-thirty, out at three-thirty. I join a local gym, start taking aerobics classes, I am in the best shape of my life. I find a small apartment in Evanston, just north of the Chicago line. It houses Northwestern University, sits on Lake Michigan, has funky and offbeat neighborhoods, shops, bookstores, restaurants, and cafes. I trade in my Celica for a small black Fiero with a sun roof. It's not New York, but I begin to feel at home here.

Chapter 10: Chicago

At the shop, the kids are only too happy to put in the extra hours that the bosses expect. They are all working fools, putting in sixty to seventy hours a week, all for a forty-hour a week paycheck. When my supervisor asks me why I am not putting in the extra hours, I ask him how many hours he is paying me for. We never much talk after that.

As you can imagine, the dress code reflects their rigid corporate attitude. Most of the higher ups have traded in their khaki camouflage for the corporate uniform ... dark suits, white shirts, solid or striped ties tight at the throat, cap-toes or wingtips. One lovely morning in July, temperature already ninety at o-six-hundred, I put on my light weight beige suit, a white linen shirt open at the collar, pale yellow tie knotted loosely, and a pair of tan Italian shoes, white socks. I walk in the front door of the shop, bound up the stairs two at a time. At the landing stands the boss man, a forty-five year old hardass who did two tours in Vietnam. He's got thick coke-bottle glasses, tight-assed in his spit-polished uniform. With legs apart, and hands on his hips, he looks me up and down, says in his most militant voice, pointing at my shoes: *"Those are not EDS issue!"* I automatically come to attention, trying hard to hide the smirk on my face. I salute him and bark back: *"Yes Sir!"* From that point on, I know in my bones that my EDS days are numbered.

So many times, I wonder what the fuck I am doing here, working at this unlikeliest of gigs. With no easy answers forthcoming, I divide my time between work and the rest of my life. I like Evanston, it's a cool place to live, the lake, restaurants, cafes, music venues. I go to Chicago to visit the museums, see the fabulous architecture, and check out their great food joints. In Evanston, there is a great little bookstore across the street from the espresso joint. They have a nice poetry section, one day I pick up a book by this guy named Robert Bly. 'Male consciousness,' now that's an interesting idea, I like what the guy has to say. The Evanston Reader has an ad for a men's group that meets at one of the community colleges west of town, I decide to check it out. It is winter '86, I've been here a year already.

I notice that when I get lonely and need someone to talk to, I call a woman, usually Annie. Although I still have some old male buddies in NY, I do not let them see my sensitive side, my body remembers the cost all too well. I think about my brother, I miss him. When I call, he tells me about his baby daughter and married life, our worlds are so different, we have been disconnected for a long time. As I read Bly, I feel something new stirring inside me. When I spend time in the men's group, I am aware that the conversations focus on the usual male talk ... work, money, women, sex, sports. For me, something is missing, something deeper, I can't name it.

I have a woman friend in New York, an old fuck buddy. I call her one day, we reminisce, catch up on the superficial stuff, I ask her if she wants to come out for a visit. I pick her up at the airport that weekend. For the next week, we go out to eat, drink, movies, museums, and fuck. She returns to New York the following Sunday. I drop into a dark funk.

> *From that inner darkness emerges a valuable insight ...* **sex is not the answer.** *How many times have I had sex and end up feeling like this, that familiar hole in my heart ... sad, lonely, empty, longing ... for what?*

In the act of coupling, the great potential for union is in that moment. Yet I miss it, over and over and over again. In the pursuit of sex, my cock participates, my head participates, my seductive creativity participates, but my heart does not participate. In that moment of disturbing awareness, I make a promise to myself ... I will not have sex until my heart is in it. Not necessarily in love, nor marriage, she does not have to be the woman of my dreams. I simply want to feel something in my heart, to feel present and connected, and not want to run away. For the next two years, I date a few women, I tell them this, they look at me strange. Still, I remain celibate. As Annie would say: *"Two down."*

It is a cold Thursday morning in early March 1988, sun just coming up over Lake Michigan. The sky is already a crystal blue, and people are filing into the cafe for their morning shots. Removing gloves, unwrapping scarves, blowing on numb hands, they dip their noses into the steaming coffee and for that one brief moment … aaahhh. The cafe sits off the corner of Main Street in Evanston right under the railroad tracks, a quick ride into the city. The cafe is always jumping, the work crowd in the morning, the mothers and kids and Northwestern students during the day, the musicians and artists and night owls at night. The place is a gold mine, always crowded. Their coffee is terrific, the foam on the latte perfect. The pastries are delicious, I love dipping my croissant or scone into the hot coffee. Reminds me of Pappy and the Caffe Puglie in New York.

Micki and I sit at a back table sipping our lattes. She teaches psychology at Northwestern. She is heavy-set, bleached blond middle-aged punk, snappy and sassy, smart as hell. I love talking to her about all kinds of stuff. She is a feminist in her politics, but she adores men, loves to fuck, and has a deeply intuitive sense of the dance between the sexes. We like to talk sexual politics, and we meet regularly at the cafe for breakfast and early morning intellectual stimulation. I often talk to her about the men's group that I joined. Being with men hits me someplace deep, makes me think about the *Halos*, athletics, I miss the male camaraderie. But this men's group doesn't touch that achy spot. I say to Micki:

"Last night I had this dream, one that I often had as a kid. It is dark and I am running away from someone. I know that I have felt paralyzed in this dream before, with my pursuer usually overtaking me. But this time I am surprisingly nimble and I outrun him. It is always a hooded man … dark and threatening, dangerous, scary. I don't know what he wants from me. Yet now, strangely, I consider that he may want to give something to me. I awaken and realize, for the first time, that I am deeply sad."

Mickie loves picking apart my dreams, especially the sexual ones. I have a pretty good dream recall, she and I have been able to decode a lot of what goes on in my psyche. I trust her, her integrity, her insights, and her ability to hold my vulnerability in confidence. Over the years, this is why I have gravitated to women to talk about my inner world, it just never feels safe with men. Guys just never seem to quite get what I am talking about, like I am speaking a foreign language. If it isn't sports or business or politics or sex, most guys are just not savvy about the inner world. It is frustrating, my current group is frustrating. I tell Mickie how this dream is familiar, where the man is often my father or Poppy, I cannot tell. She pulls out a book from her briefcase, opens to a poem, and reads this to me:

Those Winter Sundays
Sundays too, my father got up early
and put his clothes on in the blueblack cold,
then with cracked hands that ached
from labor in the weekday weather,
made banked fires blaze.
No one ever thanked him.

I'd wake and hear the cold splintering, breaking.
When the rooms were warm, he'd call,
and slowly I would rise and dress,
fearing the chronic angers of that house,

Speaking indifferently to him,
who had driven out the cold
and polished my good shoes as well.
What did I know, what did I know
of love's austere and lonely offices?
Robert Hayden

I feel an ache down deep inside me, like dropping a rock into some bottomless cavern. I think about my father, about Poppy and Pappy, about my brother … I have no men friends, I have no men friends. I hang my head, I am stunned at how deeply this hits me. I recall the camaraderie on the playground, in the gang, on baseball and basketball teams throughout my entire youth. We loved each other in a way that we did not know how to articulate. In my personal life, in athletics, in the military, I see it in every group of men who are part of a larger whole. Not only is it competitive, it is cooperative … it is both. There is nothing more beautiful to watch than men working together toward a common goal … when aligned, we are a force of nature. I see now why this men's group does nothing for me, it has no goal, it has no deep purpose, it has no soul. I crave the deep and sacred masculine.

I share this with Micki, tears fall from my achy heart. Micki smiles, pats me on the shoulder, she senses the gravity of my insight. So I ask her if she knows of any ass-kicking men's groups. She smiles, crinkles her nose and says: *"Funny you would ask me that, as a matter of fact, I do. I have a colleague, a male therapist named Dave, who has a new group called 'The Warriors' He just told me about it the other day. And here you ask … "*

That evening, I call Dave, ask him about his group. He says they are having a workshop that coming weekend, I tell him I already have plans. He tells me the next one is a couple of months away, I tell him I want to go. He tells me to send him a hundred dollar deposit, he will send me paperwork, I say okay. I ask if he could tell me something about it. He says no, see you then, and hangs up. I say to myself: *what the fuck.* I am single, forty, and celibate. I am in a deep not knowing about myself and women … open yet discerning, no urgency, not chasing. Now I am to let go of the old men's group, and step into this whole other thing, with unknown men. Something is changing in me, it is scary, it is exciting.

Mid-afternoon on Friday May 6, 1988, I drive north up into Wisconsin, to a camp in the Kenosha woods. The paperwork sent to me is cryptic … directions, arrival time, bring food for six men … nothing else. I have absolutely no idea what will happen, so I pack some layered clothing … sneakers, walking shoes, shorts, jeans, t-shirt, a sweatshirt, jacket, and a NY baseball cap. It is a warm lovely day, I am in no hurry. Listening to music, top open on my car, I wonder what lies in front of me. Told to be there between 5 and 5:30, I pull off the main road just after 5. Driving down the dirt road heading into the camp, I arrive at a crossroad. In the center, a man is standing ... six foot four, black hair, long beard, black clothing, a large staff in his hands. I pull up next to him, roll down my window. He just looks at me for a full minute, then says:

"What is your name and why are you here?"
"I'm Dene, I'm here for the men's workshop."
"What time were you told to be here?"
"Between 5 and 5:30."
"What time is it now?"
"Quarter after 5."
"Follow this road till you see that man."
"Thank you."

As I slowly drive away, my first thought is: *"What the fuck have I gotten myself into?"* I feel fear, and my exact next thought is: *"Fuck Yes ... it's about fucking time."* I feel relief and excitement, that maybe, just maybe, I have found a place where men talk about real shit. Because in that moment, I realize how much I need a change, and how ready I am for just about anything.

My initiation into this band of brothers is life-changing. I discover a capacity for leadership that has long been dormant. All my previous work on family of origin issues comes sharply into view. Challenged and confronted to flesh out my old concepts of men, opening me to feel deeply what is in my body, awakening the *'wild warrior-like nature'* of the deep masculine, pushed and encouraged to take a brutally honest look at the hidden shadows that unconsciously drive my life ... I liberate a part of me that has been imprisoned since childhood. I discover a deeper, more intelligent language and context for what emotionally moves through me. I feel alive and awake.

I notice how many white-haired men are here. I think to myself:

"If old men are here, this must mean something." There is a group of them sitting on the floor at the far end of the pit. I tumble off the working carpet into their arms. They hold me, smile, stroke my hair, wipe away my tears. One old grandfather says: *"Welcome home."* All at once, my past makes sense, my unknown future stands before me, and here I am. I get home that Sunday night, look at myself in the mirror, and smile. I think: *"Who is this guy?"*

They call themselves the *'New Warrior Network.'* Originating in Milwaukee in '84, Bill Kauth, a self-declared feminist therapist, sees the rapid growth of women and the feminine consciousness. He also sees that men are stagnant, not growing personally and collectively, the way women are. He is friends with two other men in Milwaukee. One is Ron Hering, a professor at the University of Wisconsin, the other is Rich Tosi, an engineer with General Motors and a former marine captain. Bill brings them together one night, and as they sit around Bill's kitchen table:

Bill: *"We should do a training for men."*
Them: *"Why the fuck should we do that?"*
Bill: *"Because there aren't any."*

They go to California and take Justin Sterling's *'Men, Sex, and Power'* training. When they come home, they cobble together a training, originally named: *'The Wildman Weekend.'* It debuts in Milwaukee in Jan '85, and immediately gains traction. They rename it the *New Warrior Training Adventure,* and men begin to come. It moves down the pike to Chicago in '87. I find it in early '88. I am the 300th man initiated into the *NWN.* Our network is comprised of several hundred men, each committed to helping himself and other men heal. This *'MensWork'* quickly becomes the focal point of my life. Truly, I have a new self-awareness, a quiet power, a feeling of integrity and strength, a long lost sense of belonging and brotherhood … this time with a group of men who are awake and working on themselves. This inner work moves into the foreground of my life. The Network offers a follow-up series, and an opportunity to staff the next training. I am hungry like a wolf ... I say yes to everything. I have ready access to the handful of men who are the teachers and leaders here in the mid-west. I do the *'integration'* training, then join a weekly circle with several men that I initiated with. We are alive, raw, honest, deeply emotional, with in-your-face confrontations, holding nothing back ... I have found my tribe.

I devour every book on *'MensWork'* that I can get my hands on ... Robert Bly, Sam Keen, Warren Farrell, Aaron Kipnis, John Lee, Joseph Campbell, Carl Jung. I am alive in the work, the work is alive in me. As I look around, I see very few men alive like this. I am changing, morphing into another version of myself whom I do not yet know, but am quickly becoming. My relationships with men are different, no longer viewing them through the lens of competition, more through brotherhood. I think a lot about men in general. I see them/me/us in pain, yet we deny this terrible truth. Since the crib, we have been bred on competition, fed false ego beliefs that real men are strong and in control, don't show emotions or vulnerability, are always ready for sex, are tough and successful, and never cry.

I remember my first initiation into the *Halos*, how different *this* initiation is! How many years have I spent in pain, numb in the heart, tough on the outside, big black hole on the inside, drugging, sexing, pretending? I realize that I do not have to live like this anymore. These few courageous men have chosen a different path, I am now choosing to walk this path with them. It is a path of brotherhood, men committed to resurrecting ancient values of the masculine ... real love for each other, integrity, accountability, fierce clarity, ruthless honesty, loyalty. And the modern necessity for men ... emotional literacy.

This is true MensWork, turning our eyes to the inside, shining a light into the shadowy places, discovering what broke our hearts and shut us down. Then daring to open the heart, feeling the pain, and risk getting it broken again. Coming to understand that when we let the heart break open, love comes out.

Part III: Marriage & Family

Chapter 11: Ming

She is tall and well built, bigger than my mercurial body is used to. But when I look at her face, something stirs inside me. She is a hostess at the Blind Faith Café in Evanston. It is Fall of '87, I get out of work late, stop in for some dinner. She seats me at a corner table, I take off my coat, loosen my tie, close my eyes, and take some deep breaths. The year has been hard ... my beautiful Nona has passed away, I am disconnected from family, I hate working for EDS and the US Army, I feel lonely in the mid-west cold. I can feel that old familiar achy hole in my heart. I eat quietly, and when I get up to leave, she smiles at me. I am hungry for tenderness, still searching for a heart of gold. *"Is she the one?"* I often ask myself that question. I smile and walk out the door. Over the next few months, I return to the Blind Faith often, hoping to see her again ... but she is gone.

A year later, two weeks after I do the New Warrior Training, I walk into that cafe. A woman at the nearby table turns, looks at me, and offers a sweet hello. Surprised, I smile back, she looks familiar, I can't place her. I keep looking, trying to remember, nothing lands. She is with a group of people, I hope she will look at me ... not a glance.

That Saturday, it is warm along Lake Michigan, I am walking back from the beach to my car. Down the middle of the street, I see a young woman with two young kids approaching. They are laughing and frolicking, and as I look in her face, I say: *"I know you from somewhere, where do I know you from?"* She tells me she said hello to me the other day at the Blind Faith. She says she used to work there as a hostess. Aaahhh, now I remember you. *"Are these yours?"* I say, pointing at the youngsters. *"No, just baby-sitting."* I smile, take a deep breath. Her name is Mignon Mead, she tells me that her Japanese teacher calls her Ming.

Our first date is the Chicago Blues Festival in Grant Park. We sit on a blanket, not saying much. When she gets up for a soda, my eyes follow her, I think to myself: *"I like this one. I know nothing about her, but I have this feeling, just like I did the first time I saw her."* I have been attracted to many women over the years, but somehow this is different. I feel both scared and excited.

Over the next few weeks, Ming and I go to the Mets/Cubs game at Wrigley, we see Sting in concert, we walk along the lake, we talk about our past, our families, our dreams and fantasies, what excites and scares us. She is ten years younger than I, our backgrounds and tastes are so different. While we are attracted to each other, we choose to stay vertical. I tell her I have been celibate for two years, she tells me she has been celibate for one. She has recently completed LifeSpring Advanced, I say I am equally passionate about MensWork. Courtship is the time it takes to get to know someone, to discover likes and dislikes, similarities and differences, to see if the energies align. At first, we show only the good stuff, do our best to hide the funky stuff. I'm made of fire, I like to fight, Ming's made of water, she flows away. Honestly, we do not have much in common … except our passion about the *'work.'* She is a Montessori teacher, works part-time at the Blind Faith, the lease on her rental apartment is up soon, she is scheduled to go to teach in England. I know my days at EDS are numbered, each of us is in a deep not-knowing. She lets go of England, we find an apartment in Evanston, and in six weeks, we move in together.

We struggle through the first year. I have not lived with a woman in a long time. Fighting and arguing is my love language, avoiding and retreating is hers. One day Ming says to me: *"I need to leave."* I say: *"Where are you going?"* She says: *"No, I am leaving you."* And for the very first time in my life, what I have worked so hard to protect against, my worst nightmare, worse than my mother's wooden spoon, I am left flat. Something cracks open inside me that day, my heart aches with an altogether different pain ... the real one, the deep one, the one below everything else. Since childhood, I have shut all of this down. In therapy, I talked about it, but never let myself come close to actually feeling this pain. Because I never let myself care enough about any woman. Instead, I charm the girls, hustle their panties off, then run away. Time after time after time, always managing to stay safe, not letting myself emotionally need them. Typically I'd come, shower, then walk out the door.

> *Until now, my heart has never participated in my sex ... unconsciously designed to protect me from feeling this. With Ming, I have let my guard down, let my heart open, and now I am face to face with what I have always feared the most.*

I am a zombie ... rage and tears and screaming and wailing, long periods of deathly silence. I quit EDS. Day and night I walk the streets alone, disheveled, I can't eat, can't sleep, can't do anything. I walk along, shuffling with my head down, can't even look at a woman, as everyone triggers me. I walk past where Ming lives, both praying and dreading that I will see her. I avoid the Blind Faith Cafe like the plague. My hair grows on my head and my face, I barely wash myself, I am a fucking mess. Thankfully what I do have is a mature married male therapist and my men's integration group. A thread of the work is alive in me, I know I am deep in my mother complex, and even at my ugliest, these men still love me. That they get me through this is a miracle, as each day, multiple times a day, I consider ending this horror.

Four months pass, and one Friday night, I return from a powerful therapy session. I have put some pieces back together. For the first time in a while, I have an appetite. I think: *"What the fuck, if I truly want to heal, and reclaim my own power, I have to see her again, sooner or later. I'm going to the Cafe."* I walk in, and not seeing her, ask the boss where Ming is. *"She's not working tonight."* Whew! That Sunday morning my phone rings. Ming says: *"I hear you were looking for me ... wanna go for a walk?"*

We meet in a park along the lake. She looks good, I look like shit. We walk and talk, just like we used to, we both have changed. Ming acknowledges her father issues, his judgments and harshness, her tendency to run away. I reveal my fear of abandonment, my mother's abuse, my neediness and sexual dysfunction. We know that our time away was both messy and necessary. For we have each constellated a new awareness of our underlying psychic patterns, our respective love languages, all at play in our unique dance. The question that hangs between us: *"Are we still willing to do this work with and through each other?"*

I travel to LA to visit my dear old friend Annie. The first morning, we sit in her backyard drinking coffee, I bring her up to date on everything. She looks me in my eyes, like she has a dangerous piece of truth to tell me. I shudder as she says: *"I never thought I would see this day, the day when you would give your heart away. This is your love story, dear friend, as you have finally fallen in love. I know it hurts like hell, and you look like shit. Still, I am so proud of you."* We laugh, we cry, we remember all the work that we did together, how far I have come, I am so grateful. I feel myself ready to say yes to Ming, ready to let go and see where it goes. I am forty-two years old, and finally I feel like a grown ass man.

One night a few weeks later, Ming and I are on the phone. She says: *"I know that I love you, but I don't know if I'm in love with you."* I say: *"I love you every which way, and I can live with you or without you … so I'm in. When you decide, let me know."* Really? I actually said that? I am shocked to hear those words coming from my mouth. That following Sunday morning, early like 5:30, I hear a knock on my back door. Who the fuck, I think, and open the door. She walks in, gets down on her knees, and swears to me: *"You're the one."* She continues: *"I ran away because you needed me too much, it scared me. That you can live without me gives me breathing room. I can do this."* I smile, and consciously realize that underneath my false bravado, underneath my resistance to ever need a woman, underneath my ego's incessant protection … I am needy. Now it is clear … this is my real mother wound.

We move from Evanston to Chicago that October. We are better than before, but still stuck in lots of places. Our reactive patterns continue, strong defenses resistant to change. We fight, we fuck, we make up, we dissect our patterns. I feel increasingly grounded in this relationship, trusting in our mutual commitment to the work, and to each other. Ming does the Woman Within workshop, avidly reads and talks to me about co-dependence. I talk to the guys in my group about this relationship, my growing fondness for Ming. I think about getting engaged, I am already looking for a ring. Most of the guys are married, of course they delight at my changes. That next weekend I find a beautiful antique diamond ring. I snuggle it into my inside coat pocket for safe keeping. Christmas is a couple of weeks away, Ming and I plan to visit her family in Detroit, I plan to propose.

Each of us has seen each other's parents only once. From my earliest therapy, I recollect that whenever I visit my parents, I inevitably react to something they say or do. It doesn't much matter what, the buttons are here inside me, and they automatically push them. Naturally, I get triggered. They cannot help but do this … after all, they put them here in the first place. Unaware, parents imprint their unconsciousness onto their children, with its accompanying wounds, conflicts, and hot buttons. In the absence of any defense, we cannot help but internalize them. Ming and I recognize this mechanism at play for each of us with our respective families, so we make an agreement that when we visit, we will be conscious allies. When we are with her family, I am the watcher for her reactions, when we visit mine, she is the watcher. The watcher's job is to track the other's reactions, and offer the gentle reminders that the buttons within have been triggered. We remember that this is all our core stuff coming up, the raw material for our healing and real change.

On our drive up to Detroit, we stop for lunch at a nice country restaurant, I had made a reservation. It is Saturday, a couple of days before Christmas. The weather is gorgeous, snow on the ground, a crystal blue sky above, sun warm and delicious. We sit down, Ming goes off to the restroom. I take the ring out of my coat pocket, and place it on the table. I move it around, trying to figure out how to make the best presentation. Ming is gone for what seems like an hour. With each minute, my agitation increases. There are other people in the restaurant, I tell them what I am doing, they laugh at my crazy nervousness. Ming finally comes back to the table, tells me that she's been on the phone with her sister. Everyone is quiet, waiting for the crucial moment. I take the box out of my pocket, open it, and quietly ask if she will marry me. She looks at me astonished, she had no idea. When she says yes, the whole restaurant applauds. With red face, I reach out my hand, we stand up, we hug and kiss, and take a bow together ... we are officially engaged. In my own quiet reverie, I think: *"Wow, amazing that I've reached this place, so often I imagine that this day would never happen. In my twenties, two women proposed to me, I declined immediately, I knew I was way too fucked up. Many times, I found myself resigning into bachelorhood. Now this. I have a softness in my heart that is new. I think about both my Nonas, about Annie, about my angels ... all the women who have loved me. I see them all smiling."*

We arrive in Detroit by nightfall. At dinner, we make our announcement, the family is excited and happy for us. The next day is a busy one, preparing for the Christmas Eve party hosted by Ming's mom and dad. The whole family will be there ... uncles, aunts, cousins, nieces, nephews. In the late afternoon, Ming's dad calls me into his study. He is tall, handsome, full head of white hair, very patrician, a lawyer. He is seated at his desk, invites me to sit opposite him. He says: *"Congratulations, young man, on your engagement. Mignon has told me about the two of you, but she did not tell me this. I see that you love each other, and I am glad for you. However, as her father, I have some questions for the man who is taking my daughter's hand. First, what are your intentions, and second, how will you support her?"* I am not surprised at his paternal questions, actually, I am quite moved that I find myself sitting here in this kind of inquiry. I considered that her dad might do this. I respond: *"Well sir, thank you for your acknowledgment, and I hear your questions. Please know that I love Ming very much, we are good with and for each other. I intend to love her to the best of my ability. We are both working, we enjoy Chicago, we have no plans on kids or marriage anytime soon … we're good."* Then he says: *"Thank you, I sense you are good for each other. And … I hope you realize that she is a delicate flower."* I say: *"Yes sir, I see that, and I will do my very best to treat her gently."* He says: *"Dene, you are a fine young man, and my wife and I extend our blessings to you both."*

That evening, over cocktails, Ming's dad makes the announcement. The women squeal, the men clap me on the back. They are a large, boisterous, rowdy drinking family, and they are not shy. They seem to like me, we're joking already, I feel welcomed. I have not felt this connected to family since my childhood, when my Italian grandparents and extended maternal family gathered for a wedding, birthday, anniversary, poker, pinochle … great food, lots of booze, music and dancing, dirty jokes, always some kind of crazy shit or argument. This here is not Italian, but it's way good enough. Ming and I welcome all the congratulations.

Later on, I see Ming's dad, along with her uncle and cousin, they are all standing at the bar. It looks like they are talking about tennis. I walk up and ask if they are tennis players. Over the top of his glasses, Ming's dad looks down at me and says:

"You play? Did you bring your sneakers?"
"Yes, of course, on both counts."
"We have a match tomorrow morning at eight am at the club. You and I versus these two guys."
"I'll be there."

I am not a real good tennis player, but I have good legs, and I can hold my own. That morning, I chase down every ball, returning several for winners. We trounce our opponents, as I earn my first brownie points with my future father-in-law. Over the years, we disagree about many things, but we never quarreled, we were always on good terms.

It's Christmas, everyone is drinking, everybody's shit is up, including Ming's. We go for a long walk along the lake, Ming talking through and processing her reactive material, especially the alcoholism. We acknowledge the value of this unique opportunity to be able to do this together, with each other, for each other, a practice worth repeating, which we do regularly over the years. Nonetheless, we have a good time in Detroit with her family, we return to Chicago engaged, satisfied, and aware.

One morning in early '90, Ming bolts out of bed and declares: *"My dreams tell me we need to move to the Southwest."* Ming is both intuitive and impetuous. They are often intertwined, I can't tell the difference, as I struggle to trust her voice. I know my own impetuousness, I am just learning to trust my intuition. Chicago is cold, we are tired of the mid-west city life and weather, we both think a change will do us good.

We keep talking about rehab, about our mutual co-dependence, imagining that we need help breaking these large patterns. Ming is not an alcoholic like many in her family, but acknowledges her co-dependant issues. In late January, she checks into the Cottonwood Rehabilitation Center in Tucson, AZ. A few weeks later, I drive down from Chicago for family week. After rehab, our plan is to explore the whole Southwest. Ming's parents come for the week, neither is able to acknowledge the alcoholism … in themselves or in the lineage.

When Ming gets out of rehab on a Tuesday morning, we decide to explore Tucson for a couple of days. This time of year, the sky is a deep crystal blue, the sun a warm seventy, beautiful dark-skinned students from University of Arizona walking around in shorts and t-shirt. The city is part Latino, part Native American, part cowboys and bikers, part students, part snowbirds. Rugged mountains surround the city, calling to the spirit in each of us … it's hard not to love Tucson in the winter time.

My old friend Larry from New York, along with his wife Toni have recently moved to Sedona, so we head in that direction; it's a

Thursday afternoon. I recall to Ming my dear friendship with Larry, working together, Nina and Debusschere, living in Manhattan, doing drugs and women. I tell her about Toni, a beauty from Savannah, a great cook, and a world-class astrologer. We turn right on I-10, head north up I-17. The sun is going down, the colors across the rising red landscape saturated. I look over at Ming, and even though rehab tells us not to do anything rash, I impetuously say: *"Let's get married this weekend."* She looks at me wide-eyed, just smiles with that loving look in her eyes and says: *"Yes!"*

We get in after dark, Toni and Larry greeting us with a sumptuous meal. After being thoroughly filled, we sit in front of the fireplace to stretch out and catch up. We finally get around to telling them about our wedding plans, that we want to marry in the sacred red rocks. Grinning, Toni says: *"Let me do your marital astrology chart."* Excitedly, she takes out her astro books and a yellow pad, and for a half hour she scribbles and mumbles and laughs to herself. Finally, she looks up at us with a big grin and says: *"You guys have about ten percent in common ... but that is probably enough to make this marriage work. You have a lot of work to do together, but because you truly love each other, you can do this. And here is the best part: tomorrow is a perfect day for you to do this, but you must marry before 3:30 in the afternoon."* Full bellied, and drunk on love and possibilities, we all shuffle off to bed.

Friday, February 23, 1990, we awaken to sunshine, cloudless blue sky, crisp cool air. Sitting at the kitchen table, feasting on dark rich French Roast coffee, OJ, eggs and sausage, fruit and toast, we sketch out our day. Larry calls his friend Tom, a non-denominational priest and medicine man, tells us to meet on the red rocks around 2 pm. As soon as we can gather ourselves, we head down the pike to the town of Cottonwood to get a license ... it is 9 am. The woman at the desk has a cousin named Mignon, our first sign from above.

We move fluidly throughout the day, with all sense of time and space falling away ... everything falling into place exactly as necessary. We buy new clothes, all in white. We buy rings and flowers, enjoy a lunch at an outdoor cafe. Right next door is a native jewelry store, where we buy an exquisite pair of turquoise, silver, and beaded feather earrings for Ming.

February in Sedona attracts tourists, and the Pink Jeep tours are everywhere. We are headed to the Airport Vortex, and imagine a crowd. Tom the priest meets us at the bottom, we all hike up the hill. To our delight, the top of the red rock is completely empty. And to our continuing amazement, a perfect circle of yellow cornmeal lies on the ground. With blue sky, red rocks, yellow sun, and perfect circle, we all step into the container. Tom consecrates the space, smudges us each in turn, and we all fall silent. Looking around, breathing deeply, grateful for the energies that have brought us here together, appreciating each other and the magic and synchronicity in our lives ... Ming and Dene lovingly exchange vows. Larry snaps pictures, Toni just smiles. Tom gives us paperwork to fill out ... we walk off that hill at 3:15.

We drop off the film and go home to consummate. Back out to pick up the film, we dine al fresco at the nicest restaurant in town. We sit under the stars and twinkling lights, eating, drinking, feasting, celebrating ... we are home by 9 pm. A perfectly fluid, simple, magical, loving, spirit-filled twelve hour wedding day.

Chapter 12: **Tucson**

For the first eleven years of my life, I watched all the men in my life: my father, both my grandfathers, the guys at the factory, the cronies they hung out with, the kids on the street, and their fathers act hard and tough, pretending that they don't feel pain. I saw a guy get slashed in the guts with a knife, then brag about his wound. I watched a kid get his face almost bitten off, then show off his scar. I observed young men on the battlefield of sport get legs, arms, shoulders, knees, ankles broken. Later on, I watched these same young warriors go off to war, come back shattered on the outside, broken on the inside, many didn't come back at all. These beautiful and gallant young men, across the whole culture, valiantly lived out the mottos and credos passed down from father to son, for generations.

In salute to the invincible, impregnable, invulnerable ... I see a man's life is the systematic construction of a suit of armor, spit polished, full of metals which he shows off to the world ... laying claim to his manhood. I watch our culture lay bricks and mortar in building the pantheon to Zeus and his fucking sky gods.

I remember a 50's movie about Crazy Horse, played by Victor Mature. I always liked the guy, a strong and gentle man, put into difficult situations, not afraid to cry. He has a handsome hang-dog face, with dark soulful eyes, dark curly hair, the tears stream down his rugged face. This is one of the few models of the time where a man is both fierce and tender. We have four movie theaters along Broadway. During the week, me and the guys scrub up money, hustling small odd jobs in the neighborhood, returning empty soda bottles for coin. On Saturday, we walk down to one of the theaters. There are three nearby, the other way down Broadway, near the Bronx line. Walkable, but a pain in the ass to get to.

One Saturday in late October '57, Robbie and I go to a special at the Strand Theater ... *Frankenstein, Dracula, The Werewolf,* twenty cartoons, all in one afternoon. We go in at noon, get out after six, it is dark and windy, and our houses are far away. We start walking home, we see monsters inside every shadow. We are so scared, we both start to cry, running as fast as our little legs can carry us. When we turn the corner onto our block, Robbie, who lives near the end of the street, runs into his house, leaving me alone to make my way up to the end of the block. The longest run of my life, I am crying, sweating, shivering all at the same time. Yet just before I get upstairs to the apartment, I stop. I know I can't go into the house with tears on my face. So I wipe my eyes with my sleeve, blow my nose, take a deep breath, and bop into the house like nothing has happened. My folks are watching TV and ask me if I had a good time. I give them my best cover up smile, and say yeah cool, and walk into my room.

TV in the 50's is filled with cowboys ... Roy Rodgers, Tom Mix, Hoppalong Cassidy, The Lone Ranger, Wild Bill Hickok. The good guys wear white hats, always win. Every day, I don my cowboy outfit, shirt and pants, pearl handle 6-shooters, matching boots and hat. I am the baddest little fucking cowboy on the block. In the theaters, they show lots of Cowboy and Indian movies, where the Indians are always blood thirsty monsters, the cowboys or the cavalry riding to the rescue of some innocent homesteaders encroaching on Indian land. I never quite get that one. Even though I like my cowboy outfit, I think the Indians are so beautiful ... their teepees handsome, horses magnificent, long black hair stunning. These are not really savages, there is something very wrong with this picture. The other guys usually root for the soldiers or the cowboys, I secretly root for the Indians, but they never win.

In June '90 it is my turn to go to rehab, for both co-dependence and drugs. Ming comes for family week. My parents are now living close in Sun City, AZ, so with no excuse, my mother drags my father to family week, but my brother does not come. They quietly listen, don't offer much. My family of origin work proceeds without them, no surprise.

Ming has been staying in Tucson with the friend she stayed with when she was here in January. The woman has a big house in the desert on the outskirts of Tucson. She has two grown kids, and plenty of room for us if we want to move here. Ming and I do not have to think too much about this. So in early August, Ming and I and our two cats move to Tucson. A New York street kid out here in the wild west, I say to myself: *"Wow, Tucson, I hope that real cowboys and Indians live here."* My initiation and education in MensWork is very much alive in me, but there are no men's circles here. I'm pretty sure that cowboys, Indians, and bikers aren't interested, but then again, you never know.

By the first week of September, I land a job in tech, I know it is temporary. I place an ad in the Tucson Reader, offering a New Warrior men's group. I am surprised when half a dozen men sign up right away. My skills sharpen quickly, my teaching lands well, deeper in some men. I bring both a NY edgy sharpness and urgency, with a compassionate heart. And I am a newly-married man. I am feeling this strange sense of purpose, my life is being led somewhere.

Right after Christmas, downtown Tucson has a Native American parade. It is sunny and warm that Saturday. The streets are filled with booths and food stands, native peoples everywhere. We love the costumes and jewelry, the feathers, horses, the drums and dancing and rhythms, the bright eyes and rich dark skin, and especially their hair. Long and black, straight to the waist, decorated with feathers and beads, both women and men … they are exquisite. Ming buys earrings, I buy a turquoise and silver bracelet, and I vow to not cut my hair for awhile.

In January '91, we buy our first house. It is small and funky, in a nondescript neighborhood on the east side of town. Closer to work, we turn our small third bedroom into a sacred space. I paint one wall a dark turquoise, decorate it with native pictures, books, feathers, candles and sage. We both begin to meditate regularly, we listen to spiritual and native music. Ming and I drive up into the Catalina Mountains, we bring sacred medicine. For the first time, we recognize that this is no longer recreational, it is healing medicine, done with sacred intentions. While we honor our 12-step healing, we each know that spirit is calling us in a way. There are issues in our relationship that we are peeling back, we trust that this medicine will help open us further. We find a safe and enclosed grove on the mountainside, we set up our little camp. We offer a prayer of blessing and safety for our journey, then we ingest the medicine. While we were told that this particular medicine is designed to open the heart, this is not what happens, for either of us. Ming leaves the campsite, she is physically tumbling down a dry gulch, deep in a past life regression. I sit alone in a grove of trees overlooking the edge of the mountain. This vision unfolds:

> *A small group of native people encircle me, both women and men. The chief is an older man, long gray hair in braids, feathers adorn his leather vest. He and an elder woman stand in front of me. She speaks first: "They call me Running Deer. The ancient chiefs and shamans and medicine people have been returning to the Earth for many moons, and we come now in this time of Her greatest need. Coming from the mountains and deserts and jungles and forests across the planet, we return to help the people re-member who they are, and their right relationship to the Great Mother. She has been generous, and the people have been selfish. They have forgotten the Circle of Life, they have forgotten the Giving, they have forgotten themselves. We believe that you can help others remember."*

> *Running Deer steps back and the chief steps toward me: "I am Standing Falcon. You were here with us not long ago, we are glad that you have remembered the ancient ways. Many are returning to usher the people through the End of Days. Men especially need a new medicine, one that will awaken them from their collective trance. This MensWork is your medicine for this lifetime, for it will transform you, and you will teach other men to transform. It is a dangerous time, many will perish, the outcome is not guaranteed. Please remember who you are, and do this essential work. Always remember that we are with you."*

Ming and I reconnect and exchange stories about our respective journeys. Something deep is arising in and between us, something for our individual and marital healing, and something for the healing of others. The love between Ming and me is strengthening, we know that our lives are being called. Still, much divides us. We work hard on our relationship, we see the projections and our own unresolved issues that lie at the core of our conflicts. We read many books, attend local teachings and workshops. She has her circle of women, I have my circle of men. Ming talks about having children, my warrior work is growing. While I am still working through my childhood issues, I do not yet trust my capacity to be a good father. I swear that I will never be like my parents … good luck with that! The neural pathways from childhood are etched deeply in my brain and body. They have been repetitiously traveled down, they are tried and true. And they are not going away anytime soon.

On our second medicine journey, Ming and I find a quiet space on the top of the mountain. It is late winter, the air is cold, where we sit has no wind, the sun is warm, we wrap ourselves in blankets. We sit cross-legged, opposite each other, knees touching, holding hands. We offer our gratitude and intentions to the spirit world. Our prayer for this journey is for more light in our relationship, show us the core stuff that keeps us stuck, help us heal our old fear-based patterns and projections, and love each other and our own lives more deeply. Only then can we truly help others.

With the words just out of our mouths, I feel my body contract … an ache in my heart and fear in my gut. I say to Ming: *"I am afraid to love you, and afraid to let you close to me because … "* Then I begin to name the ways that I hold back, the ways I protect, defend, avoid, deny, project. The ways I use my ego, and my anger, the ways I manipulate, seduce, misdirect, abandon, withdraw. The ways that I blame, accuse, shut down, distract, medicate. And then Ming says: *"I am afraid to love you, and afraid to let you close to me because … "* Then she names her withholds.

This goes on, back and forth, for four straight hours. We do not let go of each other's hands, we do not get up. We stay connected, through all the hurt of the raw truths that are spilling out of each of us. Finally, when we are fully drained and exhausted, with nothing left to say, we sit in silence and just look at each other. As we gaze into each other's eyes, bright and shiny, wet with tears, there is nothing but love. We realize that having rung this bell of truth, it can never be unrung. We have just recommitted ourselves to each other, and to a much deeper, more profound intimacy.

> *Of all the crazy stuff that we are doing, this is as wild and risky as anything so far. It is both a blessing and a warning. To speak a deep truth to a loved one about her is scary. To speak a deep truth to a loved one about myself is terrifying. I make a conscious choice to be open and revealing. Most men think that vulnerability is a weakness, we are well trained to stay inside the tight structures of the 'manbox' masculine. Marriages and intimate relationships suffer as a result, as both the love and the pain in the hearts are kept hidden. Today Ming and I make the most important choice of our life together ... to consecrate this marriage, to make safe this container, to honor each other's vulnerability, and to commit to our own transparency. This day, we discover that real authentic power is the willingness to speak one's deep truth with a vulnerable heart.*

In February '91, the San Diego men's community offers its first New Warrior Training Adventure. With Tucson not that far away, and San Diego the first and only training center outside the midwest, it feels almost like the work is coming to me. I have two men from my first group willing to drive with me to SD to do the training. I know many more will come. I remember Standing Falcon's words: *"Men especially need a new medicine, one that will awaken them from their collective trance."* My heart is grateful.

The training is staffed by mostly local men, as well as men

from Orange County, Los Angeles, and San Francisco. Men come from Santa Fe, I bring my two guys from Tucson. All these individual communities begin to strengthen in this MensWork. In April '91, I get a phone call from Rich Tosi: *"Dene, you are now a co-leader of the New Warrior Network."* I say: *"Wow, really? Thank you."* He says: *"Yeah, congratulations, we have lots of work to do, see you soon."* and hangs up. Prior to San Diego, my last NWTA was a year ago in Chicago. I have a twinge of fear and excitement to be back in the container again, doing the deep delicious soul work. I also know that I have been sharpening my arrows in the groups that I am running. I feel proud, elated, and ready to kick this thing up a notch.

From '85 to '90, all the trainings occur in the Kenosha woods, with Milwaukee and Chicago the only offering centers. From here, the Network Council arises. They know that the work is growing fast. The concerns are many ... leadership development, skill building for staff, integration group development for follow-up, standardized protocols used everywhere. Layer in organizational administration, finance, certification panels, the politics of welcoming new brothers across the US and even abroad, many want to offer the training in their home communities. I am one of those brothers, and Tucson is moving in that direction.

In Dec '90, Minneapolis is the first to come online after Milwaukee and Chicago. San Diego follows immediately after. The Network is in serious startup mode. The training in San Diego is a significant learning for me. Facilitating in a small group is one thing, facilitating on the *'Warrior carpet'* is something else ... this is where the real shit happens. While in Chicago, I studied with all the master facilitators, I trust the work that is alive in me. My group teaching builds more self-trust, still I am young in the work. This training offers me valuable and painful feedback.

Saturday afternoon, a man is on the carpet, I am co-facilitating with Michael, the best of my Chicago teachers. The man's head hangs down, his body carries a ton of shame. Thinking that I might be able to shock him awake from this trance, I spit on him. He raises his head, looks at me with tears in his eyes, and drops his head back down, he is deeper in shame than before. Michael steps into the process and delivers the man into a tender, quiet place. The staff takes a break. Inside the staff room, I sit in a chair in the corner, reflecting on what just happened on the carpet. Soon I am in my own deep shame. *"I can't do this, I'm never gonna be good enough ... I can't get out of my own shame, how can I ever help a man get out of his?"* The sobs are full-bodied, tears fall heavy, I am forlorn. Just then, Michael comes over and sits down beside me. At first, he simply puts his hand on my shoulder, and lets me cry. As my tears subside, he says: *"Look at me. You learned a valuable lesson out there today ... that men always reflect to us our own unresolved issues. These are the very things that we react to in each other, we constantly project our pain and unowned stuff onto the other. All us men carry the same archetypal wounds, this one is shame. Unconscious, it does damage, both to the man, and to the whole container. Conscious, it helps deliver the man, and all of us, from the throws of insidious toxic shame. Learn this lesson, for you will see it often. Learn this lesson, and you start to heal yourself, and other men. Learn this lesson, and you will be a great facilitator. Because Dene, you can do this work."*

I take some deep breaths, drink some water, and ready myself for the next round. I greet the first man who steps onto the carpet, and I deliver him through his entire healing process. Michael looks at me and smiles.

In April '92, I bring a man from one of my groups to initiate in San Diego. Ed is the first man to turn into the work as much as I. When he returns and shares his experience, the group accelerates, as now there are two of us on fire. Ed is a counselor, and shortly after initiating, he tells me that he has a contract with the City of Tucson to counsel men who are arrested for domestic violence. He asks me if I could help him create a program for these men. My mission had found me.

We open an office together, and we run a series of six-week programs for battering men. Having come from the NY streets, I have an instinctive camaraderie with these men, I know where they come from. Abused, violent, alcoholic, addicted, many uneducated … these men are in deep trouble, causing a lot of pain in their wake, and deep shame and damage to themselves. One courageous man's sharing provides an awakening that hits me the hardest, something that informs my lifelong commitment to emotional literacy in men.

He says: "In that moment, just before I put my fist in her face, I realize that I have no resources. I do not know what to say to her, I do not know how to silence the insanity in my head. I do not know how to slow the adrenaline and speed and alcohol in my blood that has me seeing red. The only power that I have left is in my right fist."

Men's violence does not arise from power, it arises from powerlessness. In the face of a woman's instinctive capacity to shame a man, and in the absence of his own internal communication resources, she renders him helpless. He is overwhelmed, under the influence, adrenaline flooding the brain, his instinctive body in a *'fight/flight/freeze'* state of unconsciousness … he calls upon the last remnant of power that is available to him. And if he has been abused, or witnessed abuse in his earlier years, he easily tends toward violence. Very few men who come to our group get it.

One man, a former Hells' Angel, comes with me to SD to do a new warrior weekend. Shortly after stepping on the carpet his rage fills the room. The muscles on his big body bulge, his tattoos dance on his back. When he is quiet, the facilitator whispers something in his ear, and the man breaks down in tears. It is increasingly clear to me that after every man's rage is every man's pain. And the medicine for that pain is grief. As my man steps off the carpet, his eyes are all wet and soft. To see his 'fierce and tender' is exhilarating.

Chapter 13: **Dakota**

When Ming and I meet, I am forty, she thirty. She is a certified Montessori teacher at the school right next to the Blind Faith Cafe. I visit her classroom, the kids ages three to six, so precious, and she is so good with them. We do not really talk about having kids, she says she is open, I say I'm not ready. Here in Tucson, we talk some more about a family. We now have a house, I have my work, we have friends and community, and we're a bit older. I do not sense her biological clock is ticking loudly, still she is thirty-three. The subject comes up more often, she has a clear yes in her body, I still hesitate. I know I have some clean-up work still to do if I dare choose to embark on this next rite of passage.

In my twenties, I declined marriage, I knew I was way too fucked up, I would only do damage. Now I am more mature, I have worked through a lot of issues. Yet I know how deep the imprints run, there are enough old patterns that keep me hesitant and untrusting. I am not troubled by this, my eyes are open, I trust my growth process, I sense myself readying.

By '92, I am in high demand to lead our men's trainings. I am in San Diego every few months, bringing more Tucson men to strengthen our home community. Since the early days of the New Warrior Network, one of the mainstays in our trainings is men smoking cigars. While it feels ancient and deeply masculine, it also feeds my nicotine addiction. I started smoking when I was ten years old. Most of my adult life I have smoked camel non-filters. So smoking cigars is no big deal. My jones does not go away when I come home. I try to hide my smoking, but Ming has a nose like a bloodhound. She tolerates this, doesn't say much. Yet I know she doesn't like it, especially now that we are in the baby conversation. I have kicked this habit before, having stopped a dozen times. Yet somehow I always find a way back to my camels. Both parents smoked throughout my whole childhood, even before, when my mother was pregnant. She had a heart attack in '75, and quit smoking. My father traded his butts for cigars, took him a few more years to kick them. I vow that I will not bring this to our baby. This is one nasty habit, and I am finally ready to break my nicotine addiction.

In September '92, I do a training in San Diego. I bring a pack of unopened camels, I do not smoke cigars at all. On Sunday morning, I make my way down to the fire pit, there are a couple of men tending the fire. I tell them my story, they gather around the fire, they pass sage smoke over my body for a cleansing. I take out the pack of camels, look at it for a moment, then say out loud:

"You have always been a good friend, since I was very young. You were always there, you never said no, you always delivered exactly what you promised ... something to fill the deep hole within me. That hole where the pain, rage, fear, shame, grief reside. That hole that I have been afraid to see and feel. Thank you for safely hiding this from me until now, the pain at the root of my addiction. I will be having a baby soon, and I do not want to pass along this curse. I am now truly ready to look at all this emotional material, I am ready to go deeper in my healing. So here, today, I declare my own liberation from this nicotine addiction. I thank you for what you have given, I am ready to be without you. And for the last time, I say goodbye."

I hear Annie say: *"Three down."*

That November, I am invited back to Chicago to lead a training. It feels like a homecoming, I am humbled and excited to be returning to my MensWork roots. I am heartily welcomed back, it is fantastic to see so many old friends and teachers. At the Saturday night staff meeting, I am sitting on a comfy couch, the room is noisy, we are all on a high from the great work of the day. On the floor are four young men, maybe eighteen to twenty, they had initiated only last month in Milwaukee, they have come to dance. They seem eager to hear what I have to say ... about carpet work, about men and MensWork, about women and marriage. The words and ideas come easily, my discourse fluid and integrated. I have this funny feeling in the moment that I am old enough to be their father.

On the flight back to Tucson, the United magazine has an article by Kent Nerburn entitled *"Letters to my Son: A Father's Wisdom on Manhood, Life, and Love."* He tells of taking his eight-year old son to Atlantic City, NJ, where his father took him as a boy. He tells about his wounds and learning, and how much he has healed his father wound through having a son. I recall the conversation with the four young men, I think of Ming, fatherhood feels much closer. Arriving home that night, I walk into the bedroom, Ming is sleepy but awake. I love that she stays up for me when I come home from these trainings. After four days with men … the raunchiness, the irreverence and the sacred, the rage and the grief, the beauty and power of men doing soulwork … I am so ready for Ming's warmth and loving. I take a warm shower, snuggle in close, we are tender and juicy. I tell her about my experience with the young men, then the article on the plane. I tell her I am ready for fatherhood. That night we are together, without any barriers between us, just she and I and our loving intention to bring forth a new life.

Ming quits her job in early '93, she's already preparing … feels like something in the unseen world is guiding us. She is comfortable in trusting spirit's collaboration, I am slowly getting there. We throw away our contraception, we enjoy our openness, spontaneity, fluidity. We know we're in Kairos non-linear time, we know we're in invisible hands, we know we're in a deep knowing, and we trust that we will be delivered through this. For the very first time in my life, my heart is wide open, and I am ready for my next initiation.

Late one afternoon in May, I come home from work and Ming has this funny look on her face. She says to me: *"We're having a baby!"* We laugh with delight, we hold each other close, we are both grateful and excited. Ming has already envisioned this, she knows she is in the Great Mother's Hands. I'm almost forty-six, and I'm scared … not about having this baby, more about being a good father. My childhood, the streets, my NY instincts, my anger … all have conditioned me to not trust. Yet my life has been held by the unseen since I was nine years old, maybe before. At times I am deeply torn, my fear is palpable. But my life right now, this exquisite woman, my MensWork … all reminding me of something else. I remember the angels, spirit guides, grandmothers, and the indigenous who have forever danced in my constellation. They have never protected me from the pain and the struggle… that is always my task. Yet they have guided me through the initiations, through the trials, wrestling with my own karmic demons and darkness, always delivering me into the light. I have moments of great terror, I have moments of awakening. In my deep soul, I trust all of this. Honestly, this feels so new, and now all too real. Fortunately, the magic guides the way, with the self-doubt never far behind.

The summers are hot in Tucson, Ming's mom and dad buy us a big beautiful air conditioner for our bedroom. The first few months are rough, Ming has morning sickness. She wants a home birth and a birthing tub. We invite three close friends to be with us; they gratefully accept the honor. We find a highly recommended midwife, Ming tells her what she wants, she is in alignment with all of it. One afternoon, I come home and Ming says: *"I have such a hankering for teriyaki chicken. The Yokohama Rice Bowl is close by, let's go now."* She scampers from the air-conditioned bedroom to the air-conditioned car in no time flat, and in ten minutes, we are sitting in the restaurant. I am unable to recall how many times we do this, seems like almost every day. My mother craved pizza with me, hot dogs with my brother. I never could handle pizza, my brother never liked hot dogs. I wonder how our kid will feel about teriyaki chicken.

Ming carries beautifully, she is plump and full, her eyes sparkle, her skin glows like the sun. Must be the chicken. Making love is slow, everything unfolds easily before us. Neither of us likes doctors, our midwife takes us to a woman naturopath. She checks Ming and smiles: *"Keep doing whatever you are doing!"*

Most of our friends are my age, their kids gone, some have grandkids. All the men who have followed me into the work, have witnessed the work that Ming and I have done to get us here. Ming has the older women who bring their experience and wisdom. They all love having a new one coming in, we feel so blessed to be safely inside this container of love. As we lay in bed at night, we place our hands on Ming's belly and talk to the being inside who has picked our lives to enter. We do not know the sex, don't really want to. Ming thinks it's a boy, I am open.

We both have learned, me haltingly, to trust that Spirit always gives us just a bit more than we can handle. Whatever it is that this being brings, it will stretch us good, me especially. I actually feel as pregnant as Ming, as I imagine that I am birthing a new me. Ming senses a Native man close by, regularly smells tobacco, sees her own past life with this tiny being within her. I sense an indigenous woman, an Amazon, as if she has been with me since I was a boy. We talk about names, Ming's body responds to boys' names better, my male ego feels proud, like I imagine that I actually have some-thing to do with this. We play music at night, a variety of genres for our baby to hear. Whatever it is, it'll be a rock'n'roller, with both a fierce and tender imprint from each of us. I sing boy songs like James Taylor *"Sweet Baby James"* and the Beatles *"Beautiful Boy."* We play spiritual music, blues and soul, country and doo wop, 60's, 70's, 80's … we play it all.

One Saturday, Ming sits in her women's circle, which includes two Native American women. They ask her about names, she says she thinks it's a boy, but no names so far. Suddenly, Ming picks up the scent of tobacco. She recalls a past life and someone named Dakota. Later that night, while lying in bed talking about what happened in the circle, Ming holds her belly and asks: *"What is your name?"* She offers some that we have been considering, nothing. Then she asks: *"Is your name Dakota?"* And the baby kicks. She asks some others, nothing. Then she asks Dakota again, another kick. Ming looks at me and says: *"I guess our baby's name is Dakota."*

We find this article to read:

"In some African tribes, when a woman knows she is pregnant, she goes out into the wilderness with a few friends and together they pray and meditate until they hear the song of the child. They recognize that every soul has its own vibration that expresses its unique flavor and purpose. When the women attune to the song, they sing it out loud. Then they return to the tribe and teach it to everyone else. When the child is born, the community gathers and sings the child's song to him or her. Later, when the child enters education, the village gathers and chants the child's song. When the child passes through the initiation to adulthood, the people again come together and sing. At the time of marriage, the person hears his or her song. Finally, when the soul is about to pass from this world, the family and friends gather at the person's bed, just as they did at the birth, and they sing the person across the river to the next life.

In the African tribe there is one other occasion upon which the villagers sing to the child. If at any time during his or her life, the person commits a crime or aberrant social act, the individual is called to the center of the village and the people in the community form a circle around them. Then they sing their song to them. The tribe recognizes that the correction for antisocial behavior is not punishment; it is love and the remembrance of identity. When you recognize your own song, you have no desire or need to do anything that would hurt another. A friend is someone who knows your song and sings it to you when you have forgotten it. Those who love you are not fooled by mistakes you have made or dark images you hold about yourself. They remember your beauty when you feel ugly, your wholeness when you are broken, your innocence when you feel guilty."

Alan Cohen, author of "Living from the Heart."
"They're Playing Your Song"

Early Feb '94, Ming is full bodied and more than ready. We rent a birthing tub, set it up in the back side of the living room. The whole space is full of soft chairs, couches, and pillows. Candles, sage, sweetgrass burn sweetly, the body oil is warm. A big music box remains on, our favorite music filling the house. While it is cold outside, our home has never been warmer.

Late Tuesday afternoon, Ming goes into labor. The midwife and our friends arrive in the early evening, I have put out some food and drink, the music is on. The energy feels safe, warm, sacred. The conversation is easy, but Ming is uncomfortable. The baby had shifted the day before and Ming has some serious back pain. Joe is one of our friends, he is a Rolfer, he is in my men's circle. Joe has the most beautiful hands that we have ever seen. He massages Ming, she has temporary relief, yet her pain grows worse. The midwife monitors Ming, says that she is doing well in spite of the discomfort. She is dilated 4-5 cm, the baby is strong, we still have a ways to go. This continues, well into the night. No amount of massage gets Ming pain free. Her dilation remains half way. Then in the wee hours of the morning, the midwife says that the baby is in distress, Ming is in serious pain, and we should go to the hospital. So at six am we take Ming to the Tucson Medical Center. We are surprised that the docs and nurses are so relaxed with us. They give Ming an epidural, and tell us that they are willing to wait for a natural birth. We both breathe a sigh of relief, and suggest that our friends go home to get some sleep, we'll call you when anything changes.

Ming is in bed, I sit next to her, we talk to our little one inside. *"We're all OK, we're safe, we are here waiting for you, take your time, just be healthy."* The nurse comes in routinely, checking Ming, checking the dilation ... we get to six cm. And there we stay till well into the afternoon. At around four, the doc comes in and suggests a C-section, the baby is in serious distress. We surely do not want this option, yet it makes the most sense. We talk it over, we honor what is happening, and at four-thirty they wheel her into the operating room. I follow shortly thereafter, quickly washing up and into scrubs. I remember that place of prayerfulness and trust, I breathe deeply, I know we all are okay.

On Wednesday Feb 9 at 5:04 pm, Ming delivers a boy into the world and into our lives. They wash him, wrap him in a warm blanket, and give him to me. I take him to Ming, place him upon her chest. She holds him close, I hold them both. He is healthy and beautiful, we are grateful beyond measure. Soon Ming and baby are rolled into a room, he is asleep, we are both exhausted. I am torn between staying in the small bed in the room, or going home for a good night's sleep. Ming wants me to stay but I need some sleep. Reluctantly, I kiss them both goodnight, I'll see you in the morning. I am more afraid than I realize, for I am a father for the first time, at forty-six years old. Oh my God!

I arrive bright and early the next morning, Ming and baby are sleeping. I sit next to them, Ming awakens, we kiss good morning. She says: *"All night I have smelled tobacco, I know this baby is accompanied by native spirit guides. He is definitely Dakota."* Of course, we both love the name, we wonder about his middle name. Later that afternoon, Ming has the TV on, we are watching our one and only soap. They have a character named James, we remember the song *Sweet Baby James,* we remember uncle Jimmie from San Diego, we both like it. Welcome to this life, Dakota James Mead-Shikaly.

Our community showers us with gifts and support. Our friend Nonine makes him a Native American vest, moccasin booties, with turquoise beads. She gives him a native blanket. I watch with delight as Ming breast feeds Dakota, they both sleep so peacefully together. I notice a twinge of jealousy in me … I push it away. As spring approaches, the weather is warmer … stroller, car seat, carrying pack, we three are constantly mobile. I love holding him, bouncing and playing, getting a feel for who this little being is. Our friend Alexandra is a hair dresser, she of the purple hair and exquisite paintings. She recommends her friend Ani, a world class astrologer, to do Dakota's birth chart. He is an Aquarius, cool, thoughtful, analytical. Often with his hand in my chest, he welcomes affection on his terms. He eats and suckles and sleeps well, he is a healthy joyful baby. And he loves music.

At home, we watch the winter Olympics, the OJ Simpson drama plays out on TV. While we paid the midwife in cash, we do not have insurance. We await a hospital bill in the mail, it sometimes keeps me up at night. I do my best to remember that we are not in charge. Late one afternoon, I had just come home from work, the telephone rings, Ming picks it up. It is the Tucson Medical Center, we both listen.

> The woman says: *"I work for the hospital, helping folks who fall through the insurance cracks. I have a stack of papers on my desk, and yours just dropped into my hands. Please tell me about your money, what kind of work you do, how much do you make, I need all of your information."*
>
> *I tell her about my work, being self employed as a coach, how much I make each month, our house and mortgage payment, savings, etc. She writes it all down, then she is quiet for awhile while she does her calculations. Ming and I look at each other anxiously, waiting to hear what is next. After a few minutes, she says to us:*
>
> *"Given your work schedule, how you are paid monthly, I believe we can work the numbers where you would qualify for support. I will fill out the paper work, then we will all meet with the adjuster, who will tell us what will happen. Keep the faith, I'll see you soon."*

A week later, we meet at her office. We go over the paperwork, we verify the numbers, we sign the docs. Then she walks us down the hall, into the adjuster's office. He is a middle age man, jovial build, with a deep southern accent. He gets up to shake our hands, and his name tag says *'James Taylor'*. Ming and I look at each other in astonishment, we smile. He reads the paperwork, and for the next ten minutes runs the numbers through his large calculator. Finally, he looks up, takes off his glasses, and with that sweet southern drawl says: *"I do believe that you will qualify!"* We sign some more papers, and leave his office. Our gal says: *"Congratulations, we're done."*

For months, we await paperwork, something from James Taylor or the woman angel or the hospital … nothing. To this day, we never received anything, and have no idea the cost of that beautiful experience. What we do realize, once again, is that we have angels in our architecture.

However, something strange is happening inside me. I continue to notice that when Ming breast feeds Dakota, I feel a disturbance down deep in my body. As hard as I try to push it away, it grabs hold of me in a scary way. I start to have waking fantasies about hurting our baby. In these moments, my anger is aflame in my belly, some deep beast pulling me ever deeper inward. I feel like I am being consumed by a dark hole in my gut, and it will not let go. I realize that I need to talk to someone … I dare not take it to Ming. The next night, I go to my men's circle, and I check in with my experience. I imagine that my inner *'beast'* will be judged or rejected. Surprisingly, one man quietly asks me: *"Were you ever breastfed?"* Angrily, I say no, and my body roars in pain. The group quietly waits as my anger melts into a wave of grief, I feel like my tears will never stop. As always, the river finds its own level, and I get quiet. Another man asks: *"What if you asked Ming to breastfeed you? Do you think she would?"* I think for a moment, a twinge of fear, then my heart softens … I trust in my bones what Ming will say.

After the group, I go home, intending to ask Ming the question. I am at once afraid yet trusting, for I know how hard we are both working on our childhood issues. She knows all about my dark relationship with my mother. I imagine she will be glad that I have awakened to this wound. I also imagine that she will tell me that she has just the right medicine. As I lay down next to her, our baby boy snuggled up close and warm, I feel such love for them both, such love for our lives together, such gratitude for my healing journey. I tell her the whole story, then sheepishly ask her: *"Ming, will you breastfeed me?"* She looks at me with the sweetest smile, and then says: *"D, I am honored that you ask me, of course I will do that for you. And honestly, I would be ever so grateful, as I have so much milk that it just spills out. So please!"* Ming puts Dakota in his little bed, and lays down next to me, offering me the mother's milk that I never had as a little boy. The milk is warm and sweet and plentiful. After I have my fill, I lay back down, tears of grief and tears of gratitude flowing out of me. I weep for a whole lifetime of disconnect from my own mother. My heart is full, my dark fantasies disappear, they never return.

Santa Fe, Los Angeles and San Francisco are all preparing to offer their first NWTA's. The New Warrior Network is expanding across the country, and beyond. All the new centers offering their first trainings have to import the leaders and co-leaders. As a co-leader, I am in demand. The circles appreciate my edge, my intuitive sharpness, my healing energy, my commitment to this deep MensWork. I now know, beyond any doubt, that this work is my purpose and my mission.

In March '94, Dakota is now one month old, and I bring him to our initial staff meeting for our second NWTA in April. Thirty men stand in a large circle, I step to the center with Dakota in my arms. The circle gets quiet, I walk around, looking at each man. I take a deep breath and say:

> *"This is my first-born son, his name is Dakota James. There will be many times when his father is unable to care for him, is distracted, will wound him, will push him away, will be stuck in his own shit. In those times, Dakota will need your deep masculine love and support. So, as I pass him around the circle, I ask that you hold him, bless him, tell him that you will be there for him, especially when his father is not."*

This is Dakota's first rite of passage. While he will not remember this experience, I pray that his little body will retain the cellular memory of having been held, blessed, and loved by men. At the same time, I realize the deep need that every little boy has for his father, and the equally important need to have a community of men, men initiated into the sacred masculine.

As Dakota comes back into my arms, my heart is wide open. I say:

"My own soul has long hungered for the blessing you have bestowed upon my son here today. I know that the day of my ultimate demise is not that far off. If, at the end of my days, I truly desire to have you in a circle to sing my soul across the river, then it is my responsibility to stay in relationship with you until that time comes. To stay open and present and vulnerable and honest, to do my best to sustain these relationships, to be a good friend and ally and brother in this work. I pray that you will be there for me in my final rite of passage."

Chapter 14: Dylan

Late '92 at a training in San Diego, I meet a brother from Santa Fe, and we have become close friends. By early '94, we both have infant sons. Our families visit as frequently as we are able, and a lovely friendship ensues. Like us, they have mostly older friends whose children are already grown. On one visit, they tell us that they have a rental property that is empty, and we should move to Santa Fe. While we love Tucson, and my coaching practice is growing, our need for commonality is strong, especially Ming's need for other women and children on a regular basis. So in the fall of '94, we sell our house in Tucson, tearfully say goodbye to dear friends, and Ming and Dakota and I move to Santa Fe.

The second week that we are in Santa Fe, the men's community offers its first NWTA. Since '91, men from Santa Fe have been coming to initiate, then staff in, the new warrior trainings in San Diego. In anticipation of our move, I have been actively orchestrating this event. It is the third community in which I take part in their first NWTA. San Diego was the first, but it was not mine to begin. I began Tucson from scratch, Santa Fe has never had a fire starter like me, I feel like Johnny Appleseed.

The first training is a magnificent affair. Each and every new warrior training follows the same structure and format. Yet it also has its own essential nature, its own organic creativity. Every time ... just like when I was a boy, and had a baseball game that day ... my tummy has butterflies. The fear is not about competence, it is the pure thrill and awe and mystery of communing with soul and spirit ... and midwifing men to heal and transform. Whenever we consciously constellate the '*shadow*', as we do on our trainings, the shadow comes ... for both initiates and staff. For me, these trainings help me continue to heal and evolve in multiple dimensions. A man steps out upon the carpet, I have read his short profile. He is my age, from Kentucky, shovels shit on the farm, gets into drugs, gets into trouble, quits school, joins the army. I walk around the perimeter of the carpet, listening with my body, waiting to see where he will go.

He says: *"Probably none of you guys remember the 60's, the Vietnam War. Nah, you're too young."* I step out and look him in the eyes. I say: *"I remember, I was eighteen in '65, I was a draft dodger, I stood on the street protesting the war."* Right away, I push us out to the edge. He's tough, I know it's risky, still I want to emotionally move him in some way. He bends over and whispers in my ear: *"You know I could kill you in less than five seconds."* I look at him directly: *"Yes, I know ... but that is not why you are here. Why don't you tell us your story?"*

He begins: *"I joined the army at seventeen. I loved being in the army, and showing off my shooting skills. It's the first time anyone appreciates just how good I am. They put me in the Rangers, eventually doing long range reconnaissance. They train me to be a sharp shooter, a sniper, a killer in a million ways ... and I am the fucking best. I could kill anything that moved, even entire villages. I do two tours in Vietnam, the last one hunting down fallen American pilots, as they tend to crack under torture. I get home, the country is torn apart. I feel guilty, angry, broken, useless ... no one wants to hire a killer like me. I get into alcohol and drugs, can't hold a job, marry and divorce twice with a couple of kids ... I am a fucking mess. I try to get sober a dozen times, nothing works. Lately, I have this repeating dream: I'm in Nam, running through the swamp to get onto the chopper. The GI's are calling to me: 'Come on, you can make it.' I make it to the opening, they pull me in. Suddenly they are all gooks, screaming, crying, yelling at me ... I'm afraid they'll kill me. I wake up screaming."*

He finally lowers his head, as tears begin to fall from his face. At this point, the entire floor, about sixty men, has gathered to watch. They encircle this man and me, and together, we all weep for that war, weep for an entire generation of men, weep for our country.

Initially, Santa Fe is a fascinating place, the art and culture, the Native American and Mexican influence, the exquisite beauty of the landscape. And it is a very strange place. Stories tell that it is an inter-dimensional portal. Sometimes I walk through the town and feel this wave of funky energy, like a darkness slipping into my body. Negative thoughts cross my brain, my heart contracts, my stomach tightens, and in a few minutes, the dark wave passes. The classism here is obvious, the racism disturbing, the spiritual pretentiousness unbearable at times. Add to that, it is always so fucking windy, and my body does not like cold weather. The Santa Fe winter pushes hard, new clients are few and far between, I do some group facilitation to make ends meet. I make some money from co-leading the NWTA's. More and more, I regret leaving Tucson.

As a couple, Ming and I are disciplined in using contraception. Other than the several months it took us to conceive Dakota, we are steadfast. Our sex life takes a serious hit in Santa Fe. One night, in the coldness of winter and the heat of longing and ache, we have unprotected sex. In March '95, Ming is pregnant. The news hits me hard, and not in a good place. A year-old baby, two cats, nasty winter, no real work, money tight ... my fear is disturbing, my trust has disappeared. My perspective on abortion is situational, my heart imagines the damage at the soul level. Still, the thought enters my mind. And the idea of sharing it with Ming is scary. We both know women who have had abortions. The toll it takes in the mind, body, spirit, and soul impacts for a lifetime, maybe more. My own mind, heart, gut, spirit and soul ... each has a different agenda. I am torn and deeply fucked up. Finally, I have the nerve to tell Ming how I feel, all of it. She is surprisingly patient, I am grateful for her understanding. Ming takes a deep breath, looks me directly in the eyes, and says, as clear as a bell: *"I am having this baby. You do what is right for you, but if you say yes, then mean it."* My heart pounds with both fear and love, I take a deep breath, and with all the courage I can muster, I say: *"I love you, I'm in, let's do this."*

The relationship with the friends who brought us to Santa Fe deteriorates. They are on the brink of an ugly divorce, she is pregnant, and their little boy is caught in the crossfire. For me, the winter is endless, the winds are relentless, work is not to be had, and we are having another baby. I continue to imagine the future, sometimes scary, sometimes trusting. I pray hard, I pray often. A brief taste of spring arrives around mid-April, then more snow, warm weather finally comes end of May. One day I get a call from a friend from San Diego. Bill and I have staffed together, I trust him, I trust his heart. He says that their new warrior community is looking to hire someone to administer their trainings, their I-groups, handle their books. They have an office in town which I can use for my coaching clients. And they are paying more than I am making in Santa Fe. I ask: *"How soon?"* He says: *"Asap."* I say: *"I'll talk to Ming and get back to you tomorrow."* I close my eyes, whisper: *"Thank you."* I walk into the kitchen, Ming sees my face. *"Are you okay? What happened?"* I tell her about the offer, she starts to cry, we hold each other. I think to myself: *"The angels have been listening, in spite of my darkness."*

The next day, I call Bill and accept the offer. A few weeks later, I fly to San Diego, and rent a townhouse in Carlsbad. The site of the ocean, the beauty of southern California, the welcoming of my family from so many men and women fills my heart. In June '95, a pregnant Ming and Dakota fly to San Diego, I follow by car with our gear. We have already shipped our furniture, it arrives the day after we get to Carlsbad. Friends come to help us unload and set up our household, they are as excited to see us as we are to see them. After Santa Fe, the warmth of the sun, the blue ocean, the love of friends, the wonderful feeling of at-home-ness, the feeling of being wanted … it is all so delicious. Our street address is Vista del Oro, *'sight of gold.'*

I settle into work easily, I find a small group of men to sit in circle with, as Ming and I prepare for the birth of our second child. Like before, we want a home birth, Ming is intent on a vaginal birth, she says it will blow her dark father energy out of her body. We find two midwifes in the local community, we make ready our exterior and interior space. Throughout our pregnancy, Ming feels like she is carrying a girl. One day we go into a department store, looking for kids' stuff. We walk toward the girls' section, and suddenly Ming's belly turns toward the boys' department. She looks at me with astonishment: *"I guess we are having a boy."* We laugh, we trust her body's wisdom, we trust what we are being given.

Ming carries beautifully, her body is full and radiant, she glows with a pink joy, just like before. The beauty of a pregnant woman ... full of life, full of love and generosity, fulfilling her primal purpose ... she consistently takes my breath away. Late one evening in mid-December, we are lying in bed, and Ming's water breaks. The midwives are there within the hour. When she is fully dilated, Ming lies on her side on the mattress on the floor, turns her leg up, and within thirty-five minutes, delivers our second beautiful boy into the world. He is born on Ming's father Hudson's birthday, December 16 ... we name him Dylan Hudson Mead-Shikaly.

Like Dakota before him, I bring Dylan to the community men's circle. I pass him around for each man to hold and bless. His first rite of passage, one that he will not soon recall in his conscious memory. Still, his body will hold the energy, and hopefully one day he too will remember it. Once again, we call upon our dear astrologer friend Ani, who now lives in nearby Cardiff. We give her all the info on Dylan, and a week later we are sitting in her living room with both boys. She says to us: *"I want you both to take a deep breath, as what I am going to tell you may very well change your lives."* We look at each other, and in the lengthy seconds that follow, we each recall the conception and all that has followed. Now there's more?

> *"This boy comes in under the sign of Sagittarius, strong willed beyond measure. You would be wise to call him 'the commander', for he is large and in charge. Dene, he comes to you especially, as his hyper masculine soul needs a heart softening. And Ming, he also needs deep mother love. He is here with other souls to rebuild 'the new Earth' ... archi-*

tects, technological wizards, builders, financiers, educators, revolutionary thinkers ... and your Dylan is the boss. He is stubborn, generous, truthful, and he will challenge everything you tell him, and will always do it his way. He is a true force of nature, and he has a very large mission to live in this lifetime."

Ming and I look at each other, stunned. And grinningly we say: *"Of course!!!"* Dakota is an easier child, an Aquarian wicked smart kid, always figuring things out on his own. But this one, I know since his conception that he will push me beyond my limits. I am excited, and already scared. Somewhere inside, I know that Dylan and I have some deep soul karma. I know that my life is about to experience a quantum change, and I fear that I am not ready for this. I still see myself through the lens of some limiting shadow beliefs. My inner strength and arrogance hide it well, I am self-critical to a fault. I work them as I am able, and I have never been able to hide anything from myself for very long. This kid is already stronger than me, my not-good-enough thread has just been uncomfortably pulled.

Dylan is a night owl, his sleeping routine difficult to adjust to. Sometimes we take him out for a drive at night, the movement and the hum quiet him. Sometimes the top of the clothes dryer serves. My anger and frustration frequently arise, I sometimes handle him with rough, impatient hands. I fear that my body is already imprinting him with my judging and abandoning energies. I am keenly aware that I will inevitably wound him. Still, it is painful to see his little body contract, painful to see my own helpless. My guilt and shame layer into my inner mess. We all share a family bed, Ming on one side, both boys between us, me on the other side. Dylan is nursing, it soothes him and strengthens Ming. Both boys are restless in bed, I get kicked often. Sometimes I leave to get some sleep on the couch. Still, being together is empowering for us all. The boys are twenty-two months apart. Dakota loves his little brother, yet when Dylan starts motoring around, their energies often collide. Already he does not let anyone boss him around. I try to remember Ani's words as often as possible, yet not often enough.

As the boys get older, Ming shows increasing signs of an inner struggle. I do not recognize it at first, as I usually have my hands full. Ming's fears arise, she imagines invisible energies at play, I try hard to listen. Sometimes it makes sense, sometimes what she says seems far-fetched, even paranoid. Often I am the problem, as she finds fault with me in a whole variety of ways. I do my best to stay open to her reflections, as our mutual mirroring is the lifeblood of our marital evolution.

While our age and backgrounds differ and our tastes and perspectives vary widely, our values and commitment to this work are our common ground. Now I am seeing my beloved in a deep descent. I feel frightened, powerless, confused, and I have no idea what I am dealing with. Ming says it's postpartum depression, I think we both know it's more than that. We go to see a doctor in town. This is a first for us, as neither one believes in or trusts the traditional medical establishment. We sit together in the patient room, we wait thirty minutes before the doctor shows. He walks in on squeaky shoes, offers a limp hand to say hello, and stands away from us at the counter. He glances at us over his shoulder, as he asks a series of questions, then turns away to write it all down. There is nothing in him that is vaguely relatable, he offers no compassionate connection, asks dumb questions, he is as tight and squeaky as his shoes. Ming and I look at each other and laugh, we know we have no business here. Finally, the doctor gives Ming a prescription for anti-depressants, says: *"There are a bunch of samples in the large jar over there, help yourself, and, you can pay in the outer office."* He turns away and squeaks out the door.

We walk to the payment desk, the woman gives us a bill for $250. I say out loud: *"Are you fucking kidding me? There is no way that we are paying this ridiculous bill."* Everyone in the office turns to look at us, I simply do not give a shit. We have been treated rudely and ineffectively by the doctor, then they add *'insult to injury.'* For fifteen minutes, I have a variety of conversations with everyone in that office, all except the doctor. I know he does not have the balls to show himself. Finally, they agree to waive the bill. *"Fucking right!"* I say, as we march out the door.

Part IV: The Unraveling

Chapter 15: MensWork Opens

Having been certified as a co-leader in '91, then as a full leader in '95, I am invited to lead men's trainings in many places besides San Diego … Minneapolis, Detroit, Indianapolis, Chicago, Tucson, Santa Fe, Denver, Portland, New York, even London. David Deida sends me his first book *"The Way of the Superior Man."* I am moved by his wisdom and words, our views on masculinity coincide, I send back a grateful testimonial. I invite him to speak at our upcoming international New Warrior Network gathering.

In early '96, the executive director of the New Warrior Network is stepping down, and I decide to place my hat in the ring. MensWork has become my life's work … my experience, organizational skills, psychological and spiritual understanding, and vision are sharp. Several very accomplished men apply as well, we all go through an extensive set of interviews. Finally, the board selects me to be the second executive director of the NWN.

Locally, California is expanding rapidly. I get a call from a group in the bay area calling themselves the Nation of Men, an offshoot of Justin Sterling's work. Several hundred strong, these South-Bay men are looking for another venue to initiate their new men. They hear of me and the Network, they invite me to San Jose to talk to their council. A month later, I fly up to meet with the dozen NoM chiefs. They are savvy men, keenly aware of the importance of initiation, and clearly moving away from their current autocratic structure. They already know that they need what we are offering … they simply want to establish a relationship with the Network. As I now hold political influence, I am committed to both the Network's growth, and to the proliferation of MensWork. I tell the NoM men about the new warrior training … they are deeply moved. They appreciate everything I have to say to them, four of the chiefs immediately enroll in the upcoming NWTA in San Diego. When they return, Ron, NoM's lead chief, calls me: *"We're in. Would you please come back here to address our entire membership?"* I'm on a plane two weeks later.

The Nation of Men meet one Saturday a month at a redwood grove park in San Jose. I am cultivating a relationship with Ron, his inner-work on the training was transformative. He wants this for himself and for his men. We arrive at the park at ten in the morning, I am greeted like a long-lost brother. Soon, I am standing at the top of a hill, large staff in my hand, as I gaze out at the two hundred plus men assembled below me. With my eyes closed and my hand on my heart, I start to speak:

> *"Brothers, I am so moved to be here with you all today, thank you for inviting me. I have been in a men's circle since '86, and this work is alive deep in my heart, bones, balls, and soul. It is not an accident that I stand here before you, for it is my destiny to be talking about MensWork. As the new millennium approaches, we stand at the edge of great change. The men who run the world are dangerous, most men are in pain and denial, the need for a conscious masculine rite of passage has never been greater. I believe that this training offers a transformative opportunity to bring forth a new deep masculine planetary consciousness for men. I pray that you come and join us."*

I speak for a half hour. The words come through me from some other place, I can feel Standing Falcon and my whispering Angelina close by, they know my destiny is here. The Nation of Men are moved by my vulnerability and clear vision, and within the next year, they come to the trainings in the West. And not surprising, my coaching practice thrives as well. I travel frequently to the bay area, working with individual men from NoM, and doing large workshops for the organization. I hear the familiar rumblings from the local men who want to do the first NWTA in Northern California, same with LA. The entire West Coast is alive with MensWork, and I am right in the middle of it.

In my position as Network ED, my primary task is to focus on the trainings. At least that is what they tell me it should be. But I have a different agenda, one that looks at the expansion of the Network across the west coast and across the globe. I am called to lead a training in London, and I excitedly prepare for this. I land at Heathrow, they take me directly to the site, it is cold and rainy. After hellos, dinner, and a surprisingly long intimate check-in, I realize that I have come here with a supposition. Since reading Robert Moore's *"King, Warrior, Magician, Lover,"* I see the archetypal nature of our work. And my assumption is that men's wounds are cross-cultural. Here in Europe, I ponder: *"What if it is not? What if it is only Western, what if it is only American/English?"* As there are English, French, German, Scottish, American men on the weekend, I see this as the perfect opportunity to test my hypothesis.

It is Saturday afternoon, the carpet work is in full swing. One is in French, another in English, a third in German. I stand in front of the German carpet, I see a man screaming at another man. I ask the fellow next to me what the man is saying. He tells me that the man is angry at his father for abandoning him. The other carpet, a man is grieving his father's death. On the third, the man is confronting the voice of his alcoholic and abusive father. If indeed these are the common themes, if men's imprinting and dysfunction are the same cross-culturally, then Moore and Gillette's work provides a useful roadmap for men's healing. Still, I have this twitch: what about the Asian and Middle-Eastern cultures, what about Black and African men, South American men?

Back in the US, for close to a year now, the New Warrior Network has been holding an open question of changing the name of our organization. In my conversations with Tosi, Kauth, and others, I take a stand for a name change. We know that the word *'warrior'* is misunderstood in this culture. Warrior is mostly held as soldier, mercenary, savage, killer. This is vastly different from the archetypal descriptions in Moore's writings. The conversations and arguments have traveled across communities, states, countries, continents. Soon there will be a gathering, and the decision will be made by the collective.

In early '97, we have our yearly gathering in Glen Ivy, CA. Men come from all over the country, from Canada and Europe. The work has seriously taken root, we are now international. Everyone feels the importance of the moment ... non-US representation, a potential name change, a major growth possibility. The name change exercise is simple: There is a very large white board upon the stage. Anyone who has a suggestion comes up onto the stage and writes it on the board. Many communities come with their agreed upon name, led by the one from the community who offered that name. After about an hour, there are maybe twenty potential new names on the board, and the leader of the process calls timeout. Everyone takes a break, as we prepare for the next step in the process. Each man who wrote the suggestion on the board gets to come onto the stage, and say the name out loud three times. The men on the floor who like the name stand up. If there is sufficient support, the name remains. If not, it gets erased. A few names get a sizable support, most get erased. Then a young man from Louisville, KY comes up, and quietly says: The ManKind Project. The room goes silent. After he says it two more times, the entire room stands up and applauds. We are no longer the New Warrior Network, we are now The ManKind Project, offering the New Warrior Training Adventure, and men's integration groups around the world. The name says so much about us, we are all so very proud.

Chapter 16: **The Unraveling Begins**

Over the next several months, things at home with Ming and the boys are not going so well. My work as the executive director is demanding. Now with NoM online, I have more clients. I am writing more, leading trainings across the country, out at least once a month, sometimes twice. On the weeks that I travel, I crunch my clients to accommodate the days away. I return home tired, go right back to work, getting sick a little too often. I watched my father's blue collar work ethic bring him to his knees more than once, I see it doing the same thing to me. In my priorities, my work comes first, my health and well-being come last, my family somewhere in between … and Ming is angry. I work too much, and I am way out of balance.

Like my father, I worry about finances. All my work is part time, the extra money from the trainings helps, but the cost is dear. Often, in the zero-dark-thirty hours of a Thursday morning prior to my flight to the next training, Ming and I argue. She says: *"Our baby boys are little, demanding, hard to manage even with the both of us. Goddamn, they are still in diapers. I know you want to be present, but honestly you are hardly ever here. If it isn't travel, you are in the office working, or you're physically sick. What the fuck, Dene, I cannot do this alone. I am losing it, and everybody is hurting."*

I know she is right, still I am defensive. I do my best to support this family, I do the work I am called to do. I have three different jobs plus writing, I loyally follow the American workingman's formula. I watched my father on payday take out his yellow pad and three sharpened pencils, and do his weekly math. How much for this, how much for that, how much toward retirement. I knew that my brother and I were never in that equation. He bought me a bicycle, he bought me a baseball glove, he gave little else. I got a full scholarship to college, my brother took out loans, our father didn't pay shit. Now I am here, stuck as fuck, and I see no way out. **Please god, don't let me be like him.**

Underneath my anger, there is fear and shame. I imagine other guys can do it, maybe there's something wrong with me. There are men of means in this community, I am envious. We struggle to make ends meet, and I have long rejected the word *'retirement.'* Even when there is some money left over, we always find something that the kids need. With aching heart, I fly out, bask in the purposefulness of the work, come home open-hearted. I walk in the door, Ming says: *"Here, take your sons, I need a fucking break."* My heart breaks, it takes a whole day for us to reconnect. Our baby boys are caught in the crossfire.

The trainings offer a glimpse of the sacred, it gives me hope. All too often, it hides my shadows with hubris ... *'It's okay that my family is falling apart, because I am saving the men of the world.'* My home life is painfully similar to my childhood ... working, arguing and fighting, fucking to make up ... repeat. My integration group offers little, I feel alone, rapidly running out of wiggle room. There is a workshop for men here in town. Run by two women, it is titled: *"Under Your Mother's Pillow."* Taken from Robert Bly's *Iron John* story, it offers men the opportunity to do deep work on mother issues. At work, I know I'm stuck in a common masculine dilemma. At home, I feel guilty, ashamed, angry, confused.

The mother work is healing, I remember the strength and power of the feminine, that she is the doorway to openness and trust. Trust is never easy for me, the NY street kid is always vigilant. In the workshop, I find a new compassion and forgiveness for my own mother. I believe this will definitely improve the quality of my interactions with Ming and the boys. I pray it will help me find a better balance for my own body. Slowly, and often haltingly, I see the feminine at play across the broad spectrum of my life. I realize that even though I was born into the crucible of the hyper-masculine, Angelina whispered in my ear at nine, reminding me of my tender heart. I sense that for my true healing, the masculine is not enough on its own. Unbridled, and often with the best of intentions, it does damage, to self and to others. It needs its complement ...

the tough needs the tender, the tender needs the tough, it is the yin/yang within a man, within all of us. I know I must follow this path towards the feminine, in spite of my own deep *'old school male'* imprint and my stubborn resistance. I sense that my marriage is on shaky ground.

For many generations, men have been programmed to resist this very idea of engaging the feminine. Even in our MensWork, many men just want a *'good old boys'* network. A couple of years back, at my full leader certification process, a panel member asked me what I would do if I were in charge of the Network. Without hesitation, I told him that I would invite a deeper consideration of the feminine in our work. I see how men are afraid, I see how I am afraid. Still, out of necessity, I commit to looking at my life from a more balanced perspective, with more emotional awareness. I do not yet see how much this will change me, but I do know that my marriage will not survive without it.

Chapter 17: **The Feminine Beckons**

Personally, I continue reflecting on my awakening from the mother workshop. Conceptually, I struggle to understand how the masculine and feminine fit together. But I am increasingly more at ease with this idea. I sense that this feminine is not a separate structure, not an enemy, not something to push away. My male imprint has been telling me since the crib … **no** tears, **no** fears, **no** needs, **no** feminine … be a good boy, be a tough man. But all these things **are** alive within me … I have tears and fears, I have needs, I have love and tender caring, I have heartache and pain. I see more clearly that in our trainings, men are finding healing and renewal just from expressing these deep feelings. I ponder:

> *Could it be, that at the center of a man's initiatory experience and the core of his transformational possibility, lies his willingness to feel everything? Could it be that the feminine is neither a 'she' nor 'female' … rather it is a man's own feeling nature?*
>
> *What if our awakening begins with a body centered awareness, where all the emotions reside? And in order to feel one emotion, we must feel **all** our emotions … from the most horrendous pain clear through to the most exquisite joy. Could this 'MensWork' include this interior 'feminine' awakening?*

Other than with Ming, I have not much personal interface with many women, and there is little information available on the feminine in contemporary men's writings. Jung writes about it, but I struggle to understand this in modern terms. During the mother workshop, I have the fleeting idea of providing a similar workshop for women to work on father issues. I think to myself:

> *"Here I am, deep in MensWork, honoring and healing both the beast and the beauty of the masculine in me. I see the next step: consciously turning my attention toward a deeper*

awakening of my emotional body, my 'feminine' side. And what better way for me to learn this then to work with women. This is crazy, can I really do this? I have so much work as it is. I think about the two women working with men, I know I can do this, but...?"

I ask Ming her thoughts, she thinks it is a bold and courageous idea, but has major concerns. She wants me to find more balance between work and home. She more than welcomes more of my emotional side, but she certainly does not want me to be intimate with other women. I wrestle with this idea for many months. It scares me, intrigues me, challenges me in many ways. I talk to other men, none are willing to step into this fire with me. In the absence of a clear path, in the presence of this deep knowing that there is something here for me, I decide to do a vision quest. I am almost ten years into MensWork, the feminine has beckoned, and in some way, I must follow.

In early '98, I travel from San Diego to Sedona, AZ, to spend five days in the desert with a medicine man. Jose is half Mexican, half Native, he and I have journeyed together when we lived in Arizona. He is a wisdom holder, I trust myself in his hands. He holds sacred peyote.

The first day is for fasting, we mostly walk and talk and sit quietly. I share with him what is alive in me, he is mostly silent, nods his head, smiles a lot. The second day, when I take the first dose of the medicine, my body has much to purge. No visions, lots of emotions, by the end of the day, I am drained, we nibble some food and turn in early. On day three, I take the next dose of medicine, and this is very different. From the beginning I am having visions, bold images, a powerful response to the nature around us. Early, my body purges ... I feel cleansed, strong, open ... I am ready for something.

I separate from Jose, hike up a hill, find a quiet place to sit under a tree. While meditating, I hear a very loud noise. Startled, I search the area to find the source of the sound. Nothing but silence. I walk up over the hills nearby, nothing there either. I lay down in the grass under a tree, I hear the noise again. This time it is loud and close by. I stand up, look around, nothing. Finally, I tell myself to let go, stop chasing, let whatever it is come to me. I lay back down and close my eyes. The noise gets louder in my ears, it sounds like a giant pile driver slamming into huge rocks. As I lay there, I feel the pile driver right above me, descending into the middle of my chest. I open my arms, preparing myself for the penetration. My physical body feels fear and wants to contract. But my spiritual body works to stay open.

The machine drives into my chest, I wince in pain. Again it comes down, pushing farther in, I feel tears come. The third time, the driver penetrates deep into my heart, breaking it wide open. The deep sobs come in waves, my body writhes, I wail out loud the grief of damage done, to me and by me, over my many lifetimes … it is almost unbearable. The penetration drives deeper, the pain feels like forever … and then it stops. I open my eyes, the machine is gone, it is quiet. I take some long deep breaths, my body slowly relaxes. My heart is achy, my hands massage my chest.

Inside my head, all manner of images expands outward. Waves of color and sound move across the sky, great palaces made of sparkling jewels assemble and disassemble. Images of angels and light beings with no gender fly in between the dimensions. Tears of joy stream down my face, my body is filled with peace.

Then I hear a feminine voice whisper:

"In feeling and knowing both the agony and the ecstasy of penetration, now you can stand before a woman who has been raped, and you will know what to do."

That very moment, as I lay supine on the ground, everything in me is splayed wide open … I surrender into the arms of the invisible.

Later, I return to our camp, Jose is sitting by the fire. He takes one look at me and knows that something serious has happened. I sit down next to him, and tell him the story. With raised eyebrow, he smiles: *"Remember what you have come here for."* Yes, I have come to be shown my next path, to serve my own awakening, and honestly, to seek permission to work with women. This feels like a blessing, and with it a warning: *"Be careful what you ask for. What comes next will change you forever."* I know that if I embark on this path, it will require more strength and courage than I can even imagine. I see lines of women, I feel the great pain that they bear, I see how I have contributed to that pain. Dare I imagine that I am now called to assist **their** healing? Will it be **my** healing? I hear my angel speak, a portend of things to come:

> *"With this blessing comes great responsibility, and a challenge that may be terrifying. Women will come with all manner of wounding from men. And they will project their wounds upon you. Are you ready to stand in the fire of those projections? Without defending, without reacting, without collapsing under the weight of thousands of years of male rule, and the horrific abuse of women, the earth, and the feminine in men? Can you hold that?"*

I shiver deeply at her words. My body is achy and exhausted, my heart is excited and terrified. Jose gets me some tea, lights the pipe, we smoke, nibble, listen to some quiet music. As we marvel at the starry heavens and stare into the fire, I am empty, I am full, and my mind reels with the infinite possibilities.

I return home to San Diego, not sure who I am or what I'm supposed to do next. The more I think about this, the more insane it seems. Yet I keep remembering … *'Ask and ye shall receive, ye have asked, this is what ye have been given.'* I share it all with Ming. She sees how drained and rattled I am, she fears for my health. She nurses me on her tinctures and teas, she cooks nurturing Ayurvedic food to help restore my energy and well-being. She encourages me to take some down time, I listen to her wisdom. There is much to ponder, much to write.

The Journey

One day you finally knew what you had to do, and began,
Though the voices around you kept shouting
their bad advice.
The whole house began to tremble and
You felt that old tug at your ankles
"Mend my life" each voice cried "Mend my life"
But you did not stop.

You knew what you had to do.
Though the wind pried with its stiff fingers
At your very foundation
And the melancholy was terrible.
It was already late enough and a wild night,
On a road full of fallen branches and old stones.
But little by little, as you left their voices behind,
The stars began to burn through the sheets of clouds.

And there was a new voice ... a new voice,
That you slowly recognized as your own,
Which kept you company as you strode
Deeper and deeper into the world,
Determined to do the only thing you could do,
Determined to save the only life you could save.

Mary Oliver

I recall years ago reading Marion Woodman's book: *"Leaving My Father's House."* It's about three women in therapy whose work is to reclaim their sacred feminine through healing their father wound. As a man, I experience my deep masculine through the father wound. Now I sense the door for me to the feminine goes through my mother wound. She is where I learned to feel, she is also where I learned to shut down. I remember the Iron John myth, telling us: *'The key is under the mother's pillow.'*

The picture unfolds before me ... my mother wound, my father wound, the cultural wounds to all of us, especially to women, the earth, and the feminine in men ... they are all right here. In my healing with and through Ming, in my own self-care and good fathering, in my technicolor dreams, here my next initiation stands before me ... working with women, healing the father wound, both theirs and mine, and the unique opportunity to heal my own mother wound. I ponder: *"Oh my god, really? Might I actually be able to do all this?"* Once again, I stand at a crossroad ... the red, yellow, and green lights flashing brightly, the angels and demons watching. Again, I remember Angelina's voice in my ear, welcoming me back home. I remember my Nonas, Annie, Running Deer, my dreams, and especially this angel's recent visit. The stakes are high, my fear is on red alert, and my heart is open, urging me onward. Once again, I say yes, and I feel all the women in my constellation smiling.

The enormity of it frightens me, I do not know where to begin. But I know that I cannot do this alone. Once again, I reach out to other men, this time more careful in how I tell my story. Many laugh, think it's a crazy idea, and say good luck. Many look at me with blank stare. I second guess myself, again and again. Still, I cannot shake this, I know in my bones how important it is. And in that moment, I decide that I will call this thing: *"Leaving My Father's House."* I ask Ming, she loves it. My whispering voice reminds me: 'It is **you** who is leaving **your** father's house'.

> *The house of the archetypal father, the house of my dark fathers, the house of misogyny and homophobia, the rejection of the feminine in all places, the rule by violence, the abuse of power. I feel the incredible rage and grief everywhere. I sense the archetypal vein that has been struck, how deep and dirty the blood, how monumental the undertaking. And I know one thing for certain: these are my wounds that I am here to heal ... I must go forward!*

At times, I imagine what David might have felt when he stepped out upon the field to do battle with Goliath. Likewise, I imagine the immensity of the beast that is the *'house of the dark father.'* With razor-sharp talons, with fiery breath that scorches everything in its way, the relentless force of oppression, at every level. So big and terrible, few whisper its name. We are all in its grasp, it's simply a matter of degree.

> *"The dragon is very much our raw psychic energy within the unconscious. The cave where the dragons live, the fire breathing kundalini Serpent, that is at first asleep, is vile, and woe unto him who does not know the process of its purification … when it is passed through the alchemical process, uniting cosmic masculine and feminine."*
>
> Iona Miller -   *The Dragon Archetype*

As all this begins to line up in my body, my inner vision expands. While I find courage in remembering that I have been called, still I tremble in my littleness: *"Why me?"* I feel the angel behind the pile driver close at hand … not sure if she's leading or pushing. To my question, she answers: *"Because you have a slingshot, because you say its name out loud, because you stand in the fire of men's pain, the often overlooked victims of the patriarchal father. For the 'manbox' is deadly, it kills everyone, everyone. And especially, because you see the true horror that kills women and the feminine."*

That night, I have this dream:

I am in the basement of an old house, stone walls, low ceiling, dank, dark, musty, cobwebs everywhere. I walk down the corridor, there is a door on the left. Old, wooden, heavy, I push hard, it stubbornly opens. The room is large, dimly lit, I see a dozen old women scattered randomly. Each one sits on a stool in front of a large pot cooking on the fire. They jabber away in some long-forgotten tongue, I understand what they are saying.

One Nona waves, motioning me to come over. She has a scarf on her head, a dirty apron, stockings rolled down to her ankles. She stirs the soup with a long wooden gourd. She smiles at me a toothless grin, full of sweetness and mischief. She takes the spoon out and offers me some soup. It is hot, I sip carefully, my whole body radiates warmth. I am safe in her kitchen, for this is a different wooden spoon.

My Nona was the woman who loved me as a boy, my other Nona died knowing that my mother was pregnant with me. All my life, it seems, the feminine has been with me. And now the grandmothers come alive in my underworld as well, feeding me soul food. It is time for me to remember, it is time for me to follow, it is time for me to trust.

Finally, I see the workshop … not the final outcome, nor the processes, just its fearless and terrifying intention … to knock on that archetypal door, to dare enter the house of the dark father where the beast sleeps in the bowels. To dare cast a light upon the wide array of human shadows … too long ignored, too long causing death and destruction, too long ruling from the shadows. My vision is clear, my inner support is deep, yet I remain alone. *'Please … someone say yes.'*

I have known Jim for a long time. He initiated in San Diego in the early days, we became good friends right away. He and Jan come often to Tucson to visit, Dakota's middle name is James. I call him up, say let's have lunch. We sit on the deck of the restaurant in Del Mar, overlooking the beautiful blue Pacific, sun shining warm on our faces. Jim and I are about the same age. He is a big fellow, a perfect *'good father'* projection. And he's got a delicious sense of humor, we often poke fun at ourselves so we don't get too inflated in our work. He took the mother workshop with me recently, we are both exploring our relationships with our wives, and to the feminine. He is on his third marriage, he has two grown daughters, he works hard on this one. He is grounded, practical, holds space well, skilled on the carpet. And thank God he's not woo-woo like me. I have invited him to this before, I want to give him an update, maybe a second chance.

I tell him about my vision quest, my angel visitation, all that is awakening in me. I remind him of the mother work we did, and its impact on this gender work that stands before all of us. As men who carry a mother wound, there are women who carry the complementary father wound, and both come from the same dark archetypal energies. I talk more about the *'dark father's house,'* tell him my grandmothers dream, I tell him everything. He sits there listening, I see him turning this over. I sense his confusion, overwhelm, the craziness of what I am asking him. I see the doubt on his face. He asks a bunch of questions, my response is often *'I don't know yet.'* Finally, he straightens up in his chair, leans in close to me, looks me in the eye, and says: *"Almost everything tells me to run far away from you, from this insane thing you are concocting, 'cause you're a fucking madman. It's crazy and it scares the shit out of me. But something, there's something about this. Maybe it's my own shit with women, maybe it's the clear multi-layered picture you paint, maybe it's your amazing heart and courage. And maybe it's because I love you, and I don't want you to have to do this by yourself. So fuckit, I'm in. What's next?"*

We smile, sit back, finish our lunch, stare out upon the huge blue ocean … my heart is quiet, I am relieved, finally I have an ally. At the shores of the largest feminine entity on planet Earth, we look at each other. We know we are about to embark on probably the hardest, certainly the most important journey of our lives. And it will take more than everything we have. We agree to take some time, think about this for awhile, begin jotting down ideas and thoughts, and especially talk with our wives. We leave the restaurant, hug goodbye, *see you soon*!

A few weeks later, Jim and Robin and Ming and I meet for dinner. Over wine and some good food, we all talk about this project, the pros and cons, we listen closely to the women's concerns. We know we cannot do this without their blessing. Both are in support of us, they know there will be great challenges, they have major concerns. They know all too well what happens when men and women get into tight spaces together. They trust us, but this is different, intense, a larger scale, and dangerous territory. We set up a regular schedule of meetings, we divide tasks among us, including the women. Building a workshop ... content, structure, outcomes, protocols, processes, music, marketing, finance, location, materials, flyers, documentation, administration ... is no small matter. It takes several months before we have an accurate flowchart of what we are doing.

Yet everywhere we go, including our own men's circles, we ask these same questions ... about women and men, about masculine and feminine, about inner work for men and for women, about the archetypes, about our individual and collective woundedness ... gathering information, trying to find the right alignment of energies that will birth this creation. Sometimes we get responses that tell us we are on track, sometimes we get blank faces, sometimes we feel overwhelmed by the immensity of our undertaking, sometimes we are just plain lost and hopeless.

We finally organize a focus group, a cadre of successful local businesswomen. We create a set of questions, about the assumptions that we have made about women and their fathers, about women's current relationships with men, about women in the world. These women all work with men, in high-powered positions, where money, power, and sex are the mediums of exchange. First, we ask them some general questions:

Q: *"Do you think that women in the corporate world are afraid of men in power?"*

A: *"Yes, for sure."*

Q: *"What are they afraid of?"*

A: *"We need men's approval."*

Q: *"Why do you think that is?"*

A: *"Because they are 'daddy', and we always want to please him."*

Q: *"What else?"*

A: *"We are very angry ... they reject us, and we act just like them."*

Q: "Do you think that our workshop would help women change this?"
A: "Yes, most certainly. But this is very scary stuff."
Q: "Why?"
A: "There is old deep pain here, and no one wants to look at it."

We ask them to create a list of the qualities and character traits of men who are successful in the business world. Then we ask them to list the qualities and character traits that have led to their own success. We ask them to look at them side-by-side. Finally, one woman shouts: *"Shit, we are just like them!"* And as we look at those traits … hard, tough, relentless, driven, determined, disciplined, committed … no surprise, these are the positive aspects of the masculine. Then a woman says: *"They are also cheating, abusive, ruthless, backstabbing, lying, motherfucking pigs!"* We follow:

Q: "How do you feel about that?"
A: "We hate them, we hate ourselves for being like them, we should know better."

Q: "At work, where is your heart and compassion?"
A: "We leave them both at home."

Q: "Is any aspect of the feminine allowed inside the offices and boardrooms?"
A: "Yeah … our bodies!"

We continue:

Q: "Would our world change if women were in positions of power?"
A: "Yes absolutely, but only if women embody more of their feminine aspects like caring, compassion, kindness, equanimity, nurturance, emotions, and strength."

Q: "How about these qualities in men?"
A: "Some men, but not the ones in charge."

Q: "What else?"
A: "And the guts it will take for us to force institutional changes like childcare, maternity leave, equal pay for equal work, no glass ceilings."

After the women leave, Jim and I sit looking at each other. Oh my, maybe we have tapped into something here, not only for women who have been abused by men, but also the struggle of women in power, who see and tolerate this male behavior every day, who toil in the belly of the beast. In our MensWork, it is clear how *'manbox'* thinking represses everything feminine in men. In listening to these women, repression of the feminine absolutely lives right here inside the corporate structures. Right then, we name our workshop:

LEAVING MY FATHER'S HOUSE:
A Workshop for Women

*Coming to terms with men, boys, her own masculine,
and the archetypal father ... through examining
her relationship with her personal father.*

Jim and I know our capacity for holding space for men. We both love and respect the carpet, yet working with women is different. We have to watch our own hubris, our own mother issues, our sexual issues, our many blindnesses. With men, the father wounds are personal, we know the male drama, we trust our technology. But working with women brings in so many other dimensions. Every aspect of the gender cultural narrative comes into play, there is much more unconscious stuff that we have to be aware of. The wounds that women carry are multi-leveled. Building this first container will be a tremendous learning experience for us. Jim and I question everything, every assumption and judgment that we have. It is challenging to stay conscious of what we see and know, for there is so much that we just do not know.

We continue to bring all of this to our wives, they are more important than ever. As we articulate our awareness of issues, especially the sexual aspect, they both relax, for this is what is front and center for them. They tell us that as long as our own sexuality is in our awareness, they trust that we can handle ourselves in a good way. Still, even though we are asking the right questions, they continue to urge great caution. We commit to keep sharing our learnings.

In October '98, we offer our first LMFH workshop in San Diego. We greet the women in a stoic way, which is what we do in our men's trainings. We offer a hard edge to bump up against, thinking that this will evoke fear or anger, some kind of reaction. It works with men, it falls on its face with women. They do not respond with fear, they simply refuse to play. Throughout that entire first training, we see how often we have it backwards ... tough where we need to be tender and tender where we need to be tough. The conversations and learning are rich for all of us, we are all teachers and students in this. The processes continue to move forward, as little by little they begin to trust us, and start to drop down into their personal pain places. Jim and I keep checking in with each other, watching everything, learning what works, what does not work, taking constant mental and written notes.

On all our breaks, we debrief what we are learning ... the dance of our own masculine and feminine energies, the reactions from our own 'manbox', the innate eroticism in the energy, what feels familiar, what feels different, how to hold both women's power and their fragility. We remind ourselves that all the darkness of the archetypal masculine is being projected on us here, and it will only increase in intensity.

Collectively, we see that:

> *Women's wounds are all the same ... a woman's struggle to have her authentic voice, and the human right to have her own choices.*

Her voice speaks:

- *to a culture that has been predominantly male run for the last six thousand years.*
- *at the heart of little girls wounded by unconscious fathers.*
- *at the heart of a woman's anger, for women who are unheard and dismissed.*

- at the heart of battered women living in shelters across the world.

- at the heart of abortion, ecology and recycling.

- at the heart of calling out rape and sex abuse.

- at the heart of calling out unfairness in the workplace and prejudice everywhere.

- at the heart of calling out male violence.

- at the heart of calling out men who still do not get it, men who have no idea what they feel, who have no ears to listen to women's pain, who carry forward the good old boys' networks, who beat, batter, and rape women in their own houses, and who still live blindly and dangerously in allegiance to the old masculine ways.

> It is a voice that has cried out for way too long, a voice that cries out still. A voice that is growing stronger ...

In the face of all this, Jim and I consciously choose a fierce accountability for ourselves ... for every hurt, betrayal, transgression, wound, rape, murder, that **any** man has perpetrated upon **any** woman ... **we acknowledge and own our complicity**. Our most challenging task is to **not** defend, justify, nor react, even if we are innocent, the actual perpetrator, or even the victim.

Jim is a father to two young women, this hits him harder. I have hurt many women in my past, I feel my own shame, sorrow, fear. I remember the message from my vision quest, I remind Jim. We trust ourselves in this challenge, and know that we will be given what we need along the way. We just have to stay open, humble, clear ... and both tender and fierce in the face of the projections. It will be a continuous learning, always a little in front of our understanding. Many more women will follow, this is just the beginning. But only if we can hold this non-reactive space. If we fall into the trap of defending and rationalizing and justifying, we will fail miserably.

How we navigate this experience will determine whether we can actually continue this work on a larger scale. Whatever reactions that arise in us must be noted, made conscious, processed and cleared. During our breaks, we energetically cleanse ourselves, we talk about our own reactions. This is exactly the inner work that Jim and I have to do, for in order to serve the needs of these women, we must do our own inner work.

We stumble through the first workshop, taking copious notes on all our mistakes. We learn from each one. We ask the women to fill out a questionnaire at the end of the workshop, we read every single word. They give us tough feedback, they give us appreciation and gratitude. Their learnings are deep, their collective takeaways transformative:

- *It's okay for me to have strong boundaries with men.*
- *I do not have to be nice.*
- *My body is mine.*
- *Fuck men.*
- *Men need to wake up.*
- *I believed it was all my fault. Now I know it's not.*
- *My voice is important, I won't be silent, I won't raise my hand.*
- *Thank God some men get it.*
- *No man has ever been as good as my father.*
- *I miss my dad.*
- *Men do bad things because bad things were done to them.*
- *My self-esteem does not depend on any man.*
- *My emotions are important, and they matter.*
- *It's okay to need and ask for love and affection.*
- *I never realized that men are afraid of women.*
- *It's okay for me to be strong and powerful.*
- *I am not obligated to give sex to my husband.*
- *It's okay to be a little crazy.*
- *I am not stupid.*

Jim and I are both good listeners, our wives have helped us

learn to listen carefully, thoughtfully, sensitively. But the messages coming forth from all these women blow us away. A clear unified voice of the feminine, a collective warrior voice that knows this time for truth has come. A message that they are willing to take back into every fabric of their lives, into the workplace, and especially to their husbands. They commit to staying connected to each other. They honor us … first for our courage in doing this. They are grateful that there are good men in the world who understand. They sincerely appreciate men who are accountable for the bad shit they have done. They are especially grateful that we own our emotional side. They marvel that men are in healing circles with each other. They are hopeful. We stay open to everything they say, both positive and negative. We know that we are all learning together here, and our own transformation will determine the future of this workshop. We rewrite the outline, over and over and over again. We do not find our real groove until we have done a dozen workshops.

In a little more than three years, we do twenty-eight workshops. Hundreds of women come, the diversity surprises us. Age, race, sexual orientation, marital status. The stories that women tell bring us to our knees. Many times on the carpet, I break down in tears listening to the horror that has been perpetrated upon these women, not only by their fathers, but by the grandfathers, the brothers and cousins and friends of the family, their own husbands. As they ask us to role-play these men, it is not difficult to find these dark places in each of us. As each woman steps out to do her work, we both stand before her, and invite her to pick one of us to play the role of her father. One woman picks Jim to play her father. Her story I will never forget:

> *"My father was the minister of the only church in a small rural western town. Our family had much standing in the community, the flock came to my father for guidance, pastoral counseling, and various community issues. My mother was quiet, deferential, always protecting and supporting him.*
>
> *I was the eldest of four sisters. When I was about eleven*

or twelve years old, my father started to visit my room at night. He began to innocently and lovingly stroke my hair, telling me how pretty I was, how I was his favorite, how proud he was of me. He told me not to tell anyone of these nighttime visits, as the others will be jealous. I agreed to keep this secret.

After awhile, his hands slowly began to move down my body. I was just beginning to develop, my father told me I was beautiful, and how much he loved me. Pretty soon, he started to touch me in all my private places. It was not long before he had me touching him. Shortly thereafter, he penetrated me, taking my virginity. This went on for a long time … first me, then each of my sisters in turn. Each was sworn to secrecy, even from each other. My mother chose to stay blind to all of this."

On the carpet, the woman speaks matter-of-factly, as she has spoken of this before in therapy. I suspect that there is something not yet revealed, probably to herself. I am gentle with my questions, I ask her: "So what do you *not* want to tell us?" Her head drops, she says: *"I hate to say this – that I actually liked it. It was the only time he ever paid attention to me, the only time he told me that he loved me and was proud of me. Now I feel so ashamed."*

Her tears come in waves. She cries hard for a full ten minutes. After the grief passes, she goes to the bathroom … and for eight hours … the poison comes out of her body, from all cavities. We place another woman in the bathroom, to watch over her and keep her hydrated. When her purge is complete, she emerges in front of the group. She is ashen like a ghost, but her eyes are bright and full of light, like an angel. She is indeed cleansed.

To be in close proximity to just a small but indicative portion of the damage done to girls and women, my heart breaks open, time after time. This is the very agreement that we make … to stand in the fire of women's pain, just like we stand in the fire of men's pain.

To be an ally to this healing is humbling, to be so sensitized to a woman's pain has consequences in the rest of my life. I begin to see women differently … many of my judgments drop away, my compassion opens wider. I recognize the struggle in a woman's experience … I meet it with my own tenderness, often with anger and outrage at the damage. I recognize the consequence to men of having the feminine in themselves shut down, contributing to our insensitivity, and frightening capacity to do this kind of damage. I see the importance of conveying this to the men in our circles and trainings. I embrace the importance of men's emotional awareness. And I see the dangerous and scary side of the feminine as well. They do their own damage. They are not without power, rather this power often lies underground.

The one constant that Jim and I observe throughout this entire workshop experience, and the one we witness in all our men's trainings, is the deep need to be loved by our fathers. In the little girl and little boy in each of us, in our true vulnerability and openness, in the places of greatest pain and trauma, there is the deep, human, essential need to be loved … by our mothers and by our fathers.

Rarely do we get enough of this in childhood, but we always get the core wound. And it is precisely this soul wound that leads us to the inner work. Here, in our nakedness and vulnerability, in the terror of our own pain, with the fire of our rage and the tears of our grief, we fashion the medicine. For the medicine is love … and it is all we need to heal.

For me personally, this creates a deeper awakening in my own marriage. I am much more sensitive to Ming, I see her and hear her in an altogether different way, I see her cultural wound as a woman. *I recognize the importance of the fierce and tender balance in both of us in the rearing of our boys.* I see my own 'manbox' more clearly. And within me, I am increasingly grateful for my intuition, my emotional sensitivity, my gift at sensing the pain of others. I remember the tough little kid who fought on the NY streets, I remember Billy, and Poppy, I recall the hard-ass competitor on the sports fields. I know the constant thrust of my driving ambition and will to excavate my own underworld. Flushing out shadows, penetrating my own heart's opening, discovering the beauty of my own masculine. And now, with my full emotional body on-line, I find balance between my masculine and my feminine. And God knows, I will need it.

Chapter 18: **The Unraveling Deepens**

In April '01, we do a women's workshop in Baltimore. I usually stay in touch with Ming when I am on the road. I call her several times, only get her voicemail, no return calls. At first, this work brings us closer together, after awhile, the chasm between us deepens. My work life brings out her hostilities, her emotional contentiousness becomes harder to hold. I see my part clearly … I am frequently traveling, busy more often than not, I still fret about money, controlling with her and the boys. Her judgments, her casting blame, and her projections grow darker. Even though she has not said it, I feel her getting ready to leave the relationship again. Throughout the weekend in Baltimore, I feel a deep heartache, I sense she has made a decision. I fear for our marriage, I fear for the boys, I fear for all of us. As hard as I try to shake this feeling, it won't let go. I get home on Sunday at midnight. She is sitting at the kitchen table, I am not surprised that she's up. She looks at me … a false smile plastered on her face, a vacancy in her eyes like no one is home. She says: "*I want a divorce.*" Then gets up and goes inside. My heart breaks again.

Since my mother's '*wooden spoon*' on my little boy's ass, I have successfully managed to avoid abandonment and rejection by women, simply by not letting myself get close to any. And then at forty, I fall in love with Ming. The long-buried heartache from childhood that I felt with her first leaving came out in rage and grief, the dam finally broke. While I was mentally unstable and emotionally crazy, it was also my first conscious descent into the mother wound. From that, we began to see the larger patterns at play, both hers and mine. While we navigated a reconciliation, this pattern repeated itself over the years … her growing judgments and blame, her distancing and vacancy, threats to leave … and here it is once again. Ming's harsh criticisms constellate my mother projections: '*It's always my fault, I am too much, or not enough, I deserve to be punished and abandoned. So she leaves.*'

Through the years of our marriage, with all the growth and transformation that we have created, some part of me is always vigilant. Watchful, not fully trusting, sensing underneath that abandonment could happen again. I see my pattern, I am not sure that she sees hers. She does not see the fear and shame in her criticisms, the abdication of self-responsibility in blaming, her own not enoughness, her father projections … *'My lawyer father judges and controls me, tells me I am not smart enough … I think it is true. I blame him for my and our failures, then I run away.'*

In my own rigorous inquiry into my childhood wounds and trauma, through therapy and analysis, on the carpet work with so many men and women, I see the core of our marital conflict … *unconscious parental projections* … for both of us. I wonder: *"Might this be all that a marriage is? Might this be why most modern marriages fail?"* With the dissolution of the glue that traditional gender roles have provided, we now have a glimpse of the underlying psychological terrain … the history of our lineages, the early childhood and continuing multi-level imprints, the personal wounds that lie beneath the watchful eye of the ego. Too deeply etched into the brain's gray matter and the body's cellular memory to be ignored for long, they eventually have their way with us. In the depth of my mother abandonment wound, with the arrows of blame that pierce my heart, I do not yet see the depth of Ming's unraveling, only my own. It breaks my heart, elicits my protective anger, feeds the shame underneath … I am shattered.

Since moving to California, which began Ming's slow yet steady decline, we now consider moving out of state. Several months prior, we visit Ashland in preparation to do a woman's workshop there. Still a small quiet Oregon town, we meet some lovely people, there is a vibrant men's elder community, a wonderful organic market, good schools, lots of kids, and a skateboard park for Dakota. Last Christmas, Dakota asks for a skateboard, we go to a shop nearby and buy him the whole regalia. Back home, he dons all the gear … helmet, knee guards, wrist guards, elbow guards … he looks like a midget gladiator. There is a skateboard park two blocks from our house. We walk over there, a bunch of older kids are flying all over the place. We find a small space in the corner, he is up on that board in no time. Cautious at first, I can see the natural athletic ability of this kid, just like his daddy. Every day we visit that park, every day he gets better and better. After only a couple of weeks, he is jumping off the steps. One day the following week, he walks up to the top of the stairs, six steps up. It's his first large jump, he hesitates just a moment, then hurls his body out. He manages to land on the wheels, but the momentum topples him over hard. Tears come to his eyes, I can see he is hurt. He comes over and sits next to me. I tell him: *"It's okay to cry, let yourself feel the hurt in your body. Let's rub the hurt together, we say 'feel better.' You are very brave to try the big jump, you have been preparing for it the whole week."* We sit for awhile, easing his pain, I see him gathering his courage. I ask: *"Are you ready to get back on the horse? Try again?"* His tears have subsided, his hurt has gone away, he's a bit skittish, but he says: *"Sure daddy."* He walks over to those stairs, gets himself ready, then without hesitation, he flies like an eagle, lands perfectly, and coasts over to me with a big smile on his face. This is the beginning of Dakota's marvelous skate-board career.

We visit Ashland several times, we all talk about moving out of California to a smaller place. The boys like Ashland, Dakota already has skateboard buddies, Dylan wants to play soccer. We quickly sell our house and buy a lovely house in Ashland just off Main St. It is now May, we are in the middle of our marital unraveling, and here we are on the road again. Ming suggests that I take the boys and go without her. I bargain for us to all go together, that we'll figure out our options there. Strangely, even though we both acknowledge that our marriage may be over, we are different with one another: kinder, forgiving, tender. Caring about each other's welfare and the well-being of our boys, we all move to Oregon.

Some old friends and several new friends show up at the house the day we arrive. Unloading boxes, moving furniture, welcoming the boys, bringing us food … how marvelous to live in a small town. We are expressly grateful to all of them, still we keep our issues quiet. Once settled, my dance around Ming is tentative. I honor her choice, yet I do not want to lose my marriage and family. I give her plenty of room to talk, mostly I listen, affirm her feelings, find my own accountability, she does the same. I know that I cannot control this. We sleep together, we hold each other, we affirm that we love each other. We do not have sex, but we are not hostile. We tell both our families that we are separating, without drama and a tale of woe. Neither one explains, we do not share details, when they question, we answer mostly: *'We don't know yet.'* The move is a big change, maybe a restart, at the very least another big distraction. Ming temporarily releases the idea of separating. We decorate our new house, meet the neighbors, get the boys grounded and enrolled for school in the Fall. We are grateful that we are no longer in California.

In September '01, we watch on TV the collapse of the twin towers. I sit on the couch with Ming and the boys, and say out loud: *"This is the beginning of the end of the patriarchy."* And I know beyond a shadow of a doubt, that this MensWork that I do is so necessary if we are to create a new healthy masculine. Regardless of what is happening with my marriage, I know the importance of continuing my work, with both men and women. Jim and I do an LMFH the weekend after 9/11 in San Francisco. In December, we offer our final workshop in Seattle. It has run its course, and Jim and I are burnt out. Along with both our wives, we grieve the loss, we are grateful for the tremendous learning, and we are so glad for some down time. It has taken much from us, and we have received gifts beyond measure. Jim and I both believe that the next time we offer this workshop, it will be with corporate women. *For me, my life is never the same.*

Ashland is idyllic, nestled in the beautiful Siskiyou mountains in southern Oregon, twenty miles north of the California border, just up from Mt Shasta. A creek running through town, long time host to the Shakespeare Festival, it has lots of old hippies, I feel right at home. As much as I have learned from the women's work, I am helpless as I watch Ming continue to decline. There are times when she attacks, blames me for all that is wrong in her life. I do my best to stay open to her reflections, they hurt me nonetheless. I lose the thread of what is hers and what is mine, and in my self-judgments, I take on more by blaming myself for her growing insanity. Perhaps this is a remnant shadow from the LMFH work. Maybe I take on too much. Has this work with women taken too much from my edgy masculine? Disturbing to ponder.

Ming's enneagram six-point gifts her with the capacity to sense danger. The downside is she finds it everywhere, even where it is not. She finds it in the outer world … environment, food, drugs, chem-trails. Mostly, she finds it in me … my anger, harshness, male power, not listening, working too much, control over money. Each judgment has a piece of truth that I am working to heal. I begin to see my own shadow masculine more clearly. Still, each of her over-reactions indicate her growing emotional decline, a slipping away from normal reality. My own inner edge gets increasingly blurry. One day, my patience finally at a breaking point, I say to Ming:

> "My dearest M, I love you more than I can ever say in words, and, you are making me fucking crazy. Your ennea-gram wires you to find danger, find fault, find flaws. Surely I am dangerous, faulty, and flawed, and that will never change. So, if you can find someone who is not these things, who could make you happy, who will love you in the safe way that you desire, then I release you to do just that. I love you way too much to hold on and see you suffer like this. If it is really me, then I set you free. However, if perhaps you choose to stay here with me, I ask that when your judgments of me arise, I want you to notice and acknowledge your own projections. Then please, if possible, shut the fuck up, and get some help."

This is the first time that I have ever said this to Ming so directly. From the beginning, I know she is the one, I desire no one else, she is the love of my life, my soulmate, and I am with her till the end of my days. But now, I am at the edge of my own sanity. As her paranoia increases, I stop listening, stop believing that we can fix this, stop trusting her decision-making around the boys, the things she rants about, and the crazy ways that she spends money. She has days of incoherence, days of manic excitement, days of darkness. The rare times that we have sex, we hold each other tight, desperately clinging to the frayed threads of our loving. In those few moments of clarity, we both know that we are under the spell of something that we do not understand. The few friends that remain close to us call it a spiritual emergence. Our abyss feels so deep and dark and personal, it is hard to see any light at all. I watch, heartbroken, as my beloved steadily slips away, and I am not far behind.

In the midst of this, Ming enters menopause, and unilaterally declares a moratorium on sex. We move into separate bedrooms, we do not have sex for over a year. I tend to the boys, they see their mom in trouble, I remind them that this is not their fault. Our friends Paul and Anya, Junpo and Sandra lend love and support as godparents, God knows I cannot do this alone. I stay grounded for them, keep their lives moving in a good direction. I know that what is happening to them with Ming is painful. As hard as I try, I cannot protect them from their own mother. Unless we leave, and not then either.

So each night I read to them … The Hobbit, The Lord of the Rings, Harry Potter, other good stories. Dakota plays baseball, Dylan plays soccer, I go to all their games. They have good friends in school and in the neighborhood. They often ask for overnights, I encourage them to go. With the boys away, and Ming in her silent reverie, it gives me some quiet moments to catch up to myself. I reflect on the insanity of my own childhood, I am disturbed and guilty to see my sons going through the same thing. The only place that I find solace is in my work.

While I still travel to do trainings, I do so less and less. My coaching practice is a good place to mood-alter my helplessness, it provides a continuing sense of purpose. I sit in the elder circle, a group of twenty plus men, most have been in the work a long time. Sometimes I bring my heartache and grief, sometimes I bring my anger and frustration, sometimes I bring my fear and fright at what is happening to the boys, to Ming, to myself. They listen with love and compassion, they do not judge. They offer to me what they can, the situation remains without solution.

Stuck in the cycle of my own insanity, I turn to my writing. I enroll in a writing class in a community college in Medford. The instructor is an old Berkeley hippie, we connect immediately. Her first words to the class: *"Why are you here?"* Ten women and two men in the class, everyone checks in. I say I have written on and off over the years, mostly dream journals, and I need a creative release for what is in my life right now. I am here to see if I have a writing voice, and to find a form. Then Berkeley says to the class: *"Write a paragraph, on anything, you have 15 minutes."* I write the opening paragraph to *"My First Initiation"* essay (Ch 1). It comes out so easily, without thought, from where I do not know. When I read it aloud to the class, Berkeley looks at me and says: *"You sure do have a fucking voice, keep writing, and welcome to my class."*

For the next ten months, I write my childhood story. It provides comfort to my disturbance, emotional release from my pain and heartache, a distraction from my real life, and a clarifying sense of my historical dysfunction that drives much of what is in my life now.

Early one evening, Ming does not come home. I make some calls, nothing. I take the boys in the car, we drive all over town looking, nothing. I call the police, give them a description of Ming and her car. A half hour later, they call back, they have found her car at the edge of town, in a ditch just off the main road. We drive there, the police are waiting. The car is open, there is no damage. Her shoes are in the front seat, no note, the police have scoured the area and found nothing. They tell me to go home, there is nothing they can do right now.

I take the boys out for pizza, we are all scared. They know she has been unstable, I tell them that mom is smart and tough, she'll be okay, she just needs some time and space. I remember how many times the cops came to my house when I was a kid, I know how scared my brother and I were. I snuggle in close to the boys, they too are smart and tough, we hold onto each other, we know it is just us now. For three days we do not hear from Ming. Early one morning she calls, says she is fine. A big sigh of relief, and underneath my fear is a belly full of anger. She is in the southern California desert, with the Yaqui medicine man that we had both previously studied with. She did not want to drive the whole way, so she left the car and hitchhiked. She is at the bus station, she'll be home tonight. I ask her if she wants to talk to the boys, eagerly she says yes. I turn the phone over as both boys talk to their mom. They all laugh and cry, they are excited that mom is coming home. I am not sure what I feel, or what I need to do next. I meditate and pray on and off during the day. I ask for love, patience, compassion, wisdom. I pray for both tenderness and fierce clarity. I pray that I do not let my anger get in the way. It seems that is all I feel these days, a burning fire in my belly. Sometimes I cannot tell the difference between my anger and my acid reflux. I am beginning to sense that they may be one and the same.

That night, we pick Ming up at the bus station, hugs and kisses all around. We are relieved that mom is home and well. Later that evening, after the boys are asleep, Ming asks if I want to hear about her adventure. Of course I am curious … my belly is surprisingly quiet. She lights a candle, and we sit down on the floor. I look at her, I see the beauty that she is, the woman I fell in love with, the mother of our beautiful boys. I see a medicine woman, a spiritual traveler, and her disturbingly splendid glory.

Her story is disjointed, no time lines, no reasons, only her internal struggle to find herself. She says she has been feeling lost and depressed, sometimes she is flying, the heavens sparkling with light. She went to see Lencho to get grounded. He fed and nurtured her, prayed for her, gave her herbs and teas, and some exercises to keep her stable. He sensed that her spirit was adrift, looking for something, not sure if it's past or future. He urged her to be careful, there is danger close by.

Ming goes silent and just looks at me for a long time. Then she says: *"D, thank you for being such a grounding force in my life, for how hard you work, for taking care of the household, for everything you do, especially for taking care of the boys. I know that this has not been easy for you, my spell has become your nightmare. Just know that I appreciate you and I love you always."*

In letting myself feel the pain and shattering at the hands of this woman, my heart cascades into love. Our Love is right here, right now, right in the middle of whatever this mess is, and it always has been. We both know that something much larger is at play, a soul activation, an initiation deeper, darker, and more troubling than anything we have ever faced. Our angels are here somewhere. Sadly, I struggle to discern their light in the middle of my own darkness.

A week later, Ming checks into a hospital, she is in the psyche ward for ten days. Honestly, I am grateful, hoping that she has hit bottom. I take temporary solace in knowing that she is safe. When I visit her the second day, I gaze through the window of the locked door, into an empty room filled with disturbed people … a dozen of them, in their pajamas and robes, wandering around in their own drugged out worlds.

I see Ming close to the door, I wave to her, she looks right through me. I pick her up the day she gets out, she is on heavy meds, not much to say. We visit the doc assigned to her, he tells me that Ming has been diagnosed with bi-polar disorder, that the meds she's on will stabilize her, he will change them in a month. He tells us that she will need to keep taking the meds, not sure how long. He is a recovering bi-polar and swears by this drug. Ming, always the purist, surprisingly agrees.

For the next several months we are mostly stable. The so called *'psychotic episodes'* diminish but do not disappear. Ming has moments of clarity, moments of disturbing distortion. It is the week after Christmas '05, we spend two lovely nights in a quaint bed and breakfast in Ashland. We are tender, loving, connected ... still, I can feel that something isn't right. Over breakfast in bed the morning of our departure, Ming says: *"I have stopped taking the meds, I cannot do this anymore, I need to leave."* Words that I have long dreaded, words that I knew would come again, words that I could never run away from.

Ming decides to move out. She finds a small apartment and gets a part time job. I stay in the house with our boys. She needs some money as she is moving out this weekend. Shocked but not surprised, my heart aches for twenty-four hours. The next morning, I wake up, clear as a bell: finally I know that she has to go, and equally clear that I need to be without her for awhile. I call my friend Tom in San Francisco, he has a house boat in the Berkeley marina. I ask if he can put us up for a few days ... of course, he says. That night, I have a dream and can't remember any of it. Simply, I awaken to the crystal clarity that this is perfect. The boys and I load the car, gas tank is full, San Francisco just five hours south down the pike. As the boys hug their mom and pile into the car, she and I stand in our front yard, looking at each other. At the exact same moment, we both say: *"I love you."* We hug and kiss goodbye, my heart feels a peace and trust that I have not felt in years. The boys and I get home that Sunday, Ming is gone, we rearrange the entire house in a few hours, and fashion it into our *'man cave'*... we know that we are okay here. And my heart knows that Ming will be okay too.

The new arrangement is good for her, it is good for us. The space between is a welcome relief, the boys are adjusting, my work and writing expand. Ming has been seeing a woman therapist, she and her husband have offered couples counseling. I go to check them out, I like both of them. They hold an open non-judgmental space, they feel safe enough that I can bring my truth. I have so much stuff to download, Ming has her share as well. I think perhaps this space and an opportunity to clear the decks will be good for everyone. Every week for ten months we go to therapy work, cleaning house from the very beginning of our relationship, seeing how our past patterns have informed our marriage. Finally, I have an outlet for my built-up anger, resentment, and pain, Ming has a bellyful to download as well. Within this safe container, and maybe for the very first time, we hear each other, we see each other, we are totally vulnerable, transparent, and brutally honest.

One Monday morning in May, we have a couples appointment at ten. Ming calls and asks me to pick her up. I pull up in front of her apartment, and as she gets into the car, I notice she is all dressed up. We have a great session, we know we are making progress. After-wards, I drive her home, we sit in the car talking, she asks me if I would like to come in for some tea. Since the beginning of our separation, I have continuously dropped off and picked up the boys from her place, rarely has she asked me in. I feel her energy, I know what she has in mind. I ask myself if this is good for me, my body answers before my brain. Once inside the door, we don't even make it to the bed. Clothes strewn, bodies askew, soon we find our groove on the living room floor. It's been so long since we had this together, it feels so good. This otherworldly connection, naked on the carpet … this love at once mysterious, confusing, yet unsullied … and by the grace of God, still fully intact. With this opening, with this acknowledgment of love and connection, we move rapidly ahead in our therapy. More truth telling, more vulnerability, more transpar-ency. Ming shares an exercise that she calls "Heart Balance." She says she has been practicing this in her *'bi-polar'* moments, she feels increasingly at peace with her internal conflicts. I am grateful that she is learning to self-modulate.

On November 3, Ming's forty-ninth birthday, in our therapy session, she tells me that she is ready to move back in. We have made tremendous progress in these almost eleven months, more than I ever could have imagined. Not surprising, I feel resistance. In this separation time, I have liberated my own voice and body, paid attention to what is good for me and for the boys, spoken both my hard and vulnerable truths to her, fearlessly. *"Not my problem if you don't like it, I do not live with you anymore."* Selfish yes, also fiercely honest … and I do not want to lose this sense of freedom. In this therapy, I realize that right next to my masculine power, there is still my feminine shadow … my own critical voice, the voice of not enoughness, the voice of shame. I see how my anger unconsciously arises in opposition to Ming's criticisms, anger that I internalize and do not express. I see my projections clearly, and I need to stay vigilant. This truth ripples through me in a whole new way.

In our session, I do not immediately respond to her request to come back home, I see that she is surprised. I simply say: *"I hear you, I need to think about it, let's talk again."* I meditate on this for the whole week, I bring it to my men's circle. Some are in favor of rejoining, some support my liberation. While having two households is costly, I feel my freedom and my integrity are both at stake. One elder recommends that I write up a list of agreements, ask her to do the same, something that we can both commit to. We call our therapists, they are in full support. We bring our respective lists to our next session, it causes considerable conflict. Ming and I both speak our clear truths, we hash out our differences, we eventually find common ground. She wants me present and available, I want her acknowledging and appreciative. She wants me fluid, I want her grounded. She wants me trusting, I want her responsible. Our therapists see the culmination of our work with them … each of us having a clear voice, clear boundaries, vulnerable, honest, negotiable with the other, each knowing when to fiercely take a stand, and when to tenderly surrender. I remember our first couples session many years ago in Evanston. In the couples office was a plaque that said: *"Marriage: To Love, Honor, and Negotiate."*

Consciously negotiating a marital relationship is as difficult a task as there is. It's not like a business deal where it's more instinctive, less emotional, the attachments are easier to see and work with … usually not that deep, probably not that personal. But marital intimacy is a whole different game. For eons, cross culturally, marriage has been the singular stabilizing institution that keeps community in place. Its power cuts across many levels and dimensions, family is sacred … feminine energy is the internal anchor, masculine the external. No longer a survival necessity, these days the institution is on shaky ground, family structures in great flux. Women are not so much at home, families not so solid. With Pisces receding into yesterday, and Aquarius unfolding into tomorrow, old values are upended, new values as yet undefined. Within this family structure is where the core wounding occurs, where the soul's purpose gets seeded, where the brain circuitry is imprinted with mother, father, familial, and cultural wounds. Now the disintegrating container adds the next layer of complexity. At the very core of the family dysfunction is the unconsciousness of these textures, themes, patterns. Thankfully, Ming and I see our multi-layered conflicts, we work the seams separately, we work them together, we find the paths of light, we work the shadows.

There is a dark gray Russian Blue cat that hangs around Ming's apartment complex. Sometimes she lets him into the house, feeds him, gives him some love. Her lease is up the end of November, she wants to move back in on Thanksgiving weekend. And she wants to bring the cat. One of the agreements that Ming and I make is to read some books for couples. She buys a book by John Gray, we have both read 'Mars and Venus,' we like his perspective, we appreciate his humor in the challenge of intimate relationships. This one is titled: "*What Your Mother Couldn't Tell You and Your Father Didn't Know.*" Written specifically for couples, it reveals the imprint of gender roles that our parents played, roles no longer relevant or appropriate for our modern times. The stories are poignant and funny, Ming and I see the myriad mistakes that we make. All the couples in the book could be us. One night, we are reading this book together and Ming asks if we can keep the cat. I chuckle, remembering the joys of our previous feline friends. I say OK, but I have to name him. She asks what name I have in mind. I say: *Dr John Gray.*

Ming moves back in the day before Thanksgiving, all four of us are happy and grateful. Over turkey dinner we have a lively conversation about how to rearrange the furniture. The boys and I like it the way it is, we have made it work for us. Yet we know that Ming's moving back in necessitates a change. Each of us respectfully listens to the wants and desires of the others. By the end of the day, we have a mutually agreed upon schematic that we all can live with. On Friday morning, we get bagels, cream cheese, and lox for breakfast, then set about moving the whole house around. We are done by late afternoon, we sit down to rest and assess our new space. We all agree that we like it. I light some sage, smudge the whole house, shush out the shadows and ghosts of our painful time in Ashland. Then invite in the love and light and hope for better days. We sit back down in front of the fireplace, hold hands, we give thanks that we are back together ... weary yet empowered by the long struggle, and immensely grateful for our healing. The boys are happy that mom is back, relieved to feel mom and dad lovingly together.

Ming's return is sketchy ... sometimes fluid and graceful, she brings much needed *'mother love.'* Sometimes she is erratic, offbeat, disconnected, non-rational. The boys and I look at each other, I smile and remind them that we are okay, that some things take time. In bed at night, Ming and I are close, she recognizes that she has more work and integration in front of her. She acknowledges that the boys are struggling, commits to pay more attention. We keep reading John Gray, his humor keeps us light. Ming poses the possibility of moving again. While Ashland felt like a godsend when we moved here, indeed it has become a living hell. As challenging as it might be ... and god knows where we will go this time ... it makes sense to move. We share this with the boys, they do not like this at all. They have friends, they play sports, play music, they like school. They say: *"Please do not do this again!"*

Our entire ordeal in Ashland renders it impossible to stay here, Ming and I are clear that we have been initiated again, it is time for the next change. The Ashland energy feels stifling, the triggers are everywhere, the memories painful, the boys are wounded. Ming and I work hard to be clean with them. We do not badmouth each other to them, we do not let them get in between us, and we stay deeply connected and committed to good parenting, regardless of the marriage. Too often, struggling or divorcing couples play the kids as weapons. In their own unconsciousness, they are blind to the damage that they do, blind to their own damage doing the damaging. The kids are caught in an untenable place ... *"Who do I be loyal to?"*

Dakota is twelve, Dylan is ten, each bears the deep Ashland wounding. Yet somehow I have managed to keep this grounded and real for them. Having Ming back reinforces our sense of unity. They have learned and persevered through some hard lessons, matured probably way too soon. And they have strong feelings, opinions, wants, and needs about everything, including moving. Ming and I know that we must listen and attend to their perspectives. Still, they are boys, they do not understand the complexity of marital challenges, the deep emotional, psychic, and spiritual issues in our lives ... these are all beyond their comprehension. Ming and I know that there are forces at play beyond our own awareness. Whether it's the energetic influence of Mt Shasta, the high rate of divorced couples in Ashland, or our own family karma finally having its way with us ... we know that soon we will have to put Ashland in our rear-view mirror. We create a vision board, with pictures of different places and space for positive/negative attributes of each. We include all the places that we lived in before, and add a few like Seattle, Denver, and Sedona. Even though both boys resist, we include them in the entire conversation, doing our best to make this a family adventure. Ming's sister, brother, first cousin, and families all live in Denver. They are professional corporate types, not our tribe, but we are in good rapport with all of them. We float out the idea of relocating. They know our story, they honor our journey, they love us and are all too happy to have us. We visit over Christmas, and in the middle of a twenty-four-inch snowfall, we fall in love with Boulder, Colorado.

Chapter 19: **My Brother**

During my year-long separation from Ming, I reach out to my brother Al much more often. As boys, he does not incur the family damage that I do, but he does incur damage from me. My own childhood abuse and pain that I try so hard to bury comes out sideways ... my teenage anger, angst, and testosterone come down hard upon him. When I leave for college in '65, I am eighteen, Al is thirteen. It is the last time we live under the same roof, I rarely look back. When I find MensWork in '88, as I take a deeper look at my family of origin issues, I awaken to the parts in me that have been damaged. But I also start to feel the damage that I have done to others, especially my brother. In cultivating new relationships with men, I feel the heartache of my estrangement from my blood brother.

After my first initiation, I call him, tell him about my experience, suggest that he might consider doing the training. He is respectful, but distant. I imagine he thinks: *"Why the fuck are you calling me now? You never really gave a shit about me, now you want me to do some bullshit workshop with you. Go fuck yourself."* He lives in Florida, married with a baby girl, he has a life that works for him, and that life does not include me. Although I understand his perspective, my heart hurts nonetheless. I feel sad, guilty, ashamed. I make a decision to do everything I can to heal my relationship with my brother.

Across the next eighteen years we talk often, usually I initiate the calls. I suffer his distance, I ache with his unwillingness to reach back ... still I persist. After our boys are born in '94 and '95, we start to visit each other. Al and family live in the East, Ming and I and the boys are in the West, the personal contact is infrequent. After awhile, he acknowledges the efforts I am making, he sees my sincere attempt to heal our relationship. He appreciates my vulnerability, but he is not interested in doing the training. I begin to describe the carpet work, the incredible healing potential for him, for us. He tells me he remembers some of what happened in our youth, but he does not feel it with the depth that I do. Clearly, I want this healing probably more to ease my own pain, yet I sense that he has more pain here than he lets on. I am careful not to push too hard, which is hard for me, I tend to push.

Our phone conversations deepen. I share my struggles in Ashland with Ming, the difficulty in fathering two boys when their mother ... and their father ... are unraveling. I share my health issues, I am open with him like never before. He shares his own difficulties with his family, work, health. We have not been this connected since childhood. I continue to advocate that we both do the men's training together, he begins to see the healing possibilities. There is one coming up in Portland in September '06, I am the weekend leader. His wife investigates MKP and finds all sorts of shit online. She is staunchly against his attending, especially having to fly across the country. In spite of her protest, Al signs up for the NWTA, and books a flight to Ashland. We are on, and we are both scared and hopeful.

The initiation runs from Friday through Sunday, staff are onsite on Thursday. I find Al a place to stay in Portland on Thursday night, and a ride to the site on Friday. I fear that he will bail, I trust that he will show up. When he gets to the site, I breathe a deep sigh of relief. Even though I am the weekend leader, and responsible for the one hundred men on this training, I am in my own emotional and spiritual descent. In the staff circle, I check in with all my personal baggage ... fear, shame, incredible pain and grief with my brother ... of my own childhood, of our early relationship, of the years of distance and disconnection. I imagine that Al might do his inner work around our father, I fear that he will do his work around me.

The pit is a large gymnasium, there are four carpets spread across the entire floor. In the center of the room there are two large adjoining picnic tables, and a half dozen folding chairs atop. The leader and co-leaders rotate sitting in watch over the four working carpets, making sure that everything is safely moving along, and on time. Soon enough Al steps out on the carpet. I overhear some of what he opens with, I know he has chosen a staff man to play the role of his brother. As hard as I try to stay cool, I am crawling out of my skin. One of the co-leaders and another staff man grab me by the hand and take me outside. In no time, I am deep in my own process:

"I have come to MensWork for my own soul's redemption, to heal my karma for my many lifetimes of having inflicted pain and suffering upon others. I know my brother and I have past life history, I have wounded him before. This is my payback, and his opportunity to heal … if he can get through his rage at me for the lifetimes of perpetration."

I weep uncontrollably, my body will not stop shaking.

David is a black co-leader from LA, a dear brother, and he is leading Al's process. I know David well, we have worked together on many trainings, I trust him. Over the years, we have many fathers and sons, and brothers and brothers attend the trainings together, either as initiates or staff or both. As each man does his carpet work, the relative stays out of view to give the man room to work through his issues on his own. The rule of thumb for facilitators is to allow the relatives to reconnect on their own. Every once in a while, the facilitator, at the conclusion of the man's work, invites the relative to connect with the man on the carpet, in real time. I pray that David will be gutsy enough to ask Al to invite me onto his carpet after his process. After what seems like hours, a man comes outside and says: *"Your brother would like to see you now."* I am still a blubbering mess, but here we go.

As I walk back into the gym, the room is unusually quiet. Most of the men have encircled the carpet where my brother is. I step into his space, my brother looks at me. He is drenched with sweat, his hair and clothes are a tangled mess. But his eyes are glowing, tears streaming down his face. He opens his arms to me, I step into his embrace, we hold each other and weep hard ... for our childhood, for our family, for our father and grandfathers, for the unexpressed pain and suffering that all the men in our lineage were never able to heal like this. I know in my bones that this healing goes in all those directions, irrespective of time and space. Other men stand watching and weeping, for their fathers and brothers and the pain in their own male lineages. We say that one man's work is every man's work. It is surely true this day for all of us ... men grieving together, men healing together.

Al and I spend several days back in Ashland ... unpacking and integrating what just happened for each of us, marveling in the closeness that we both have missed and longed for, and just laughing and being together. Dakota and Dylan enjoy hanging with uncle Al, Ming joins us for dinner, we bask in the deep feeling of family. We make a commitment to stay connected, to keep working on our issues together, and to see each other more often. His wife is relieved and grateful, that Al did his healing work, and that he has reconnected with his brother.

I take him to the airport, we hold each other for a very long time. We know that mom and dad are close to the end, then there will be just us. We acknowledge the blood that flows in our veins, we came through the same hole into this family container, we suffered in the same places in similar ways. Our karma is intertwined, our souls are now in harmony. In our tearful gratitude, we hug and kiss and say see ya soon, brother.

Chapter 20: **Out of the Frying Pan**

In the late summer of '06, my own body sharply declines. One day I awake to incredibly hot pain in my groin muscles. I see a chiropractor for a few months, without much success. Finally I get X-rays on my hips, the results show bone on bone on both sides. The right one is more problematic, we set a date for surgery in April. Our plan is to move to Colorado in June. The week prior to surgery, the day before the visit to the doc, Ming and I are talking about therapy and the second surgery. She innocently asks: *"Why don't you get them both done now? You won't need to come back here, nor will you need to find another orthopedist in Colorado. What do you think?"*

Logically it makes sense, physically it feels crazy. The next day I ask the doc, give him all the reasons, and to my surprise, he does not say anything. I ask if his silence is a serious consideration. He sits down and looks at me, then says: *"I rarely do two hip replacements at one time. You are on crutches for a good while, therapy is harder, recovery is slower, and the body remains in shock for many months. That being said, and given your circumstances, if I **would** do double, it would be on a body like yours. You are young, strong, healthy, with very little body fat, you could handle it. If you really want this, I will do it."* I tell him that Ming and I want this, let's do it.

On Tuesday morning, April 3, '07, I have double hip replacement surgery in Ashland Hospital. Our friend Anya comes to visit, she is a medicine woman with great depth and vision. She tells me: *"You have just cut out of your body all the toxic masculine energy that you have carried in your bones, both personally and collectively, in this and many lifetimes. This will open your heart in a way that nothing else could. As difficult as this is, and might be, it is an important spiritual initiation for you."* Little do I know just how prophetic this is.

I cram as much physical therapy as I can into the next two months, and on June 15 we depart for Colorado. I navigate carefully through the move, it is challenging to sit and watch other people work. We rent a lovely three-bedroom townhouse in Boulder, twenty-five miles northwest of Denver … close enough to, and far enough away from Ming's family. Dakota is thirteen going into eighth grade, an upperclassman in the middle school. Dylan is eleven going into sixth, the first year of middle school, and a newbie like his class-mates. They both did the *'Boys to Men'* program in Ashland, they are smart and savvy, we trust they will find themselves here. Still, they both are angry. Even though we remind them how exciting a new city, new school, new friends will be, they remain stubbornly angry for the entire summer.

In the past, I have led a number of New Warrior trainings in Denver, I know several men in the community. I find a men's circle in Boulder, I attend the MKP Colorado leader body meetings as well. My coaching practice is mobile, thankfully, many of my clients follow me. Ming is open like a new flower, bright and shiny, creative, delightful to be close to. We find a new groove, a new level of intimacy, the doom and gloom is gone. She is off all meds, she visits a psychiatrist to challenge her bi-polar label. He studies her history, asks her a series of questions, then tells her that she is not bi-polar, those docs in Ashland were mistaken. But it certainly was something.

Boulder is very different. Ashland is laid back, artistic, edu-cationally fluid, varying ages in the same classroom, familial, and nature focused. Here, there is much more attention paid to grades, status, clicks, colleges. Even in middle school, there are drugs every-where. Relatively quickly, both boys are drinking and smoking dope. Having engaged in all manner of mood-altering substances since I was a teenager, I know this stage, I know this mindset, I know this need. Ming and I have good conversations with the boys, we share our own experiences in this area, we offer sufficient cau-tion. We both know that this is *'normal'* here, that we must make room for this, and that we can handle the degree of difficulty that it will invariably present. Over time, Dakota gets busted for underage drinking in a car, gets his license suspended for two years. Hard earned lesson for him. Dylan gets busted in school for carrying weed. We are in school often, with teachers, counselors, principals. We hear them tell us the Boulder drug stories from a larger perspective. We hear them affirm that both Dakota and Dylan are good kids, intelligent, friendly, with good manners, not any real trouble. They encourage us to keep our eyes open. We pay close attention.

Upon arrival in Boulder, my left hip heals rather quickly, but disturbingly, the right one shows no signs of recovery, it hurts like it did before the surgery. I call the orthopedist from Ashland, he says: *"It takes some time. I have your X-rays, structurally you are fine. Do another round of physical therapy, call me then."* I do another round, no change ... a constant throbbing pain in the very center of my right hip. The Ashland doc writes me a prescription for Percocet. I do a Rolfing series, nothing. I call Ashland doc again, he does not know why I am not healing. Eventually, he tells me that his liability lawyer told him to not talk to me anymore. I am angry, frustrated, adrift, in pain, on opioids ... as fucked up as ever. Most nights, I awake at three in the morning, the meds worn off, the shadows dancing at the foot of my bed. My darkness takes over more and more psychic territory ... *"This is all your fault, this is why your kids do drugs, you should have never done both hips, maybe you need to find a way out of this. If you can arrange a suicide to look normal, Ming will get your life insurance. They'll be okay if you are gone."*

I reach out to Ming, reach out to my men's circle, pray to my guides ... can't find any peace anywhere. Still in pain, I do deep tissue massage, Feldenkrais, yoga, chiropractic, acupuncture ... nothing fucking works. I eat Percocet like candy. I tell my chiropractor about my opioid consumption. He laughs, tells me many of his patients use ten to twenty times more than I do. One day, I am talking to my friend Paul in Ashland. He tells me a man has just done the New Warrior weekend there, he is a medical intuitive, insightful and powerful. I call him, David and I have immediate rapport. For the next six months, we unpack and uncover everything at every level ... physical, intellectual, emotional, spiritual, familial history, past life karma, attitudes, language ... everything.

Finally, one day David says: *"We have done everything that I can think of, still we are unable to establish a cause to your condition. My intuition says go get a new orthopedist, get a whole new set of X-rays ... I think it's structural."*

It is early '09, almost two years since the surgery, I make an appointment with an orthopedist in Boulder. They do a dozen X-rays, I sit in Dr Steve's office while he looks at the pics on his light board. For fifteen minutes he just looks, I sit here twitchy as fuck. Finally, he turns to me, takes off his glasses, and says: *"I know why you are in pain."* With that simple sentence, the fears and grief and tears from down deep in my body come flooding out. For so long I have needed to hear these words, nobody could tell me. He says: *"The cement that holds the prosthetic into the femur has come loose, offset a half inch. Yes, I can fix it, we'll take out the old, roto-rooter the bone, clean up the tissue, put in a new and larger prosthetic."*

The second week in February, I have a right hip revision. Immediately after surgery, I stand up with weight on my right leg ... the deep untouchable bone ache is gone. Yet the pain and weariness of two surgeries, the physical and psychic invasion, the upset across multiple body levels ... this burden remains heavy. I feel at war with my body, it has betrayed me like never before. I am fragile, constantly achy when I walk, balance is shaky ... I feel like an old man at sixty. I struggle with the Percocet. The *'druggie'* in me likes the high, I tell myself this is why the boys are doing drugs. A month after surgery, I go cold turkey ... I have chills and sweats and body ache on and off for three months.

Dakota turns eighteen in Feb '12, graduates high school in June, gets into the University of Colorado, does the NWTA in September. His carpet work is splendid. At the conclusion, the facilitator has Dakota invite me onto his carpet. He confronts me with my bossiness, my power and authority, my arrogance and control, my conflicts with Ming, making him grow up too fast, and how deeply I have hurt him. With a full and tender heart, we hold each other, and through my tears, I say to him:

"Dearest Dakota: My first-born beautiful son, I know all too well how much I have hurt you, and from the bottom of my heart, I humbly and sincerely apologize, please forgive me. I am so proud of you ... your honesty, your intelligence, your heartfelt sensitivity, your good moral compass, and the good man that you are, that you have always been. I have awaited this day since before you were born. You are such a gift, and a blessing in my life. Thank you."

Dylan is on a different trajectory, doesn't give a shit about school, couldn't care less. And he does not need my approval. I push Dylan, hard and demanding sometimes, still in my own stuckness in mistaking school for real education. I fear his failure, I fear my failure. The harder I push, the more I try to exert control, the more he juts his jaw and silently says: *"Fuck you."* Somewhere along this path, I remember Ani's comments: *"He is stubborn, generous, truthful, and he will challenge everything you tell him, and will always do it his way. He is a true force of nature, and he has a very large mission to live in this lifetime."*

In that moment of remembering, I feel the depth of my soul commitment to Dylan. That as his father, I am here to lay the groundwork for him, so that he may cross the threshold, fully empowered, into his true mission ... whatever it takes, no matter how hard it gets.

In and out of classrooms and schools through all of his high school years, they all say the same thing: *"Dylan won't listen to anybody or anything. If he doesn't want to do something, that's it, he does not negotiate. He smokes a lot of weed, is mostly checked out, does the bare minimum. Otherwise, he is a good, kind, quiet, smart kid."*

David, my medical intuitive, and I have become good friends. He and Susan visit us in Boulder, we do not visit them in Ashland. They are journeyers like us, she from Chicago, he from Toronto. A continuous thread in our ongoing conversations is the idea of moving out of the US. They have researched Uruguay and Ecuador, Mexico seems to be the closest and easiest to get into. In early '12, they move to San Miguel de Allende, a small city in central Mexico, six thousand feet high plateau, a five-hour bus ride southeast to Mexico City. Back in the 40's and 50's, it was an artist community, still is, with a fairly large ex-pat population. The weekend after Dakota's NWTA, I fly down to SMA. I spend ten days there, fall in love with it. The architecture is Spanish, a cathedral in centro, the streets European, the shops quaint and funky. It has been voted the best city in Mexico, it has charm, style, and it has first, second, and third world conditions. I return home, tell Ming about San Miguel, encourage her to visit.

In early '13, Dylan moves into heroin. We do not know this at first, he is out of the house more often than not. Distant and silent when he is around, he has essentially disappeared. We do our best to nourish him when he allows, we let go of school issues, as it only causes conflict. The guys that he hangs with are seedy. Our trust level diminishes, we tell him not to bring anyone into the house. He finds a girl, brings her around, we give them safe harbor, she proves more dangerous than the guys. During the year, he has two over-doses, everything has spiraled way out of control. I am unraveling again, deeper and darker than ever.

I have a colleague in Boulder. He is sponsoring a medicine couple from Brazil, they offer a series of workshops and individual sessions. The woman is an ayahuasca curandera, I sense she has medicine for me, maybe more than I realize. I have this dream:

I'm in the desert ... Mexico or the southwest or South America ... with the ancient people. There are many women dancing, one dances up to me and looks into my face. She is my size, voluptuous, dressed in colorful garb. From her wide set purple eyes, she looks deeply into mine. She is radiantly alive with healing medicine. Without saying a word, she tells me to let go of the white man's ways. She offers me a piece of cloth, like a blouse. I am flying through the canyons, sharp red and orange rocks, narrow passageways, bright sun. I hold onto the blouse as it carries me up on the wind. We are all trying to get out of the grasp of the white man.

I am walking through the town. All the ancient people are shamans, all in altered states ... peyote, ayahuasca, mushrooms. I see a white man in a black military uniform, taking videos of the whole town. He moves fast, has powerful cameras, weapons, sophisticated technology. We know that he is the enemy, yet I am not afraid. I know it is possible for all of us to disappear.

In the town, I see a very old medicine man, cutting open a white snake down the middle. He tells me that I must drink the snake's blood or venom, not from its head but from its body. I feel a twinge of fear. He reassures me, he tells me the medicine will stop the shakes and take away the fear.

I forward this dream to her through my colleague, she responds positively, says that ayahuasca is snake medicine. When they arrive in Boulder, we spend considerable time together, she tells me that Dylan is safe, protected, deep in his own initiation. She confirms his power and mission, tells me that I need to expand **my own** perceptual apparatus, and trust the spiritual evolution of my entire family. They invite me to come to Brazil, spend some time with them, allow the ayahuasca medicine to initiate me into my next level.

In June '13, Ming visits Susan and David in San Miguel. The plan is to stay a month, I will fly down, stay a week, then we fly back together. The second week there, Ming calls, tells me that she is not coming back. My heart feels that all too familiar ache, I just listen. She tells me: *"This is not about you or us, it is about the burden of parenting, the plight of Dylan, the darkness of the US, the struggle to make sense out of this life. I love San Miguel, you do too. I want us to move here."* I fly down in early July, indeed Mexico is enticing. The complexity of a move at this time is simply too much. Dylan is almost eighteen, hopefully he graduates high school next year. I anticipate resistance from both boys again but even more so, this feels like wrestling with a bear. Ming remains committed to her own inner world journey, logic eludes our conversations. I come home deeply uncertain of the future. Once again, I hold the container as best I can for me and the boys. But this time is way different. With Dylan in darkness, Dakota in school, Ming in Mexico, I focus on **my own** upcoming journey to Brazil. My prayer is that whatever may happen for me there, it will bring insight and strength, in order to consciously navigate these familial complexities. Ming stays in San Miguel for four months.

In November, I fly to Brazil, and spend two weeks with the curanderos in their compound. They are hospitable, somewhat pre-occupied with house reconstruction and community, I have lots of alone time. The husband and I walk and talk often, he teaches me about the ayahuasca plants. He cuts the vines, makes the brew, then accompanies me on my first journey. His container is beautiful … walls adorned with much art and artifacts, room painted in an array of colors, with couches, carpets, pillows, blankets everywhere, and a terrific sound system … definitely a masculine energy room. He doesn't say much, wants this first journey to be all mine. We sip the tea together, he turns on some exquisite music, and within a short while, I am in my journey:

> *I am a priest during the Inquisition, in Spain or Portugal. I am in the cellar of the castle, where the dungeons and prisons are. The screaming is deafening, the whip's loud crackle landing on flesh. The smell of shit and puke and urine is nauseating, the smell of fear and despair overwhelming.*
>
> *I walk along the corridors, the inmates moan, some beg me to pray for them. They know that killing themselves is a mortal sin, yet they cannot bear the pain anymore. I dare not hear their confessions, I am too full of my own guilt and shame. I am a part of this horror, the 'inquisitor' who finds the reasons for their heresy, who condemns them to prison or burning. The scene changes.*
>
> *I am in a square austere room … single bed, small table*

with candle, a Bible. I pull out a whip from under the bed. I remove my heavy wool garment, and the lighter shirt underneath. I kneel at the foot of the bed, staring up at the crucifix upon the wall. And slowly I begin the rhythmic swing, the thongs and hooks find my flesh. Bearing the pain outside quiets the pain inside. I do not remember passing out.

The nausea rises in my body, I step outside into the night, the sound of insects a symphony to my ears. I puke out onto the trees, the jungle welcomes my poison. I purge for a long time, it is cleansing to body, mind, spirit. I reenter the container, my guide sits quietly in the corner, eyes closed, swaying to the music. I write down my vision, there is plenty of time to talk. I place a pillow on the thick carpet, and lay back down. Immediately, the music captures me, producing visions in my head:

Castles made of precious gems of varying shapes ... pink, turquoise, ruby red, sapphire, emerald, gold and silver ... the walls moving up and down, everything weightless, etheric, non-corporeal. The percussive rhythms move my body, I stand up, feel like I can fly. An angel appears ... feminine, large white feathered wings, white robe with a gold sash, a sword in her raised right hand. She smiles at me, left hand extended, beatific and merciful ... the heaviness in my heart is gone. I feel light, cleansed, forgiven. Tears flow gently down my cheeks.

In no time, the first light breaks. Each of us awakens from our dream state, tired but coherent. We gather ourselves and step outside to greet the sun. We share our experiences, I tell him that this priest in me has been looking for redemption for a very long time. He says that the journey always belongs to the medicine. It finds the wounds within, administers accordingly, sometimes offering agony, sometimes ecstasy. Today, the ayahuasca has blessed you with both.

I sleep into the afternoon, there is fresh fruit and lemonade in the kitchen. Dinner is sumptuous. He is quiet and introverted, I do not get much conversation about my process. She is more outgoing, offering me insights into past lives. She explains: *"The time signatures mean nothing. It is our karma that carries the soul's themes and threads of unresolved psycho-spiritual lessons, across time and space. When we are ready to confront our transgressions, the medicine knows what to do."*

With Ming's unraveling, with Dylan's fall into heroin, with my own guilt and shame and self-flagellation, this piece of forgiveness is more than welcome. Once again, my *'angels'* find me, especially when I am in my darkest darkness.

I spend most days on my own … walking, reading, writing, listening to music. People come by daily, most do not speak English, and surely I do not speak Portuguese. A beautiful language, I find a music station on Pandora. We go into town every other day, I buy some things for Ming and the boys. Soon I will journey with the woman. I enter her container three days before the medicine. This one is different, it is not what I have imagined. The room has a thatched roof, stone walls open at the top. It is a distance from the rest of the compound, deep in the jungle. There are paintings of mermaids and angels and pixies on the walls, and large breasted dark-skinned women, in various states of undress. It is spartan, hardly decorated, a couple of mattresses, a single pillow and blanket, no bathroom, a box of tissues, a large candle. I am without electronics, without reading or writing materials. She brings me only fruit, three times a day, she is silent. In preparation, I walk, meditate, fantasize, dream.

The night of the third day, both she and he enter the container with two large congas, I am surprised that he is here. With very little fanfare, we drink the tea. They lie together on a mattress, I lie upon the other. The candle is dim, I can hardly see them across the room. The music is loud, pulsing percussions, singing, screaming, grunting, groaning in ancient tongues. I imagine the couple is fucking, I cannot see. After a while, she gets up, naked to the waist, large pendulous breasts down to her round belly. She goes over to the congas and starts to pound the skins. And for a full hour, she pounds those drums relentlessly, never stopping to take a break, hardly to take a breath, sweat pouring down the front of her body. I lie down on the mattress, close my eyes, and this comes:

It is a parade of the snake people. Snake heads on human bodies, human heads on snake bodies, snakes coming out of cocks, snakes coming out of breasts. Giant snake men with giant snake cocks, snake women riding upon them, heads thrown back, in screaming unbridled ecstasy.

Right down the middle of the street, the King and Queen of the Snake Parade ride upon a gigantic snake. The king steers the snake, the queen rides upon the huge snake cock of the king. Everything is pulsing, pumping, everyone is fucking, all the snakes are writhing ... a fucking snake orgy.

This is the primal thrust, the original seeding of life, the unsanitized garden of eden. It is in each cell, each heartbeat, each life form, each in-breath and out-breath ... it is life constantly birthing itself through us.

Then suddenly she stops drumming. Together, they stand up, bow to me, and silently walk out the door. With cocks and cunts and snakes swirling in my head, I walk out into the jungle to purge. The milky white liquid keeps coming out of me, wave after wave, I feel my core innards coming out of my mouth, I can't stop coming. When it finally settles, I feel clear, empty, full, relaxed ... post coital. I lie back down, I sleep and dream, I awake at first light.

I fly back home on Thanksgiving weekend, greeted by Dylan's third overdose, he is just out of the hospital. Ming is fearfully disturbed, Dakota is numb, I am completely exhausted, and far from integrated. In my absence, my men's group has been in support of Ming throughout Dylan's ordeal. I visit with them the next week, they hold me in my disheveled mess. In their arms, I wail from my gut, weep from my broken heartedness, quiver and shake from the fear and terror and powerlessness that is my life. I tell them that suicide is never far from my conscious thoughts.

PART IV: *The Unraveling*

I visit the ayahuasca community in Boulder for support. I share my dreams and visions, I share my learning, I share my disappointment at the limited integration time they made available to me in Brazil. They invite me to do medicine with them. I know that I need some deep integration, I imagine that journeying with the community may foster that end. That weekend, I do another ayahuasca journey, it is a horror. My darkness deepens. I say to Ming that I will not survive another Colorado winter. We have spoken in depth with Susan and David, they invite us to move to Mexico. I now want us to consider this, as I know that I cannot handle much more.

Chapter 21: **Running Out of Room**

In early '14, I get a call from school. Dylan is busted with drugs and needles, he is incarcerated at the sheriff's office, ready to be released, come get him. Ming comes to pick me up at the office, I wait downstairs in the bright sunlight. I think of Dylan, then I see his energy body vibrating right in front of me. Directly above this apparition, I see a swirling white energy dropping itself around Dylan's energy body. In that moment, I remember the curandera's words that Dylan is safe and protected, I remember that he is a force of nature, I remember my soul commitment to him. In a nano-second, all my fear and concern and worry for Dylan disappears from my body. In its place, I feel the love, the protection, and Dylan's good karma surrounding him, and me as well. Ming arrives, I tell her my vision, we both breathe deeply.

We drive to the jail, Dylan is out in ten minutes. Surprisingly, Dylan is humble, honest, apologetic, he says the drug was ketamine, and the needles are not his. He has been selected by his drug community to hold the clean needles, as he is the most trustworthy. Tears come to all our eyes, for in that moment, we all bask in love and compassion. And even some trust, maybe not for Dylan's actions, but a trust that there truly is a healing arc in Dylan's multi-dimensional initiation, one that I am powerless to fix or control. All I can do is hold the energy.

The next week, we are called into school by Dylan's principal. A bright and beautiful woman, Joan gets who we are, she gets Dylan, she gets our essential goodness, and she gets the magnitude of all that is unfolding in our family dynamic. She has good news ... Dylan has enough credits to graduate. In fact, he has enough credits to graduate early ... like now. They want him out, he wants out, we want him out. There is an in-patient rehab center in downtown Denver, we offer a month to Dylan, surprisingly, he agrees. The following Monday, we drive Dylan to rehab, it will be two weeks before we can visit. On our way home, Ming and I weep, we laugh, we are relieved that Dylan is safe, at least for now. We are humbled to have a ray of hope, and blessed with a glimpse of the unseen forces at play in our lives. Ming and Dakota and I go out for sushi that night, we all drink a little sake, it's been so long since we have laughed and celebrated.

With some time and distance from the immediacy of Dylan's addiction, Ming and I consider a move to Mexico. We share this with Dakota, ask him if he wants to go. He is completing his second year at university, he tells us there is nothing here in school for him. He will get a job, has an apartment lined up with friends, he wants to stay in Boulder. Even with rehab, we have no illusion that Dylan is ready for sobriety. In our long walk these days, I share with Ming my inner conflicts:

> "If we stay here under these conditions, death feels close at hand for me. Ayahuasca has been both illuminating and dark, I am done with it. How can we leave, how do I live with myself abandoning our eighteen and twenty-year old sons? I am at the most serious existential crossroad of my life. I have always been the enabler, having needs and putting myself first so very hard for me. My father did nothing but put himself first, I swore I would not do that. Instead, I unconsciously deem myself unworthy, and put myself last.

Wrestling with this, considering every possible scenario, trying to find the both/and options, balance eludes me. Finally, the terrifying statement that I feel close by, the decision that I do not want to make, the brutal truth that is right in front of me: *"It is better that I stay alive in Mexico and give our sons an abandonment wound, then stay in Colorado and give them a dead father wound. Oh God, please give me the strength to do this."*

We call the Mexican embassy to apply for two visas. A woman named Blanca Luz (*White Light*) gives us an exhaustive list of documents and forms, says that if we do all these things, we will be granted the visas. It takes us many days to assemble everything.

Even though the truth has been revealed, living it is terrifying. We sit on the paperwork, I just cannot call for the appointment at the embassy. A couple of days later, Tom, an old friend from San Francisco calls me, I have not talked with him in a couple of years. He says: *"I met a man recently who calls himself an 'astro-cartographer' … someone who tracks your astrological lines across the grid of the earth. The map he creates tells you where all your planetary lines are located … health, wealth, love and romance, mysticism, healing, conflict, transformation, etc. I have been thinking about you lately, I know you guys have moved a lot, thought this might be useful. His name is Dan, here is his contact info, let me know what happens."*

We call Dan the next day, he does the mapping for all four of us in three days. We print the maps, they are revealing. Neither of the boys have lines going through Mexico. Ming and I both have a number of very powerful lines going through western India, and interestingly right through the middle of Mexico. Dan confirms that San Miguel will be deeply healing and transformational for us. He says that the boys will be fine, as they have good lines going through Colorado. And he points out something that shocks us: Ming has a Mars line going down the entire west coast of the US. We tell Dan about Ming's difficulties in California and Oregon, in her unraveling across twelve years. We long suspected that something invisible, unknowable, something mysterious was pulling the strings, and we were just the puppets. And here it is finally revealed, all these years later, the missing piece to this puzzle … that Ashland was the final unraveling, an initiation personal, familial, celestial. I wonder if they all aren't.

This is also the final confirmation that San Miguel is the right place, this is the right time, and this move will be healing for all of us. We call the embassy the next day. A week later we meet with Blanca Luz. We have filled out every page requested, and there are many. We make a duplicate set, and walk into Blanca's office at 8:55 am on Friday. By 10 am, we walk out, each with an ID, and a six-month visa, renewable in San Miguel for a full year, temporary and permanent residence available.

That weekend, we talk with Susan and David, tell them we will come in the summer. They tell us they had been planning to go south then, and their house is available to us. That weekend, we talk to the boys, invite them both to come with us, they both decline. In some strange and unexpected way, they handle this much better than I imagined. I do not tell them about my own inner struggle. Instead, I tell them about the astro maps, I describe the larger dimensions at play, that each of us is on a growth path, and we are all in this together. And while this will be challenging, this will also be good. Dakota has his plans, I imagine that Dylan is relieved, he is now on his own, he can do his thing, whatever that is. We buy plane tickets for July.

In June '14, Dakota finishes his last class at CU, and moves out that weekend. Dylan, just out of rehab in time to graduate with his class, wants to move into a sober house. We get him moved, we pay three months' rent in advance. On July 13, both boys take us to the Denver airport. Through wet tears, hugs and kisses, and deepest love, Ming and I board a one-way flight to Leon, MX.

Part V: Mexico

Chapter 22: Renewal

In high school, I took three years of Spanish; in college, two years of French; on the road, five months in Italy; and in my heart, I have my Sicilian Nona's sweet and funny broken Italian/English. Far from fluent, I commit to taking Spanish lessons. I trust I'll get by just fine here. Susan and David are driving south in August, we have more than a month with them to get grounded. Their house is lovely, thankfully a soft landing in a foreign country. I have no clients for a few weeks, we have plenty of time to acclimate. We live just outside of town, and for the first time in a very long time, we have no car. Many of the streets are cobblestone and uneven, walking for me requires conscious attention. While my hips are stable, ambulation on these streets remains a challenge. The exercise feels good, walking throughout this town opens our eyes wide, opens our hearts wider. Seeing wealth and poverty in close proximity awakens us to our own privilege. Lots of places speak English, another privilege. The Mexican people are friendly, kind, even welcoming. People say hello to each other: *"Buenos días,"* and reply in kind. I notice that when I initiate the hello, Mexicans reply. When I do not initiate, neither do they. I continue to notice that I am in a whole new world.

Coming from New York, where my first learned instinct on the streets is vigilance, I feel much more at ease here. One night, I am walking home alone at dusk. As I pass through one barrio along the way, I hear some male conversation not too far behind me. I feel my shoulders rise, my hearing sharpens, my breath quiets, I prepare my body for potential conflict. As they pass me, I see a father holding hands with his early teenage son, they are laughing and joking and carrying on. I smile, breathe a sigh of relief, and say to myself: *"Yes, you are in whole new world. This is not New York, not the US, not as dangerous as you imagine. And here, in this country, there seems to be a greater appreciation for the feminine. Guadalupe is everywhere, fathers and sons hold hands, family and friendships are their core values. These are loving people, and for the most part, it's time to relax your guard."*

This change in perspective, this conscious shift from a deeply imprinted instinct, initiates a monumental shift in me. The very idea of surrender, at any and every level, is always predicated on trust. I realize how much I have not trusted, that as much as I consciously practice emotional literacy, as much as I advocate for feminine consciousness in men, as much as I feel compassion and tenderness in my relationships, I acknowledge that in the deeper textures of my body, building trust is still a practice.

David tells me about a men's circle in San Miguel, I visit my first week in town. A half dozen men, middle age and older, they are new in the work, yet welcoming, willing, and vulnerable. I check in, offer my background in MensWork, they are grateful to have someone with experience. During the work round, I drop into my grief around leaving Dakota and Dylan behind. Afterward, several of the men express appreciation for my clarity and especially my tears, that it gives them permission to express their own deep feelings. They ask about MKP, I offer a brief history, I tell them that I have been disconnected from the organization for awhile. I commit to coming every Tuesday afternoon.

During that first month, Ming and I are introduced to many people in town, both Gringos and Mexicanos. We are grateful that most are friendly, sensitive, evolving, and happy that we are here. Ming and I start Spanish lessons, I get my office and necessary connective apparatus organized and functional. I ask the boys to set up Skype so we can video regularly. We call them the first weekend, we all miss each other very much. They both have jobs, and are okay where they live. Dylan says he is working hard to stay sober. We tell them about San Miguel, we invite them to come visit soon, maybe Thanksgiving or Christmas. Ming seems stable in our new environment, she is accepting of our family situation. At times, I am emotional ... the guilt, shame, fear still visit. Thankfully, the grief flows easily, for my heart has never been this open.

Chapter 23: **Who Am I Now?**

When I am born, my mother wants to name me Albert, after my father. My father wants to name me Dennis, after singer Dennis Day. They name me Dennis Paul Shikaly. When he was small, my brother Al Jr lisped, so he calls me DeeDee. The kids on the street all call me Denny. I never liked the name Dennis, it does not quite fit my imaginary picture of myself. And once rock'n'roll comes along, I envision way cooler names then Dennis. When Ming and I marry, we join each other's name. At midlife, my legal name is Dennis Paul Mead-Shikaly.

My childhood neighborhood is multi-ethnic. I have dark skin, I am drawn to the dark-skinned boys … Charlie the Greek, Robbie a Sicilian like me, and Guy, John, and Bobby the black boys at the end of the block. The rest of the street is white, most are Catholic … I feel myself an outsider. Just before junior high school, we move into a Jewish neighborhood. I am one of very few kids in the neighborhood who is not Jewish. All my boy friends are getting bar mitzvahs. Even though I am in classes throughout school with most of these kids … I feel myself an outsider. A quarter of our high school is Jewish, a quarter black, a quarter Italian, a quarter assorted white. I have friends in all four quarters … still, I feel outside.

In '65, I go to a left-wing liberal arts college in upstate New York. Very few kids of color, the NY downstate kids are mostly Jewish, the NY upstate kids are mostly Christian white. In the summer of '66, I get turned on for the first time. Within the year, I am fully psychedelicized. My music is soul, blues, doo wop, acid rock, Beatles and Stones. I grow my hair long, we are a loose affiliation of freaks, sikkies, hippies, drug addicts, weirdos. Here outside the mainstream, I no longer feel like an outsider, maybe this is my tribe. After graduating in '69, working as a first-grade teacher in the Bronx, no white kids in my class. Alienated in most places, I feel strangely at home here. In the classroom reading, writing, dancing with the kids, the parents invite me to their parties, I drink and smoke and dance with them, one mother makes me a dashiki. Yet as much as I love it here in the Bronx with my kids, I feel trapped in NYC. There is a similar Head Start program on a Hopi reservation in northern Arizona. I apply, they have no resources to bring me on board. The road is calling me, I cannot stay … another lost boy in America.

Like Parsifal, I wander for almost twenty years. When I find the men's network, it is an oasis, a resting place, a rarely felt at-homeness. Then finding Ming, becoming a father, initiated every which way, and here I am, another twenty years later … and still on the move. From New York to San Francisco to Europe to LA to Chicago to Tucson to Santa Fe to San Diego to Santa Clara to Ashland to Boulder … and now Mexico. Here, south of the border, in an ancient land of sun and tequila and plant medicines, a culture of family, a people close to the land, gentle, humble, open. Everything seems slower, I am slower, I feel at home here.

I am moved by the names of the Mexicanos, they use a naming structure like the Spanish. The first two names are both surnames, there is no middle name. The third name is paternal, the fourth name is maternal. Typically the paternal name is used, and just as often it is dropped and the maternal name is used. To hear a woman or a man speak their full name opens my heart. It is lyrical, poetic, full of pride. There is a culture here very different from anything I have experienced. There is a richness of history, of both light and shadow. The Mexicanos are a *'conquered'* people, having been colonized by the Spanish since the early 1500's, when the native Aztecs were conquered. The poverty, the *'noble'* suffering of Catholicism, the acceptance of reinforced second-class status … renders a people passive, they do not know how to say no. Yet with their closeness to the earth, their embrace of family, their open heartedness … there is a peacefulness here, a joy to be alive. Ming and I are grateful to be in their country, in their company, and especially to be welcomed into their homes.

Just up the street from where we live, there is a stone sculpture of the Lady of Guadalupe, or Virgin of Guadalupe, a Catholic title of the Blessed Virgin Mary. The story dates back to 1531, when an indigenous Mexicano peasant claims to have seen the Virgin Mary five times. The last thing Mary said to him: "*¿No estoy yo aquí que soy tu Madre?*" ("*Am I not here, I who am your Mother?*"). Like the Mother Mary, Guadalupe's supernatural image is Mexico's most popular religious and cultural symbol, legitimizing their own indigenous Mexican sacred origins.

I think about my lineage. I have no family tree on my father's Persian side, I have much more information on my mother's side ... Sicilian, Greek, Albanian. My Nona's name was Sebastiana Nanina Tine, my mother's name was Vicenza Maria Cusimano. In this feminine land of Mexico, within this matriarchal family structure, within my own endeavor for masculine/feminine balance, I honor my maternal lineage and take the name Dene Maria Sebastiana.

That night, I dream:

I walk into a room, there is a woman dancing alone in the middle of the floor, the music is Spanish or Portuguese ... slow, sensual, soulful. She is exotic, neither young nor old, long black and white hair, parted in the center. Her clothing is dark, with bursts of color. I step onto the dance floor, she turns to me, opens her blouse. From her left breast, a rainbow-colored snake emerges, and rises to eye level. The she-snake is powerful, opens her mouth to reveal long sharp fangs, dark eyes ... I am unafraid. I open my mouth, she splashes warm sweet milk down my gullet. I have never tasted anything like it, never felt more deeply satisfied. The snake returns from where she came inside the woman's chest. I awaken in the sweetness.

Chapter 24: MensWork Reunited

During my years in Boulder, I stay connected to MKP mostly to have my sons initiate. I formally take a sabbatical in Jan '11, I am now a Leader Emeritus. I have very little relationship with the organization, minimal involvement at the local level. Dakota initiates in '12, Dylan in '14. Our move to Mexico puts MensWork in my rearview mirror.

In March '15, I receive an MKP broadcast email, announcing the first NWTA in Mexico that following weekend. I am totally shocked by this, I have no idea that there are initiated men here. I know the three men who are leading the weekend. I quickly send an email to them, stating that I now reside in San Miguel de Allende. All three write back, and invite me to come staff in Cuernavaca. That next Thursday morning, I am on a bus to Mexico City, connecting with a ride to the site two hours west.

The Thursday night staff meeting is a home coming for me, I know several men from the US who are here to support this first training south of the border. They introduce me to all the other men, telling them about my storied past with the Project, and that I reside in San Miguel. Jaime Valdez and Carlos Legaspy are the prime movers in Mexico, we connect deeply, they are so glad to have an experienced man in their country close by. Men are hungry here, Jaime and Carlos know they need a good teacher. Several of the Mexican staff men have recently initiated in the US, a few have staffed once or twice, most are rookies. This first meeting, designed to build the container, focuses on the cultural issues between Mexico and the US. The Mexicano men are both grateful and angry. The heart and power of these men move me deeply, their clarity and language skills surprise me. Their willingness to confront the out of balance status quo says a lot about them. A Venezuelan man offers to translate for me. There are a couple of men I feel drawn to, I reach out personally and vulnerably, they reach right back. Falling in love with men in this work is a continual joy, being back in MensWork feels shockingly wonderful, that it is in Mexico delights me.

PART V: Mexico

I gratefully accept the invitation to join the leadership team as emeritus. The conversations are focused on the now, yet far reaching about the possibilities of tomorrow. Jaime and Carlos have a large vision, not only for Mexico, but for all of Latin America. I tell them that I am no longer certified to lead trainings. I also tell them that I am open to coming to Mexico City as often as necessary, I'd be honored to teach what I know. I know all three weekend full leaders, we have worked together in the past. Each speaks to me over the course of the weekend, catching up and seeing what my intentions are. This is a brand new community, much in need of training. They are also without any certified men, my credentials would give them some immediate gravitas. Each in turn, and all of them together, encourage me to recertify in July back in Chicago. Ironically, the site of the certification weekend is the same camp in Kenosha where I first initiated. I tell them a bit about my recent past, the unraveling, the integrating time that I am in, the healing energy of Mexico that I feel already. I tell them that I will ponder this next step, talk to Ming, and let them know when I do.

Ming is not surprised, actually quite happy for me. She knows how much I miss the trainings, how important the work still is for me. We talk about my going to the US in July, about the ambition of Jaime and Carlos, the need in the community. Ming reminds me of the importance of my boundaries and my own healing. She knows all my past conflicts with the organization, she encourages me to go back to Chicago, see what happens.

The three leaders write letters of support, and forward them to the MKP Certification Chair. Each letter expresses both the urgency of support for this new community, especially one as important as Mexico and the entire Southern Hemisphere. And the request that I not get trapped in the political tentacles of certification. Still, I know the Project and its propensity toward formality. Its rules and my 'rule-breaker' have clashed in the past, I make no assumptions about how they might handle this. I go to Chicago to once again sit before a panel.

At home, I am relishing in the beauty of the land and people, at the slower pace of my life … and now, at the resurrection of MensWork. Jaime lives in the heart of Mexico City, he and I become instant friends. He speaks fluent English, we have much in common, there is an urban ease and elegance in our relationship. He visits us in San Miguel, Ming and I visit him in Mexico City. Once or twice a month, I travel down at his invitation. The bus lines are first class, I come to enjoy the journey … the quiet time, the reading time, the nap time, the music time. I feel a deeper integration in my body and soul, and a rising sense of purpose. I view my MensWork journey from a larger dimension. My position as an emeritus gives me a unique space on the trainings. No longer burdened with the responsibilities of a certified leader, I open to the non-rational part of this work … the spiritual, cultural, global, archetypal … the transformational potentiality at the core of this work.

I see my own initiatory trajectory. This is the eighth time being present at a community's first NWTA. Right here in my own backyard, right in the middle of Mexico. Ming reminds me of the astro map, all my power lines are right here. I am at ease, at-home, I belong, I am in mission. My masculine and feminine are in balance, there is room here for both. Teaching this work to younger men fills my heart with joy and humility. My distance from the Project was necessary, I pray that I meet it again from a different mindset. In communicating with the panel, not surprising, the attitude of the certification chair is strictly by the book. I have been on sabbatical for more than four years, I must fully certify. No quick way through the process. Still, engagement with authority brings out my defensive arrogance … a cover for anger, fear, and privilege. My shadows are clearly in front of me.

I need not fight this, I know who I am. I commit to myself to stay ever-present throughout this entire process, to not react, to focus on what is before me, and to control only what is within my immediate sphere of influence. The institution's shadows are well known, the leaders have been grappling with this since we institutionalized, it's what institutions do. With surprising ease, I honor my *'inner rebel'*, and commit to following the rules.

In July '15, I fly to Chicago, and make my way up to the Kenosha woods. Twice a year, the North American Leader Body of MKP offers a formal opportunity for leaders to certify, and every two years to recertify. A man sits before a certification panel, made up mostly of other certified men. Each man is questioned, challenged, and invited to state his case for certification. The inquiry is rigorous, insightful, brilliant in its own way, MKP is an institution learning and evolving:

How rare does an organization question its leaders, how rare does it hold its leaders accountable, how rare does it evaluate the leadership skills of its leaders, how rare does it acknowledge the 'shadows' at play beneath the surface of everything.

The panel is fierce out of necessity, the work we do is life changing, dangerous, it requires conscious rigor at all levels. The panel's primary directive is to certify men who are awake, capable of orchestrating and holding space for archetypal initiation. It is a unique time and place, where a man gets a momentary glimpse of his true deep masculine, in all its joyful, pulsing glory.

The panel consists of ten men … diverse, skilled, vigilant, experienced, curious. As much as men bitch about the process, especially those men who do not pass this muster, rarely does the panel err. I ask Mariano, one of the leaders from the previous Mexican NWTA, to be an ally to my process. He and I walk in together and take our seats opposite the panel. I know most of the men on the panel, one man I have had previous conflict. That issue is stated at the beginning, so as to keep its shadows from influencing the process.

It is twenty years since I have sat in this seat, I feel butterflies in my belly. I close my eyes, take a couple of deep breaths, then look directly at each panel member. When invited, I tell them who I am and why I am here. I have worked with most of these men over the years, we have much history, much familiarity, much respect. Their questions are good, thought provoking, a couple rattle me. Since '10, the Project has had multi-cultural diversity clearly in view. First the African American brothers spoke out, then the GBTQ brothers spoke out. The new leadership pathway requires all leaders and pro-spective leaders to do a series of diversity trainings. Awhile back, I did the Project's first diversity training, but I admit to not having a working knowledge of the concepts and language of the recent train-ings. However, I state that I now live in a very different culture, and I am aware of my own privilege every day. I tell them of my name change, and of my conscious embrace of the feminine … in women, in the world, especially within men. I share my sincere intention to become more literate in both Spanish and diversity issues. Mari-ano tells the panel of my recent experience in Cuernavaca, that I am here at the request of my new community, as all the MX men need training. The exchange lasts for a full hour. The panel takes a recess to deliberate, they return shortly. Mariano and I stand up, and the chair says: *"On behalf of MKP, we declare that your time to be certified as a Full Leader of the New Warrior Training Adventure is now. Wel-come back, Dene, we trust you."*

While it feels good to be acknowledged, it is strange to be here after all these years. Even with this certification, things are not the same, I am not the same, the Project is not the same. Leading an NWTA training is an incredibly challenging endeavor, requiring a multi-leveled skill set, and a strong supporting cast. It is a great and humble blessing, it is a heavy burden. I now reside in a different country, a different culture, I am not fluent in this native tongue. And I am at a different stage in my life, I have lots of miles on this machine. Many things to consider, much unknown territory ahead. Still, this resurrection feels congruent with the trajectory of my life's work. These days I have more interior space, and more exterior room to consciously choose what I do next. Being in Mexico feels different in so many ways, there is so much on the table for integration. And there is something profoundly different in being in the men's circles here. I feel loving and loved, I belong in a way I never have, I feel at home. Almost akin to the *Halos*, a belonging at an instinctive level, at a blood brother level. Once again, this work is alive in my bones. Mariano hugs me, tells me how glad he is to have me at his side in Mexico.

Mariano is Cuban born, lives in Florida, the only Spanish-speaking full leader in the entire Project. He says to me: *"I will be leading every training in Mexico, at least for awhile. With Torres and Maldonado certified, with Jaime and Carlos both brilliant and impassioned to actualize this cultural awakening, and on their way to certification, with me on point and you behind, we can do this, we can help build MKP Mexico ... and who knows where else."* I fantasize that this might be the seed of MensWork in Latin America. I feel the ancient native energy in Mexicano men, the robust women carry the earth-based feminine. They are both here, in equal measure, the veils are quite thin. In downtown San Miguel, the five-hundred-year-old art and architecture are alive. The Christ statues and paintings in La Parroquia de San Miguel Archangel carry both the nobility of suffering, and the deep sadness of oppression. I visit the ancient sites in Mexico City, I feel the Aztec influence. Beneath the robust life-affirming joy of the Mexicanos, I feel their deep heartache as well. And I feel the rising need of a new freedom. I do not come as a fixer, a new age colonial, or a bleeding-heart helper. My brown skin has finally found a home ... among the ancients, among the indigenous, among these earth-based, good-hearted people.

Four men constitute the first Executive Council (Concejo Ejecutivo) for MKP Mexico: Mariano Guas (Florida), Jaime Valdes-Neri (Mexico City), Carlos Legaspy (Chicago), Dene Maria Sebastiana (San Miguel de Allende). Houston is the mentoring center. Richard Torres is our connection to both Houston and MKP, he soon joins the concejo. MKP USA is excited with the potential growth of MensWork in Latin America, they make it financially viable for MKP MX to get off the ground.

The four of us also form an I-group, we call ourselves *'Jodi-*

dos pero Contentos' … fucked up but happy. We meet every other week by phone or video, we talk about ourselves individually, we talk about the far-reaching implications of this planted seed, we talk about the trainings and developmental trajectories, we talk about the men and the communities across the entire country. I remember the film *'Field of Dreams,'* I remind us … *"If we build this, they will come."*

We carefully lay out a growth plan, it is a year before we do another NWTA in Mexico. In between, I visit Mexico City regularly, convening a variety of circles. Jaime wants me to do leadership trainings, I tell him it's too soon. We need to talk about why we are here, and what MensWork is. I remain vigilant of my privileged places, I share many of my stories, my vulnerability engenders their trust. We talk about the multi-dimensionality of MensWork, we talk about the values of integrity, accountability, responsibility, emotional literacy, diversity … we do lots of carpet work. Their excitement to get on the carpet delights me, their willingness to do mother work surprises me. The colonized suppression of Mexicano men births a macho culture, with its own unique version of the *'manbox'*. The women take charge of the household, out of necessity. Each day, I see up close the depth of the cultural wound of Mexico. I also see the modern Mexicano with two clear personal wounds … the abandoning, alcoholic, violent father, and the controlling, dominating mother. To each he has learned to surrender his voice, quietly or silently saying yes, even when he wants to say no. Accountability and boundaries are repetitively challenging themes.

Between March '16 and March '20, we do ten NWTA's, including a GBTQ training. Early on, a man comes from Argentina, he is a medicine man. He immediately sees the depth of this work, the transformational possibilities that it is. Like many men before him, Jose Luis says: *"I have been looking for this my whole life."* He and I connect immediately, our limited language skills notwithstanding. We quietly relish the ancient soul connection that we share.

He returns for each training, bringing men from Argentina and Uruguay. Men come from Venezuela, Colombia, Brazil, Costa Rica, Spain, all over Mexico ... then returning home to start men's circles in their communities. Then coming back to Mexico to staff, bringing with them more men to initiate. Soon, we fill every training, as word gets around ... MKPMX is hot !!!

On our *'Jodidos'* calls, we talk about the cultural issues more than anything else. While one of the primary values within the MKP culture is accountability ... *I do what I say I will do* ... it is not the same in Mexico. Many times, men say yes, and do not follow through. Reinforcing this value by confronting its absence gives us great pause, and deep concern for this work moving into Central and South America. After much debate, we agree to hold this issue with a conscious not-knowing, trusting that we will find resolution, or resolution will find us. On our third training, during our first staff meeting, the accountability issue surfaces immediately. Mariano stands up and the room is quiet. He gently talks about the importance of men being honest with each other, and reminds us of what happens at multiple levels when we lie. He asks the entire circle:

1. *¿Quieres ser un hombre de confianza?*
   (Do you want to be a trustworthy man?)

2. *¿Quieres confiar en otros hombres?*
   (Do you want to trust other men?)

3. *¿Estás dispuesto a dar tu palabra a otro hombre?*
   (Are you willing to give your word to another man?)

4. *¿Estás dispuesto a decirle:* **"Mi palabra es oro, puedes contar conmigo?"**
   (Are you willing to say to him: **"My word is gold, you can count on me?"***)*

The room is dead silent. Then one man quietly speaks out: *"Mi palabra es oro."* Then he says it again, and again, and soon every man in the circle is saying it in unison: *"Mi palabra es oro."* This becomes the mantra for the entire weekend. It is the accountability teaching thread in the trainings and in all our circles. This weekend, we take a giant step toward healing a centuries old cultural wound. It is the weekend when the first man from Spain comes to Mexico to initiate. Six months later, on our next NWTA, the Spaniard comes to staff, he brings three men to initiate. He is the first man to address the circle:

"Vengo de España, vengo de un linaje de conquistadores. Los hombres de mi linaje pueden haber matado y esclavizado a hombres de su linaje. Si bien este crimen se cometió hace más de quinientos años, veo el impacto de esa atrocidad en todo el país de México. Muchos de mis hermanos españoles y yo todavía sentimos el impacto. A mi manera, he venido a hacer las cosas bien. Pido que todo hombre que tenga raíces indígenas o que haya sido afectado negativamente por los conquistadores, por favor se presente."

Más de cuarenta hombres salen. El español les pide que se paren en fila frente a él. Cuando cada hombre ha ocupado su lugar, el español se pone delante de la fila y se pone de rodillas. Y con los brazos abiertos de par en par, dice:

"En mi nombre de mi padre, mi abuelo, todo mi linaje de hombres que te han hecho daño a ti y a tu linaje, y en nombre de todos los hombres de mi país de España que te han hecho daño a ti y a tu linaje … humildemente pedir disculpas. Y les pido perdón: perdónenme por favor." Agacha la cabeza, las lágrimas caen de sus ojos al suelo.

Todos los hombres de toda la sala se conmueven, especialmente los hombres de la fila. Muchos sienten que surge la vieja ira, luego sienten la verdadera humildad del hombre de rodillas ante ellos. Las lágrimas llenan los ojos de todos, mientras la fila de hombres avanza hacia este hombre. Y uno a uno, cada hombre coloca sus manos sobre la cabeza del español y dice: "Te perdono". Todo hombre llora, todo hombre está abrazado, todo hombre siente el horror de las atrocidades, todo hombre siente el poder curativo del perdón.

"I come from Spain, I come from a line of conquerors. Men of my lineage may have killed and enslaved men of your lineage. Although this crime was committed more than five hundred years ago, I see the impact of that atrocity throughout the country of Mexico. Many of my Spanish brothers and I still feel the impact. In my own way, I have come to make things right. I ask that every man who has indigenous roots or who has been negatively affected by the conquerors, please come forward."

More than forty men come out. The Spaniard asks them to stand in line in front of him. When each man has taken his place, the Spaniard steps in front of the line and kneels. And with arms wide open, he says:

"In the name of my father, my grandfathers, all my lineage of men who have hurt you and your lineage, and on behalf of all the men of my country of Spain who have hurt you and your lineage ... I humbly apologize. And I beg your forgiveness: please forgive me." He bows his head, tears falling from his eyes to the ground.

All the men in the entire room are moved, especially the men in line. Many feel the old anger rise, then feel the true humility of this one man on his knees before them. Tears fill everyone's eyes as the line of men advances towards this man. And one by one, each man places his hands on the head of the Spaniard and says: "I forgive you." Every man cries, every man is embraced, every man feels the horror of atrocities, every man feels the healing power of forgiveness.

Over the years, I have often wondered if indeed this MensWork that we do might help heal the world. I have chosen to believe that it could. I did not know how, until tonight.

Chapter 25: **The Gift of Heartbreak**

Back in Boulder, Dylan's sobriety does not last long. He moves out of the sober house, couch surfs, can't hold a job. He gets busted, does time in jail, gets out and promptly has another overdose ... he's in deep shit. Dakota cuts him off, encourages us to do the same. Ming seems more detached, less in pain, somehow she has already spiritually released her baby. I am exactly the opposite ... I feel responsible for leaving him behind, for his addiction, for his struggles. Long ago, when Ani told us of Dylan's power and the immensity of his mission, I committed to being his ally, no matter what. Regardless of what Dylan's current circumstances look like, I never lose sight of his essential life force, I never question the good values that he has and is. I still believe in his mission, and I remain committed to ensuring his survival, to the best of my ability. The weight of that almost buried me in Boulder, it weighs heavy again.

Usually beneath Ming's awareness, I give Dylan money ... for rent, food, bail, pocket money ... and as much as I hate to admit it, unknowingly pay for his heroin. Ming and I go see a therapist, Arthur is a tough, grizzly old fucker from New York, living here in San Miguel. He reads me the riot act, telling me how full of shit I am, how inflated, deluded, arrogant ... it's this psycho-bullshit that fuels Dylan's addiction. His words penetrate me like a knife, I yell and scream and argue with him, he brings me to my knees each time. I hate that he is right, he calls me out on all my shadows, he sees right through me. I know how fucked up I am, I know how much energy I expend, I know the cost to everyone. And worse, I know that my enabling only keeps Dylan weak. Still, I refuse to let go.

In one therapy session, Arthur asks: *"Dene, why do you keep punishing yourself? What do you get from all this suffering?"* I am unable to answer him, yet I feel rattled by the depth of his question. So simple, so clear, so staggeringly obvious, been my shadow theme for a very long time. Some things are so small as to be rendered invisible, some things are so large to be invisible as well. How could

I be so blind? Shortly thereafter, I dream of the black priest of the Inquisition, the figure from my first ayahuasca journey in Brazil. On his knees, whipping himself bloody … now I see the smile on his face. I wake up in a sweat, I say to him: "*It is you who has long haunted my psyche. The guilt and shame and self-punishment that I have inflicted upon myself, across my whole life, always disproportionate to my imagined 'crime,' always so hard on myself … it comes from you. I carry your crimes, I carry your punishment, I carry your need for redemption. It has been here with Ming all along, it was here with my brother, now it is here with Dylan. This is my soul's karma, maybe even my lineage karma. My task now is to finally cleanse and transform this. God help me.*"

In the circles and trainings here in Mexico, I take refuge in the carpet work, my place of transformation. In my formal role on the trainings, I focus attention on the staff men. I remind them: "*When we summon the shadows, the shadows come. Not only for the men who are initiating, but for each of us in our own continuing initiations. In our service to the initiates, we often forget that we too are in the crucible, that our own shadows come forth as well. I commit to holding an open carpet for any staff man to do his deep work. And, I need to do my work here as well. Let us do our work together, so we no longer bring these unworked shadows home to our families. So our progeny does not have to carry our sins, so we can bring to an end this cycle of destruction. For in the face of our woundedness, the only real sin is pretending that it is not there.*"

It is rare that I-groups or other training circles offer skilled carpet work … there is no other place but here on the initiation weekends. From the beginning, we know that the transformational aspect of the NWTA lies upon the carpet. Now thirty-plus years in, it still retains that magical power in this initiatory experience. In truth, I come here to work the carpet, the center of the crucible. From here, the teachings are pure. As I know the intricate weekend structures, I see the times to frame an '*open-ended moving carpet,*' that staff men can easily move in and out of. The Mexican men are hungry for this, they come in waves.

The *'carpet'* is a metaphor, a way to describe a place of magic:

It is archetypal, mythological, fraught with demons, dragons, the beasts of the underworld. A crucible, a terrifying heat, a precipitous edge ... a bare thread hangs between 'life, death, rebirth'.

It is a unique and rare opportunity to see oneself undistorted. It's deeply fearful: the revealing of the naked self behind the ego's carefully-crafted curtain which hides the shadow of darkness that lives inside the psyche.

The 'magic carpet' brings the world of soul into conscious- ness, offering up the long-forgotten images in deep memory, of the unnumbered conflicts layered beneath. It is a portal, a timeless view of the soul's journey.

One's conscious task is to work that imagery through art, music, journaling, active imagination, dream work, voice dialogue, and carpet work ... to bring the conflict into awareness.

The soul does not offer a solution, only a map, upon which lies the totality of one's journey.

Here stands all that has been imprinted into my psychic terri- tory ... since conception, since before, since the beginning. If I am courageous, if I have the heart and guts and balls to feel my own pain and suffering, layered in the cells of my inheritance ... I may re-member myself. And in my remembering, I discover a place of healing, integrating, transformation, wholeness.

On many trainings, after serving the other men, I step upon the carpet to do my own work:

I bring forth my sons, my father, my grandfathers. I bring forth my marriage, all women and the feminine. I bring my whispering angel, Standing Falcon, the grandmothers. I bring forth the cultural fathers, the windmill institutions, and the bad men who run them. I bring the institution of MKP. I bring forth the black priest, the bishops and popes,

*the entire Catholic Church. I bring forth Sicily and Persia ...
I bring forth god.*

*I stand before the entire vertical architecture of the deep mas-
culine ... in all its light and darkness. I pour out my fiery
rage, my razor-sharp anger, and my harshest judgments of
our collective crimes. I pour out my guilt, shame, my arrogance, my helplessness. I pour out my blaming, judging, my
perpetrator, victim, and rescuer. I pour out the suffering
fatigue of many lifetimes ... my rage burns hot, my grief is
a river of endless tears. My heart breaks open ... again and
again and again.*

*Ultimately, each time I grieve, each time I surrender, each
time I let the water wash over me, each time I let the river
take me down ... she is there, in my heart, in our collective
hearts, in this healing space. My deep masculine holds the
crucible, protects the sacred safety, stands watch for shadows, refuses to go back to sleep. Its strength allows this softening, this tenderness, the forgiveness of letting go. I fall
into her arms ... she offers a smile, a comforting body, a
compassionate heart.*

At once, I am peaceful, clear, integrated. I share my inner gold
within the circle. Each training, more men step forward to do their
work, I am fierce and tender on the carpet. Each time I return home
renewed. Ming and I visit the hot springs frequently, sometimes I
go alone. Here in San Miguel de Allende, the home of the Archangel Miguel, Mexico's sacred feminine offers herself. We bask in the
perfection of our journey, in the good fortune and hard work that
brought us here, and how it prepares us for the next step ... surren-
dering Dylan to his soul's journey.

'La Gruta' means the cavern, a collection of hot-spring pools
several miles west of San Miguel. It is cloudy and humid, warm but
not hot. Entering the large pool, I feel at ease in the water, relaxed in
my body. The pool is half full, mostly women, a few families with

small children. A young man is holding his one-year-old daughter, whose face radiates delight as her papi moves her gracefully through the water. The man is well muscled, amply tattooed, the power in his arms in loving service to the protection and safety of his daughter. To see the fierce and tender sides of a man is to appreciate the beautiful paradox of masculinity. The faces of the Mexicanas, dark hair and eyes, rich brown skin … is pleasing to my senses. Not just their sexiness, more their soulfulness. The teenage girls laugh unselfconsciously. The older women are more secretive, having discovered the subtle nuances of the mysterious feminine. Behind the fan, behind the eyes, behind the smile, suggested, never fully revealed.

Toward the back of the large pool is an opening in the side of the hill, a passageway carved into the rocks. I make my way toward the mouth of the cave and enter the corridor. It is shadowy and snake-like, twenty yards long, water waist high. I wade slowly through, emerging in a darkened circular cavern. The water is warm, the air cool, shafts of light enter through a small window at the top of the cave. On the left side, just below the ceiling is an open pipe, eight inches in diameter. Once per hour, *más o menos*, the water from a hot spring pours out for a short while. No one knows the next outpouring, no one knows how long it will pour. I wait patiently.

There are several people inside the cave, some swimming slowly in a circle around the large post at the center, others leaning up again the wall. People whisper, most are silent, young couples share wet kisses. I lean back, near the pipe, waiting. My mind is quiet, wandering occasionally, coming back to my breath, to stillness. With hands clasped, I ask for all fear to be removed from the cells of my body, that all my unconscious patterns be revealed and cleansed, that my solar plexus be quiet, that my heart may rest, open and loving.

A short time passes, I hear the rumbling of the coming water. I stand and turn in its direction, a line of people begins to form. I am the third one to receive the water. It comes out fast, intense, hot but not too, hitting me in the middle of my chest. I am pushed back, yet hold my feet firm to the floor. I step into the gushing water, allowing it to play over my head, my heart, my gut, my loins. I turn around and let it cleanse my back, hitting the muscles from top to bottom. The water is holy, my entire body is purified, I am baptized. That night I have a dream:

> I am in a city, nighttime, buildings darkened, shafts of light casting long shadows. I am being pursued, dark forces and betrayal at every turn. I enter a basement, a woman with face obscured cuts me with a razor blade. I fall into a stupor, half unconscious. I raise my head to look for Sherlock Holmes to solve this dilemma. Another woman enters the room, cuts me again, my head lolls slowly. A phone rings, it is my brother and another man I do not know. The stranger asks me if I have ever spoken to Jesus. The question startles me awake inside the dream, I call out Jesus' name.
>
> I am outside, the sky dark, lightning crackles, large clouds rumbling and unfolding. A fiery lion appears among the clouds, a large shaft of light comes down from above. I step into the light, open my arms, and begin to ascend. There is a brilliant light in the heavens, my heart feels tender and loving. I look up and see Jesus floating above me, his body in a loincloth. A cloud obscures my vision, I cannot see his face. My heart aches, feeling the shadow of my own doubt. The dark cloud opens, Jesus has his finger raised upward, his lion heart pulsing in his chest.

When I go home, I call Dakota, and he tells us that Dylan has fallen deeper. We call our dear friend George and share our utter despair. I brought George into the work many years prior and have been dear friends ever since. He is thirty years in 12-step work, he knows addiction, he knows MensWork. He becomes our "consigliere" with Dylan.

George says: *"The first thing you need to do is accept the real possibility that Dylan will die, and there is nothing you can do to stop it. If you cannot accept that, if you cannot let go, if you cannot surrender Dylan to his karma, you will continue to suffer greatly."*

He looks directly at me when he speaks. I am the one holding on, I have always been the one holding on, I am now the one, finally, ready to let go and trust. The very next day, Ming and I call Dylan. We tell him: *"We will no longer send you any money, we will no longer contact you, and you can no longer contact us. Initially, this boundary is for 90 days. We love you, we wish you the best."* The words are barely out of our mouths, we hang up the phone … our hearts ache, and through our tears, we breathe a deep sigh of relief.

My seventieth birthday is the 24th of Aug '17, there is an NWTA in Cuernavaca the weekend following. Ming and I invite George and Jan from Tucson, Francis from Santa Cruz, all the Jodidos, a few friends from Mexico City, we're all staffing the training. Plus friends from San Miguel … about twenty of us here in town for my birthday weekend. On Friday, we book a small elegant restaurant in downtown SMA. We are the only ones there, they wait upon us with grace and spectacular food. We laugh, we sing, we eat and drink in celebration and connection. We bow our heads for the fullness of our bounty. On Saturday, Ming and I host a party at our home.

Prior to our meal, George invites us to sit in circle in our living room. He speaks to the group:

> *"First, I want to thank Ming and Dene for having us in their beautiful home here in gorgeous San Miguel. I also want to once again wish Dene a happy 70th birthday: 'Happy Birthday, Old Man!'*
>
> *Within this small and intimate circle, old friends and new friends, we who know and love Ming and Dene … we all know the struggles they have suffered with their son Dylan, you all know the depth of love they carry for him. And we all know the spiritual necessity of letting go.*

PART V: Mexico

This past week, Ming and Dene formally severed any and all ties with Dylan, for a period of 90 days, setting all of them free from this bind they have been in for more than five years. Tonight, they are asking us to hold Dylan, hold Dylan's spirit, hold him in the light, so he can find his way back home. To Ming and Dene: 'Please join hands and together offer up your son Dylan to this community. We agree to hold him for you, and to hold you when you are in need. We are ready to receive him.'

And through tears of pain and tears of joy, Ming and I surrender Dylan into their hands.

In the absence of funding, Dylan's life falls apart. No job, no money, no support, he is on the street. He moves up into the foothills above Boulder, a tented community of mostly drug people. We are relieved that he has a place, our pain of disconnection eases as time slowly passes. We think about Dylan often, we practice letting go ... again and again and again.

Ninety days pass, we have been completely sober the entire time. We consult with George about reentry, he urges caution, watch the multi-dimensional hooks. We agree to not give Dylan money. After that, we call him. He is hurting, deeply alone, wants out. He cries hard, it breaks our hearts ... but it does not break our will. We know we cannot rescue him, for the only time that this changes is when Dylan chooses sobriety. It is late fall, his birthday is coming up soon. We ask him what he needs, we tell him no money. He says it's already cold, he could use a good sleeping bag. We find something on-line, send it to an address of a friend. He gets it, he is grateful. A week later, he calls screaming, tells us that his sleeping bag has been stolen. He is beside himself with anger, grief, and fear. I ask him softly: *"Are you done yet?"* and quietly hang up.

Two weeks pass without contact. The insanity of: *"Is he alive, has he eaten, is he half frozen, is he dead? Has he found some place of warmth and comfort?"* still creeps in. For Ming and me, this is a dark time of not-knowing.

One evening he calls, he is calm and clear. He says: *"Mom and dad, I am okay, I am staying on a friend's couch in Longmont. I have been sober for almost a week, I have gone to a meeting every day. I feel strong, but this is really hard, I am scared. The pull from this community is unbearable. They see that I'm trying to be sober, they want to pull me back in. They are jealous, ashamed, resentful, and they do not want to be abandoned. It is hard to stay sober, harder to deal with my using friends. I have to get out of here, I can't stay sober here. Dad, will you get me out of here? Please?"*

He's been five years in this heroin addiction. We have heard many stories from him, mostly lies, we are always suspicious. Still, we ask ourselves: *"Has he finally gotten the monkey off his back? Can we trust this ... or is it just another hustle?"* We so want to believe him, we call George. He tells us that indeed community pull often leads to relapse, it is easier to quit the drugs than quit the relationships. I remember my birthday party back in August when Jan told George and me about Del. Jan said: *"I know a man in Tucson, been sober a long time, his brother overdosed on heroin years ago. Del lives alone, often takes in a young man recently sober. He runs a tight ship, zero chances, clear boundaries and agreements, a mini boot camp. I trust him, and I am here to watch over this. You should do this, it's worth the risk."*

We call Dylan, he is holding onto his sobriety, literally for dear life. We tell him that we will get him out of Boulder, under one condition ... he must choose sobriety. He says to us: *"Mom and dad, I have lied to you so many times, I know how hard it is for you to believe me. I am so done with this lifestyle, so done with drugs. If you give me a fresh start, I promise you, on my life, that I will stay sober. I beg you ... please get me out of here, please."*

And he starts to cry. Of course, we cry right along with him. I tell him about George's suggestion, about Del, about zero chances, Dylan says: *"Perfect!"* I buy Dylan a one-way ticket to Tucson, a week later he is at Del's house. Ming and I have spoken with Del, he is clear, we support him. Del gives Dylan a fifteen-point set of agreements ... complete sobriety, getting a job, daily meetings, work around the house, etc ... no bullshit. Dylan surprisingly agrees, he quickly sees that the discipline does him good. A couple of times, he calls, bitching about Del. I listen, tell him that Del is your drill sergeant, shut the fuck up, and do what you're told. He pisses and moans, then does what is necessary. Six months pass, this is the longest that Dylan has ever been sober. From a dream I write this poem:

> *Inside a metal and glass building,*
> *the Armani uniform splits open.*
> *Naked flesh no longer hides,*
>
> *I stand on the outside.*
> *Disenfranchised, dirty, disturbed,*
> *Fighting for life, freedom, sunlight*
> *and air, breath and music.*
>
> *I stand in my street clothes,*
> *Clapton playing in my head.*
> *A big, broken, bass lies on the ground.*
> *Hopper says: "Listen to Springsteen."*
>
> *I hammer the rhythmic beat.*
> *I sit in a circle of men on the street,*
> *Speaking of my son's wound which I inflicted.*
> *Hopper says: "And an old school bus honked,*
> *And woke him up, just in time."*
>
> *I see my son, deep in the land of the disenfranchised,*
> *Right where he needs to be.*
> *I surrender him to his journey, for his,*
> *like mine, has to cross*
> *The barren and jagged terrain,*
> *where life is lived at the edges.*
>
> *A young man lies next to the broken pieces,*
> *His hair long, his face clear, his eyes grateful.*
> *Some return, some do not,*
> *And some are awakened by the honking school bus,*
> *just in time.*

Chapter 26: **Adios, Mexico**

At the end of '16, we buy a 750 Suzuki Quattro Moto ... a big, black, fully loaded, open air 4-wheel, we call her *"Beastie."* She is the perfect vehicle for the bumpy and uneven streets of San Miguel. Bicycles, small motor bikes, four wheels of all sizes are popular here. Lots of women drive the four wheels ... they sit up high, proud, big bodied, and ready to rumble. Finally having the Moto under my ass feels empowering, and relieving to my legs. Beastie hauls ass everywhere ... up the hills to the far reaches of the city, out the small highways to the baths and old family restaurants, along the country roads to the ranches and farms and remote crumbling churches.

In '17, we rent a house south of town, our barrio is all Mexicanos, save for us. As poverty and thievery go hand in hand, some of the nearby neighborhoods are sketchy, there is an iron gate and a stone wall surrounding the entire property. American politics has taken a right-hand turn, rumors of the border wall invade the collective conversations. However, Ming and I are well received by our neighbors, most think I am a Mexicano anyway. We notice how San Miguel has changed in our short time here. It is voted Best City in Conde Nast magazine two years running. More housing developments are being built, more Gringos moving down from the States and Canada. Downtown venues increasingly crowded, parking tighter, prices rocketing skyward, pollution spreading outward. San Miguel is hot, and getting ugly.

Members of the Cartel have second and third houses up here in San Miguel and nearby Querétaro. Maybe once a year, we hear about a murder in downtown. The few who venture to sell drugs on the streets get one warning from the Cartel, then *boom.* With El Chapo's capture, and the uncertain bloody struggle for power, the small time dealers slowly come out of the woodwork. Along with all the other growth, crime grows as well.

By '18, San Miguel is a mess. Gangs from the neighboring towns come in masked, heavily armed. They stick up the airport shuttles, they invade the homes of the wealthy. In a nearby gated community of about two dozen homes, there are seventeen robberies within a six-week period. While our immediate neighborhood has been safe, our house is vulnerable. There is no 911, we have no weapons. We are not fluent in Spanish. We feel exposed, uncertain, frightened.

Ming and I start to think about leaving Mexico. We anxiously await the results of the US '18 midterm elections. In November, when the House turns blue, we know it is time to leave. The very thought brings great sadness. We have thrived here like no place before … reweaving our marriage, reviving my MensWork, finding peace and sobriety, navigating through Dylan's dark night of the soul. The idea of returning to the US is disturbing. It is ugly and expensive, all the beautiful places where we once lived are now crowded and over-run. Still, Dylan is a year sober, and we have missed so much of his younger years. Tucson is attractive, we have lived there before, we have our old friends George and Julee, Jan and Sheri, Nonine and Charles. We make the decision, we are moving back to Tucson.

Ming and I research Tucson, it's almost twenty-five years since we left. Surprisingly, the population has not exploded, the air is not polluted, and housing prices are still reasonable. Sheri is a real estate agent in Tucson, she and Jan FaceTime us through several houses, we find one that we like at the right price. Sheri connects us with a mortgage company, we fill out the voluminous paperwork, and by mid-December, we are in escrow with a close date of December 27.

A friend of a friend is an agent who helps us sell Beastie. He says that San Miguel has never been like this. The new police chief admitted that he did not have the resources to stop the influx of gangs and crime. He says you are getting out just in time. Moving money between countries proves a challenge, but with a lot of help, and a zillion calls and emails, my tenacity pushes it all through. Ming is a master mover, and under her directorship, we pack the house, connect to a shipper, pack our personal gear, close the house. We have two one-way plane tickets to Tucson, departing at 4 pm on Monday, Dec. 24, 2018.

We tearfully connect to all the beautiful people in Mexico who have befriended us. We have left many places behind, we know the attachment and separation, we feel the love and the loss. Friendship is not about location, but rather the place in the heart where we allow someone to reside. With modern communication, friends are only a video call away, saying *'see ya soon'* is no longer a sad lie. Our life has been a gypsy life, here we are moving the tent once again. My body is no longer young, the journey no longer easy, the expenditure of energy no longer easily affordable. Please God, let this be the last. While I hold a quiet sense of finality, I know that our destiny will have its own way with us.

After my initiation in Chicago, Tucson was my first step into seeding MensWork, Mexico my eighth start-up community development. Thirty years, eight communities … I like the numerology. In the swirl of swift changes, I remember the astro-cartography maps. Ming has a distant Neptune line west of Phoenix, east of California. Neptune is about the mystic; dreams and visions; conscious spiritual practice; meditation and idealism and delusion. I have a Saturn and a Pluto line going right between Tucson and Phoenix, straight down my pike. Saturn is the *'bringer of old age'* … illness, separation, solitude, death; spiritual study and metaphysical wisdom. Pluto is about transformation and regeneration, mass consciousness, secrecy, political power, codes and charisma. This very well could be the completion of a large cycle, a spiritual return or homecoming. Tucson could be my *'transformational'* place, or my *'regenerative'* place, it could also be my *'end of days'* place … Oooohh baby!!!

Easter and Christmas in Mexico are beautiful, sacred, Catholic … and crowded. The León airport is far, an hour and a half through the hills and small towns, via a pretty decent shuttle that does its best to be on time. But the day before Christmas, all bets are off. We spend our last night in an Airbnb, the shuttle comes for us in plenty of time. There are others to gather, and they will bring us to a depot on the edge of town to catch another shuttle. Uh-oh.

On each and every street that we turn onto, there is traffic. Usually, traffic moves slowly through town, there are few traffic lights or stop signs. There are *'topes'*, speed bumps every twenty or so yards on almost every street in town. The taxi drivers are gracious, they know it's all about give and take, and honorably taking turns. It seems to take forever to get to the airport, and time is already tight. If we miss this flight, we are fucked. We arrive less than forty-five minutes before flight time; there are long lines with tons of luggage. We have used United Airlines in and out of this airport, they are quite good here. A woman comes through the line and asks what flight we are on. When we tell her, she kindly moves us up to the front of the line, we get through check-in quickly. Security in León is also pretty loose, usually just a quick wand and we're through. Randomly, I get flagged for a deeper baggage search, they take forever. We rush to the gate, the boarding line is long, flight takes off in twenty minutes. Thankfully, the line moves quickly. Ming goes through, down the gangway, I get stopped for another search. I wonder if I look like a drug dealer ... twice in one day? The search is quick, I rush onto the plane, take my seat, we're off the ground in five minutes.

¡¡ *Adios, Mexico, y gracias por todo* !!

Part VI: Full Circle

Chapter 27: A Rude Welcome

It is Dec '18, we have not seen Dylan for a year, talked sparingly since his move to Tucson. Ming and I are a bit nervous when he comes to Christmas dinner at Sheri and Jan's house. They are such dear friends, our chief allies, and our grounding force in this *'great return.'* Dylan walks in the door ... young and handsome, clear and clean, powerful and loving. He is as glad to see us as we are to see him ... we hug for a very long time. He is well, struggling to be sober, not so much of drugs, but more of the addict's attitudes and behaviors. Del is a tough task-master. When Dylan complains, I tell him: *"Take it to Del."* I am in my own recovery, my enabling is shifting to clear boundaries. It feels a bit harsh sometimes, I have such a soft place in my heart for Dylan. Yet I know it is good for me, and it surely is good for him. Not just good, but absolutely necessary.

Thursday morning we all go to the title office to finalize our home purchase. All our money successfully transfers from Mexican banks to US banks. We wire the down payment, sign a zillion pages, and wait for funding. Thursday nothing, Friday nothing, Monday nothing ... Tuesday we get requests for information from the lender that we have already answered, multiple times. Where did this money come from, what about that money, is Ming's name on the loan, which one is your business account? What the fuck? Our loan officer, Sheri, Ming and I, the seller's agent are all baffled, we have no idea why they are asking all these questions again.

This continuing parade of questions goes on for two weeks. The seller's agent wants to pull out, then wants us to pay his client for the inconvenience. Sheri steadies him, telling him that we are good, this loan will go through, just be patient. At the end of the second week, I get a request to turn over my client list, and I very politely tell them to go fuck themselves. After I hit the send button,

I imagine that this loan and this house are gone. Our household shipment from Mexico is on its way, may be here in a few days. We rent a small storage space, start looking at rentals, our occupancy in Sheri and Jan's place uncomfortably extends out ... we have nowhere else to go.

With less than a day left on the seller's extension, our loan officer gets word that we have been approved! The lender had previous issues with business from Mexico. When the government gets wind of the movement of funds across the border, they stick their nose into the vetting process. They are the ones asking the repetition of questions, even asking for my client list. Rightfully, they are vigilant about potential money laundering. I laugh, it's not like we are transferring millions. Still, we are all relieved that the house is finally ours, it's been an ordeal. A week later, we are in our second Tucson house ... it's good to be back home again.

Chapter 27: **The Men's Circles Open**

There is an open men's circle every Thursday evening in downtown Tucson, outdoors under a gazebo, a firepit, been going on for a number of years ... sometimes there are thirty plus men. Early on, the new warrior network allows only initiated men into the I-groups, which suffer from both attrition and lack of skilled leadership. A follow-up integration group is a great idea, but its built-in limitations cause community erosion.

George Daranyi is the first man at the Project level to recognize the intelligence of opening the circles to all men. He puts forth a Project-wide initiative where I-groups can bring in non-initiated men, and communities can form their own open circles. In '99, Tucson was the first community to expand open circles. George says: *"Cast the next wide, and men will come. Once in the circle, being in relationship to men who have been trained, men are more likely to self-select in. Let the work sell itself."* He introduces me as the founder of the Arizona community, Tucson specifically. He tells the story of our first meeting in late '91:

"I am a few years sober, married with an infant daughter. I have been in a men's group before. I live in a man's body, I have all the marking of success, but I do not feel like a man.

My wife and baby and I go to church, there is a meeting with the pastor after the service. I see this couple sitting at the other end of the table. He has long hair, feathered earrings, he and his wife introduce themselves as new to the Tucson community. He says he does 'men's work.' I am drawn to him. After the meeting, I walk over and ask him: "what is men's work?" He gives me a rumpled up business card, says to me: "call me, make an appointment, we'll talk."

The next week, I am in his office, and for one whole year, we do inner work. In the middle of that, Dene takes me to San Diego to do the New Warrior Training ... changes my entire life, I discover who I truly am as a man. On the plane flying home, Dene turns to me and asks how my weekend was. I tell him: "Absolutely incredible."

He says: "Good, we have lots of work to do."

Dene and I have been friends ever since. Across all these years, all the places we have traveled, and right here in this small circle in Tucson, we do this MensWork ... helping men heal, helping men open their hearts."

G's words touch me deeply, I am grateful and humbled by his acknowledgment. It reminds me of how far I have traveled, how many men's communities I have helped open, only to be brought back here, twenty-five years later, to the place where this work truly began for me. I look around the circle, I see the younger men, I am an elder now. I hear their struggle, I hear their pain ... my task is to listen, and simply share my own journey ... from when I was their age, to where I am now. I am excited and motivated to support young men in need of this work.

In early '19, Dylan moves out of Del's residence, into a sober house with several other young men. G knows the young man who runs the facility, who asks us to start a weekly circle at the house for young men in recovery. Not a normal 12-step meeting, yet sobriety focused, more a men's circle where men find support to drop underneath the behaviors, and ferret out the root causes that drive addiction. It is well received, the circle meets every Tuesday. A dozen young men come from all over Tucson, men come out of rehab to attend our meetings. Dylan and I have staffed a warrior weekend together, now we are sitting in a sober men's circle. He and I are both transparent, we each share stories from our respective experiences, the circle knows we have a primal family history. I am moved by the depth of Dylan's vulnerability, the raw honesty of his experience in his dark heroin addiction, his awareness of the impact that his addiction has on others. I see the beautiful little boy, the angry, wounded teenager who stopped giving a fuck about everything, the years when Ming and I lost him. And here stands this exquisite young man in recovery … in his integrity and power, his depth of caring, his commitment to heal and support others to heal, someone who knows first-hand the depths of hell. My tears flow with joy, gratitude, and pride.

Quietly, on the inside, my heart once again feels the tenderness that comes from heartbreak. I recall Rumi's words: *"You have to keep breaking your heart until it opens."* Gone are the agonizing sleepless nights when he was on the streets, the heartbreak of seeing him in jail, the terror of seeing him hooked up in the hospital, the pain and rage and grief felt in Mexico, both in the therapist's office and on the carpet. And finally the shame of my weakness enabling him for so long, and the cost on everyone. Feeling all of that, feeling my heart having shattered into a million pieces … I am now on the other side. I have honored the commitment I made to him when he was a baby, I honor it still, and I honor it as long as I have a breath in my body.

Sitting in two open circles in Tucson, staffing as emeriti on the new warrior weekends, G and I see the men in need of deep process work … both the new men in the circles, and especially the veteran men in the community who staff the trainings. These are the ones who sit in less than skilled I-groups. Rarely in the open circles do they get the time and attention for deep work. We have the staff carpet on the trainings, but we only do one per year in AZ. G and I talk about doing a carpet training in town, a 1-day workshop, reasonably priced, we *teach* carpet work by *doing* carpet work.

In May, we do our first *'Day of Deep Process' (DDP)* workshop … we have twenty-two men come to my house for the day. Every man does not get to the carpet, but every man does get to do deep inner work. G and I realize that we are in a very unique position to impact our entire community, maybe even our Southwest Area that includes New Mexico and western Texas. We have the depth of our love and friendship, we have the compatibility of both our respective skill sets, we share the cultural and archetypal view of men's inner work. With a combined sixty years in MensWork, we see an expanded path appear in front of us, one that *'thinks globally and acts locally.'* In August, we celebrate my birthday and our homecoming at our new Tucson home. Ming and I love potluck brunches on a Sunday morning, we offered them often in all our previous communities. It is our first such gathering here, and we are delighted to serve.

Mostly old and dear friends, we have known these folks since we were here all those years ago. We all sit in a circle, share a meal, and remember … each other and ourselves. In the familiarity of my own daily life, within the struggles of aging, health, the political climate, the climate climate, I tend to forget who I am. In the body's decline, the memory gets hazy, distorted, exaggerated in either direction. I remember my Saturn line, I increasingly realize that *'death'* has many forms. Sometimes forgetting is good, time heals all wounds. But in the triumph of time and gravity, I want to create an ascending arc to my life. Something that says I was here, that I lived, that perhaps I made a difference, that my soul can trustingly ride into whatever is next. The pebble drops in the pond, it does not know the outer reaches of its ripple.

The beauty of this circle is that it rekindles my memories. They reflect back to me our shared experiences … where we've all been together, what we've done together, our impact on others and on ourselves. They celebrate my light, they laugh and poke fun at my shadows. This is a place for truth-telling and laughter, for re-connecting to our shared love and sorrow … a place to re-member, a place to make whole. As Gurdjieff said: *"This Work is simply to re-member yourself."* Ming and I feel back home now, having returned from our many glorious adventures, to live out whatever days we have left, hopefully there are many. We are grateful to still be circling the Sun, to have lived this life, to be home among friends, to look back and know that it has all been good. And to look forward.

G and I talk about creating a legal entity for our collective bodies of work. I remember back in '92, when Ed and I ran programs in Tucson for battering men. We had formed a legal business entity named *Desert Wisdom LLC* … I wonder if that name is still available? G makes some calls, and voila, he resurrects that very same entity, with him and me as equal partners. In October '19, we offer our next workshop … *Desert Wisdom 1*. G has a lovely ranch about an hour out of Tucson, the Black Hawk Ranch, we host a dozen men for four days. While the 'DDP' is strictly about carpet work, the 'DW1' is much different. It is a deep inquiry into the sacred masculine.

While carpet work offers a jolt of electricity to the emotional body, and often leads to a significant emotional and behavioral shift, we offer here a deeper and wider inquiry. We fashion masks as a metaphor for our shadows, those things which we hide. We create walking sticks from the prolific local yucca plants. We do a daily meditation, a lodge to honor the feminine, we watch 'Braveheart.' And for the first time, we offer an inquiry into both our conscious and unconscious relationship to women and the feminine. Naturally, the meals are healthy, delicious, and nutritious. However, the check-ins are exquisite. A space of deep respect and safety, a space of shared vulnerability, a space where each man shares his journey, free of other men's judgments. And a space where men love each other, where emotional connection and shared wisdom lead us to beauty, truth, oneness. G and I know we have something special here, and we know we are just beginning.

Chapter 27: **My Father Dies**

At 2:30 in the morning of January 8, 2020, my father dies in a hospice in Phoenix, AZ. Albert John Shikaly Sr passes at ninety-eight, leaving behind two sons, two daughters-in-law, and three grandchildren. Some say he was a good man, mostly those who did not really know him. Sometimes even I say that, only because I know where he came from, and the abuse and hardships he endured. And I have been working on this shit since I was twenty-four years old.

He was handsome, charming, sweet at times, even loving. But his narcissism, his relentless concern with his own instinctive needs, his unwillingness to give true consideration to others, his absolute bull-headed stubbornness made him difficult to love. I grieve the loss of my father, but the truth is, I never really had a dad ... my brother and I were orphans.

What I still remember most is the violence of my early childhood. The screaming, the physical fights, the disgusting language, the accusations of infidelity, the damage to my mother, the regular visits by the cops. The constant rage of my father, the frozen fear and anger of my mother, the distorted viciousness and pathetic self-pity of my grandfather. The never-ending warfare between the two men that I so loved as a boy ... deeply imprinted from conception, along with the violent and misogynistic heritage from my Persian and Sicilian lineage. This wound ... this father wound ... was the first focus of my own inner work. From *"The Rag and Bone Shop of the Heart" – Poems for Men* – Edited by Robert Bly, James Hillman, Michael Meade:

> *"Walking into the house of fathers means beginning in questions and ending in mysteries. Questions abound about our 'real fathers'. At the root, our fathers connect us to a mysterious spark that flared between ancestors and two living people, when we were conceived in this world. After that conception, walls stand between father and the child to be.*
>
> *When an infant comes struggling from the warm body of*

mother, it begins to fall into the expanse of air and light and the world of innumerable things. And the infant falls into a realm of questions: "Is it a boy or girl? Is it okay? Intact? What's its name?" The child is leaving mother, falling in questions toward father.

Before the umbilical is cut, questions surround the new-born. Cutting the tie to mother increases the uncertainties that attend new life, and begin the shaping of that life from outside. Father may be in the hands that catch the child and ease the fall, but father may be kept back by custom or fear. The father may be in question himself: "Where is he? Is the father here? Who is the father? Is the father known?"

Whether in the hands waiting or long gone, the father inevitably brings distance to the child's world. *And sadness. He is somewhere beyond the falling, the reaching, the calling of the child. And later, whether the father moves closer through the efforts of love, or disappears in some struggle, he will always be present in the distance between one thing and another."*

Whether the wound is from his fist or numbness or ignorance, or from his absence or death ... there is this distance. Beneath our rage, our terror, our shame ... all the layers of pain that our little boy carries ... there is this distance. There we find the sadness, for we have lost him. Maybe we never really had him. At the edge of this loneliness, the grief awaits.

The previous December, my brother Al comes to Arizona, we know our father's time is close. He stays with Ming and me, we all go out for dinner. Al hasn't seen Dylan since before his sobriety, he is shocked and delighted at Dylan's growth. Both Dakota and Dylan saw their grandfather last summer, they have said their goodbyes. The next day, Al and I drive up to visit dad and his second wife. Neither Al nor I are fond of her, still we are respectful. We arrive at lunchtime, they are seated in the dining room. We sit down, dad hardly recognizes either of us. He has a couple of moments of lucidity, then it slips away. He is angry, belligerent, demanding, self-absorbed in feeding his hungry machine with fried chicken, mashed potatoes, red wine. His wife tries to comfort him, tries to feed him, but his hostility is almost unbearable. We are out of there in forty-five minutes. We drive over to the Starbucks nearby, get a coffee, and sit down to process what just happened. I close my eyes, take a deep breath, then I say to Al:

> *"Wow, he has been just like this all along, for his whole goddamn life, hasn't he? You called this out often, I did not want to see it. I've aggrandized his wound, made it mine. In chasing my own demons, I've chased his too, like windmills. But when I see him like this, purely instinctive and absent of personality, I see his raw ugly selfishness. Rarely a thought about someone else, always thinking he is right, can't ever remember him saying 'I'm sorry'.*

> *The truth of it, Al, is that in his self-absorption, he was never there, for any of us. He had a zillion opportunities, and failed a zillion fucking times. Today, I see who he is, maybe for the very first time. And I see the ghost that I have been chasing.*

> *Today, my illusions are shattered. I have raged and grieved for so goddamn long. But right now, I am empty. He's close to the end, his time is short, I wish him well. Maybe it will be easier for us when he passes ... I sure the fuck hope so."*

Al looks at me and smiles. He, too, is complete with our father. We have been good sons, and because of him, we are better fathers. We sit quietly, basking in the spaciousness, there is nothing left to do.

The first week of January, a friend sends me a YouTube video. I watch it: James Blunt sings of his father's impending death. I send it to Al, we watch it and weep together. The grief never seems to end, not from what we lost, but from what we never had. The next day, I get a text from my father's wife ... he is gone. I call my brother, there are no tears today, no sadness, no anger, no grief … just relief.

For weeks, I am quiet inside. I am the eldest now, the next one in line. My Saturn line reminds me of my mortality, I take my place, I stand fearlessly, welcoming death to walk beside me. I trust my time is not now. One day, surprisingly, I wake up angry as fuck.

We endure the weight of his hand, the wreck of his rage,
and the bitter ring of his words to learn his touch."
– Michael Meade

No one knew my father was eating his children...and yet
as he lay snoring, our lives slowly disappeared
down the hole of his life."
– Sharon Olds

In my father's house, I learned to be angry. On the streets of my youth, it saved my life. I left my father's house at eighteen, marching off to the beat of rock'n'roll, the drums of protest, the pounding of speed-laced acid, my hair growing longer by the day. I cannot tell the difference between my personal father, the cultural father, and the patriarchal father … they are one, their betrayal is the same, I am angry at all those motherfuckers. Back then, I did not know about the *"manbox"*, a repository of all things felt and denied. But I sure did feel something ugly in my bones. And I say loudly to all the fathers of this house: *"No thank you!"*

My head still fantasizes all the things that coulda been, shoulda been, mighta been. My heart sometimes still projects an innocent unconsciousness upon the man who was my father. My spiritual bypass voice wants to believe I have forgiven him: *"It was not his fault, he was an abused kid, he didn't have the tools … let it go, it's OK."* But my gut says: *"Fuck no, I'm angry still, I know it will pass, but not today."*

His wife does not invite us to the ceremony. Just as well, I am in no mood to blow smoke and bullshit up anybody's ass. The following Sunday, Ming and I drive to my father's house in Sun City, just up the pike from Tucson. His wife moves out quickly, his condo is now our responsibility. I am calm, I imagine what I might feel, what ghosts might be waiting. This is not the house of my boyhood, as my parents came to AZ in '84. I love the desert, I do not like Phoenix. It is flat, windy, dried up, ugly brown everywhere. Their house is in an over fifty-five elder community. Years ago, visiting the old folks was boring and comical. As I walked through the dining hall this time, I realize I am their age. The apartment is empty, in need of repair. His wife leaves a few things … the box with my mother's ashes, a pile of photo albums, pictures never seen or not seen in years, most in black and white … the ghosts are afoot.

The next night at home, photos splayed upon the dining room table, the past opens wide. Seeing the pictures brings back the nauseous anger, the ridiculousness of costume and hairstyle, remembering how stoned I was when no one knew. I left my father's house many years ago, leaving the violence, the racism, the misogyny and homophobia, the inflexible and unbearably stubborn narcissism. My scar tissue is exposed, the ghosts draw blood, but only a few drops. My father's house is many houses, across many generations. A lovely reminder from the Eagles: *"You can check out anytime you like, but you can never leave."* Maybe there is no leaving the father's house … *it is a beauty, it is a beast, and we have to deal with it, one way or another.*

These days, I see myself aging, my black hair fading into silver, my once smooth olive skin deeply-creviced by time, the desert sun and wind … my whole life is etched onto my face. Time and gravity inevitably win, from crawling to upright to laying back down, to dust we all return. From Don Henley:

> *"I look in the mirror now,*
> *I see that time can be unkind.*
>
> *But I know every wrinkle,*
> *and I earned every line.*
>
> *So, wear it like a royal crown,*

when you get old and gray.

It's the cost of living,
and everyone pays."

Both my mother and father live inside of me. In my face, my laugh, the inflections in my voice, their unconscious pat phrases deeply imprinted from a thousand repetitions. Sometimes, when I grin at Ming over the top of my glasses, she says to me: *"Hello, Mary."* At first I cringed, now I just smile. For so long, I saw them as *'enemy,'* at first the need to run away, then the desire to heal, over-come, transcend … and now to include. Today I accept the wisdom in this endeavor. I own what is mine, I make room for the inevitable imprint of my lineage. Sometimes I feel peaceful and grateful and sometimes I feel angry and sad.

More and more, I welcome the unfolding. Lifetime after life-time, different roles, different configurations, changing combina-tions … the family soul as a repertory company, playing out its unending drama. I see my own karma, I see the soul's generosity in the lessons that it offers to me. I move more slowly these days. The life-long Mercurial insistence of immediacy now gives way to a quiet and trusting acceptance of what is. Broken things remain broken, dishes in the sink stay dirty longer, the feather on the floor no longer merits my attention. The constant urge to push the edge feels unimportant.

While I cannot yet see it, I can feel my own end of days. I have long sensed that I will not *'cross the river into the promised land.'* The world is not mine to fix or heal. I am making peace with my own limitations, I accept my successes and failures as nothing more than school lessons. My memories of childhood are alive in vivid color, often I can't remember what I had for breakfast. I imagine seeing my Nona when I pass through the gates, and my heart is warm with love and gratitude. If indeed there is a gate to heaven, I imagine the only real question asked at the portal: *"How well did you love?"* I believe that the day of my birth and the day of my death are etched in the stone tablet of some cosmic calendar ... everything in between is discretionary. Death no longer frightens me, instead it intrigues me. As my Angelina bid me welcome at nine, now she silently whispers: *"We're waiting for you."*

I have a deep trust in my loving nature, the true voice of my eternal soul. While my outside is gray and wrinkled, the inside is warm and glowing. There is a sweet sadness in knowing my days are numbered. What comes next feels loving and full of light. What I leave behind squeezes my heart. How much love I have for my beloved Ming is more than words could ever describe. Our souls have held hands across many lifetimes, I imagine we shall see each other again. I am so humbled and privileged to have fathered Dakota and Dylan. They are such good-hearted men ... strong, smart, and kind. Even though they are in their 20's, and still struggling until their right path finds them, I trust that the soul of each one will someday tap them on the shoulder, and lead them to whatever their mission is on this plane. Perhaps the gods will grace me with a glimpse of that, perhaps not. The archer can never go where the arrow flies. He can only hope to be a stable bow, and launch them with a heart that knows love, courage, beauty, and truth. Their lives will do the rest. I feel there is so much more for me to do in my remaining time. My writing opens a new pathway, it is leading me somewhere. The other night I have this dream:

> *"I am in the future, being tested, another initiation ... an opportunity to integrate a higher intelligence. I do not quite trust those who are conducting the tests. People are disappearing, strange occurrences, planetary climate is changing rapidly.*
>
> *I have a secret ... a stone in a pouch that I have managed to keep from them. I am surprised that I have gotten this far without their detecting. I am about to enter a chamber for my final test. Will I have the presence, the clarity to not react to the illusions, to stay focused, to see the truth? The test begins, the chief tester is a tough man, looks like the*

actor Chris Cooper. I have placed my secret pouch outside in the high grass, I go in empty.

I see the animal essence of the tester ... a large green cobra. At first, I am frightened. Soon, I feel its soul, its depth, its intelligence, even its warmth. I no longer fear it, I can actually love it. A chamber opens, I step in, the room is filled with banks of light cells. One cell moves into my brain, right behind my eyes. The entry is simple and painless ... I feel ease, peace, simplicity, completion.

I leave the chamber and go outside into the night. The lights are dim, the moon is bright. Ming and the boys are waiting for me. A truck's wheel has pushed up my pouch from its hiding place, I put it in my pocket.

Do I share this with them? I remove the stone from the pouch, hold it in my open hand. It is a round crystal ball, it begins to glow. It radiates up my right arm and enters my brain behind my left ear. I am glowing with warmth and love.

Chapter 30: **Covid**

The day after Thanksgiving, '20, Ming visits her friend Nancy in Utah. Unbeknownst to either one of them, her friend's mother has been sick, and says nothing about it. When Ming returns the following week, she thinks she has food poisoning, but she has the virus. That Sunday, I am full blown symptomatic.

My writing is going well, I had planned to write during the holidays. This virus comes along and levels me … no yoga, no writing, no working out, no meditation … I stop doing everything that is good for me, I lose my entire discipline. My body is weak and feverish, I can't get out of bed to take a fucking piss. This is a nasty flu, not the worst I've had, but it's pretty serious. The fever is not high, still it makes me shiver. This goes on for the whole month of December. While this is not life-threatening, I am face to face with the inner horror of my entire shadow life.

Covid is an initiation like no other, ushering us all into a darkness of global proportions, fear is everywhere. Years before, Paul Levy writes about 'Wetiko,' the Native American term for darkness in the world. We have known these times before, our planet knows catastrophe and calamity, this virus is just the tip of the iceberg. Perhaps the Hopi's 'end of days' may indeed be upon us.

> *Covid reflects our global 'virus of unconsciousness'…*
> *the sum total of our individual and collective unowned shadows that each one of us projects into the world.*

Levy says that 'evil' is the abject refusal to acknowledge our own shadows. Gandhi says: "The only devils in the world are those running around in our own hearts. That is where the battle should be fought." I reflect on my own dark caverns while under the spell of 'wetiko'. Having the virus triggers another personal initiation, a descent and separation that so deeply turns my view of 'normal' upside down and inside out. Ripping away all my comforts, attacking the mind, body, spirit and soul, turning me against myself at every level, evoking fear across every dimension. Outside of me, the media relentlessly broadcasts the horrors on a never-ending news cycle. Confined to small quarters, the Hollywood Squares of Zoom move to foreground. Personal interface becomes taboo. All the warrior weekends are canceled, all the in-person groups shift to online format. Disinformation sets the growing diversity of groups against each other. Long-standing businesses and institutions disintegrate overnight. This is a whole new world, it is dark, ugly, lonely, and I am in my own hell.

My ordeal shows up at the foot of my bed, where the shadows do their dance of doubt. I have suffered some pretty dark psychedelic trips in my time, but this one takes the cake. It's like wrestling with an invisible octopus in the fun house of horror. How do I make sense of this insanity? What do I do with these feelings of terror, helplessness, hopelessness, shame, rage, grief? When I do have the energy to get out of bed, and dare to look in the mirror, I see darkness covering my face. Not only do time and gravity win, this virus claims the remaining psychic territory. Vanity takes a terrible hit … what was once a swarthy and handsome face is just an old man. I foolishly ask where the time has gone. I remember how much life this face has seen, I never thought I'd end up in ***this*** place. Where once I believed Don Henley's counsel' … *to wear your face like a royal crown'*… I just can't seem to muster that courage. They say that a bad day for the ego is a good day for the soul. Today I say: *"Bullshit! A bad day is just a bad fucking day, and my ego loves to bitch."*

The ego is a splendid psychological mechanism. It drives us to achieve marvelous heights of success, fame, fortune, notoriety. It also has a capacity to lie, deceive, misdirect, and deny the truth of my experience. Its emergence in early childhood is to protect and defend … anything to avoid pain and discomfort. How often the ego overreacts to the trigger. Here the little boy within perceives a *'threat'* with much more emotion than the grown man. And a man's ego defends disproportionately to the actual threat. What got anchored as *'software'* into the psyche at two to four years old, having repeated the same dysfunction for a whole life, is now in desperate need of an upgrade, maybe an entire overhaul. Mine sure does.

This virus is a monster, attacking the body at all levels. The physical, intellectual, emotional, and spiritual bodies are impacted, each in its own dimension. The poison oozes out everywhere. Physically, this virus knocks the shit out of my body ... the endless coughing, a lingering sweaty fever, nausea and diarrhea, no appetite, mucus, exhaustion. Just a sack of bones with a fragile skin cover, the innards gurgling and smelly, the heaviness almost unbearable ... my body is such a fucking mess.

Intellectually, my thoughts are dark, beliefs and attitudes totally negative. Full of self-doubt, I judge every choice I have ever made. My Saturn death theme is alive and well:

"Who the fuck do you think you are? Such a hotshit, so full of arrogance and vanity, so fucking 'holier than thou' ... you are such a fraud. You will never write this book, you have absolutely nothing of value to say. You have always been weak, faking it, and making it look good. You keep making fucking excuses like you've always done. You are barely ordinary, and you are going to die sooner than you think, unfinished, and no one will give a fuck. You should just crawl into a hole and die, you worthless piece of shit."

In my emotional body, I am numb, checked out, shut down, not caring a shit about anything. When I do feel, it is angst and fear, shame and self-pity. I feel no light, no hope, no enthusiasm, only despair ... just this dreaded helplessness and powerlessness. I see suicide as a viable option, I wish it were homicide. Spiritually, there is nothing, no one home ... no god, no soul, no spirit, no connectedness, just the simple reality that we are born and then we die. Dust to dust, nothing else ... the existential horror of nothingness. Then in comes the ego, accompanied by the evil twins of arrogance and shame ... one that hides the insecurities, the other that wallows in misery and self-pity, poor fucking me. This virus has opened my inner hell, where I store all my precious darkness, I am swirling in Dante's inferno.

In our month-long down time, Ming finds a documentary on Prime Video called: *"The Healing."* My first thought is *'What the fuck do they know?'* The du jour New Age teachers: Marian Williamson, Gregg Braden, Joe Dispenza, Bruce Lipton, all speaking about mind/body healing, epigenetics, nature's wisdom, and the one thing that impacts me the most: ***how our thinking influences the body at the cellular level.*** What we believe and think, especially in our unconscious mind, has a direct impact on the cells, tissues, and organs. The cells listen, and respond. Collectively, the teachers are suggesting that:

> *'Whatever I think and believe about myself …*
> *is who I become.'*

Charles Darwin and Newtonian physics, as well as modern medical science, have us believe that it is our genetic inheritance that rules what happens to the body, over which we have no control. No surprise, the less control we believe we have, the more we are likely to surrender to the *'doctors who know.'* The new quantum viewpoint suggests that *'the environment'*, including our own thinking, imprints us more than we realize: *"I am what I believe and affirm, conscious or otherwise."* In my viral downward spin, this is the last fucking thing I want to hear, cause if it's true, I am heading straight to hell. The virus finally exits my body on the last day of December, I greet the new year grateful that the horror of 2020 is gone. As the virus leaves the host, my body, mind, heart, and spirit re-illuminate, turning on the neural switches of appetite, showers and baths, meditation, healthy food, walking, working out, writing, positive attitude, inner work.

I read Bruce Lipton's *"The Biology of Belief,"* and quickly realize that I have been carrying a negative, fear-based attitude about my body since boyhood. I have digestive issues since birth. I have a hiatal hernia, so did my father. I've got arthritis in my thumbs, so does my brother. I have had two hip surgeries, my father and both grandfathers walked with canes. Up till now, I have believed that I am a victim of my lineage, and there is nothing I can do about it. In this realization, I ask myself:

- *What if my believing and verbalizing this is indeed what makes it true?*

- *What if I believe and articulate something different?*

- *What if I affirmed my own good health and well-being?*

- *What if I affirmed my own good enoughness in all areas of my life?*

Lipton's work helps me see that this early conditioning is actually software, my initial operating system, layered into my brain and neurological pathways before any real conscious memory.

Gurdjieff spoke of the four energy centers in the body: intellectual, emotional, instinctive, moving. If we look at the **speed** of each of these *'brains,'* we see that the emotional center operates at a speed beyond our control. Emotions arise quickly, intensely, powerfully, with very little choice in the matter. So too with the instinctive and the moving centers. Only the intellectual center is slow enough ... not only to see thoughts as they arise, but to influence and control what we do with them. In other words: *We only have direct influence over our thoughts, beliefs, and attitudes.* While this takes practice, mental discipline, and conscious self-awareness, before now, the choice has been unconscious. Now that I realize that I have creative choices, what does this mean for me in this next stage of my life?

It is increasingly clear to me that the horror of Covid is actually a gift, a catalyzer for profound change. As my shadows and negative beliefs move to foreground, I see their folly. I feel able and willing to bring more light to that darkness, to actually create meaningful change. What if the challenge of Covid is indeed my opportunity to awaken to a whole new way of being?

Covid has brought me face to face with my own darkness, a gift of immeasurable proportions. For the first time, all my shadow beliefs are right here, boldly written out in capital letters, one by one across my inner billboards. I see them, where they come from, how long they have been with me, how long I have believed them, how I believe them still. Unconsciously, repeatedly, since childhood, over time, I have concretized them as my reality. Wow, the realization hits me hard.

My shadow beliefs were not born in me, they are not fixed, they are not a permanent function of my hardware. They were imprinted in my psyche somewhere between conception and eight years old, when I had no real choice but to take them on, when I said yes because I had no defense, and my survival depended on it. The adults had the power, I did not, could not say no. Maybe now, I can.

Chapter 31: **Medicine**

"I'm no wino but I'm no saint either. A medicine man should not be a saint. He should experience and feel all the ups and downs, the despair and joy, the magic and the reality, the courage and the fear. He should be able to sink as low as a bug, or soar as high as an eagle.

Unless he can experience both, he is no good as a medicine man. You cannot be so stuck up, so inhuman that you want to be pure, your soul wrapped up in a plastic bag all the time. You have to be god and the devil, both of them.

Being a good medicine man means being right in the midst of the turmoil, not shielding yourself from it. It means experiencing life in all its phases. It means not being afraid of cutting up and playing the fool now and then. That is sacred too."

John Fire Lame Deer, Lakota Medicine Man

The first week of January '21, our men's group for young men in recovery meets in person here in town for the first time since the lock-down. The work we do is deep and profound. We talk about Covid, sickness, addiction, recovery, and the right use of *'medicine.'* The Native Americans believed that medicine is any object or practice regarded as having magical powers. As each of us has a core wound, we choose a vehicle to administer *'medicine'* to that wound. Some medicines are toxic or misused … heroin, alcohol, nicotine, illegal drugs, prescription drugs, recreational psychedelics, food, work, sex, pornography, violence, control … it is fear medicine. This medicine works, for a short time, delivering relief from the pain, offering a fantasy that we are okay, providing a temporary satiation in that moment of reprieve … like magic. However, this medicine wears off quickly, the wound roars from its hungry hole, and once again, we fill that hole with the same medicine. Naturally, the same results, repeated, recycled, perhaps for many years, an entire lifetime, many lifetimes.

Other medicines are healing ... naturopathic, nutritional, herbal, organic. Conscious attention, inner work, art, music, journaling, therapy, plant medicines, healing circles, bodywork, service, perhaps a mission in the world. However, these medicines do not offer the same immediate relief, no quick magic. This is long term medicine, requiring continuous application, discipline, patience, trust, support, care ... it is love medicine. Love medicine is often painful, it asks us to make friends with the wound, to find right relationship to it, to use the pain as a teacher. Pain is a necessary part of life on this planet. Suffering, however, is optional.

This pain, the core wound underneath all addictions, is always emotional. As children, we have legitimate physical and emotional needs that our caregivers fail to meet, despite their best intentions. It is simply impossible for them to attend to everything a hungry, screaming child needs. More often than not, they are unconscious about their own wounds and needs, rendering them unable to pay attention to the child's needs. And thus, unconsciously, they wound the child. By age four, the false personality is concretized.

By eight, we have been fully imprinted, our inner psychic territory is no longer ours. With the ego driving the personality, constantly vigilant for pain and discomfort, it does not want us to touch the pain underneath. So it protects, defends, deflects, denies, projects the pain, staying away from the more vulnerable feelings, hiding who we really are underneath. While everyone has an ego, those who stay away from their underlying pain, those who opt for short-term medicine tend to live **from** their ego. Those who choose to acknowledge their pain, who choose long-term medicine, tend to live **with** their ego. One is false, the other is a serious endeavor to be real.

It has taken me a lifetime of deep emotional work to reach this place of relative inner-peace and self-acceptance. I sit with my young brothers, listen to their stories, I feel their pain. As much as I want to soothe them, I know that the only way out is through. So I push them into the work, I push them deeper into their own pain and struggle, all the while promising them that if they have the courage to let themselves feel the pain, that if they resist the temptation to temporarily medicate, they might emerge on the other side, whole and intact. So they keep coming back, most keep staying sober, they keep turning into the work ... and I keep pushing them. Sometimes they go back out, because their internal pain is too great, opting for the short-term medicine of choice. Some stay out, most return, starting over again at day one. I have such love for them, and great hope. Little do I know that another initiation, right on the heels of Covid, will soon pull me down. One that will rock me to my core, one that will bring me face to face with my own mortality. How will I administer my own medicine ... literally, physically, emotionally, spiritually?

Ming and I travel to Denver in late May, the plan is to stay at her sister Cilla's house in Washington Park for six weeks. Colorado is familiar territory, I know many men in the work. I run two *'Day of Deep Process'* workshops, a dozen men each day coming to do carpet work. The process intention is to access the stuck parts within, the places where the pain hides, the places we medicate, those areas in our psychic territory that were lost, taken away from us when we had no power. Rather than deny the pain, inside this safe container, they choose to feel the ache of that loss.

The only real question in any inner work is: "What broke your heart?" For this is where the real emotional pain resides.

Through acknowledging and feeling each loss, through each reclamation of lost psychic territory, more power and agency is accrued, more being is affirmed. The more we acknowledge and heal the pain that is, the more we stand fully in the Now. Inside our MensWork circles is the simple affirmation:

Vulnerability + Truth = Authentic Power

I have always been an avid reader, but from moving so many

times, books have become a burden. I have lost or given away many junks and gems, and just as many have been left on the shelf half-read or not read at all. Sometimes just the title and intention and idea bring value, sometimes just the picture of the author on the jacket. The books that remain in my library are keepers, I don't really know why. While browsing through the 'Tattered Cover' bookstore in Denver, I find a book by NY Times bestselling author Michael Pollan, who writes about the places where nature and culture intersect: on our food plates, in our farms and gardens, and in the built environment. The book is titled: "How to Change Your Mind: What the New Science of Psychedelics Teaches Us about Consciousness, Dying, Addiction, Depression, and Transcendence." Right up my alley.

Over the years, Ming and I learn to be selective in what we put inside our bodies. Being organic and vegan is an important aspect of our good self-care. Having learned the true value of plant medicines in Mexico, I now include psychedelics as potential healing medicine, based upon the time, intention, and circumstances. Seemingly not by accident, I come upon this book. I remember as a much younger man, my use of psychedelics was illuminating, yet recreational, I did not really understand their true worth. Over the years, the sacred value of deep healing has become the motivation, as the ego, no matter how well worked, remains too well defended. This book literally blows me away. I see and sense the spaces within me that are still lost psychic territory. Covid shows virtually all my shit, and I know there is still inner work to attend to.

Michael Pollan tells the history of psychedelics, from legal to illegal to the more widespread understanding of their potential healing capacity. Psychedelics were initially designed for long-term sufferers of mental illness, addictions, obsessive compulsive disorders, and to those facing death. Many are now looking to transcend the deeply imprinted programs that carry the 'separation/survivalist/ instinctive/egoic' perspective of binary thinking. Psychedelics facilitate a shift to the more 'quantum non-egoic consciousness' perspective of non-binary thinking. Confucius, when asked about the secret of life, said: *"To be true to yourself and kind to others."*

Yes, of course, how simple ... yet how challenging the paradox, which the ego does not understand. Some passages from Pollan:

> **"By temporarily disabling the ego,** *the psychedelic molecules quiet the part of the brain called the Default Mode Network, thought to house and govern the ego function. Psilocybin (Sacred Mushrooms) seems to open a new field of psychological possibility, symbolized by the death and rebirth reported by many. At first, the falling away of the self feels threatening, but if one can let go and surrender, powerful and usually positive emotions flow in ... along with formerly inaccessible memories and sense impressions and meanings.*
>
> *No longer defended by the ego, the gate between self and other is thrown wide open. And what comes through that opening, for many, in a great flood ... is Love. Love for specific individuals, yes, but also love for everyone and everything. Love as the meaning and purpose of life, the key to the universe, and the ultimate truth."*
>
> Michael Pollan, "How to Change Your Mind" p. 353

In a very honest and vulnerable way, Pollan describes his initial reticence to the use of psychedelics. He describes the very controlled methods he deployed, using trained therapists and under strict logistical conditions. He speaks from interviews with many, and from his own personal experiences. Personally, I know my darkness all too well, I know the deep shadows, accrued over many lifetimes, and I realize that I cannot do this next level of healing on my own ... for my New York street kid ego is too stubborn, too powerful. I feel my heart opening when I think about once again dancing with this kind of *'medicine,'* but under very different and controlled conditions. In reading this book, in feeling Pollan's wisdom and deep humility, something comes alive in me. An old and familiar doorway reopens, but in a new way. I see a pathway of potential healing and expanded transformational possibilities. Finally, I see where my Saturn line points to loss, sickness, death. And how my Pluto line points to regeneration.

A psychic death always precedes a transformational rebirth.

During the six weeks we spend in Denver, most evenings Ming and I go for nice long walks in our neighborhood. The mature trees offer cool shade, I like to wrap my arms around the old oak trees. I feel grounded, safe, and trusting of my current life's trajectory. And then I start to notice a pain in my right hip. Not every night, but regular enough to get my attention. I call the orthopedist in Tucson and make an appointment for right after we get back home.

I have my first appointment with the ortho doc in July '21. Over the next couple of weeks, we do X-rays, an MRI, and a blood draw. This is the hip that did not heal from the faulty first double hip replacement in '07. After almost two years, all the while on Percocet, I had its first revision. This surgery cleared the bone pain, but the deep muscular invasions, the pain in ligaments and tendons, the incessant clunking in the right glute … I never forget that I have five pounds of metal in my ass. The new X-rays show no bone damage, the MRI shows no apparent tissue damage. However, the blood draw shows an abnormally high content of both chromium and cobalt. I ask the doc what we should do. He says we need to replace the metal-on-metal prosthetics in both hips, for they are leeching these heavy metal ions into my body. In other words, I need two more fucking surgeries. He also says I have osteoporosis, a softening of the bone tissue. In addition, I have arthritis in both thumbs, and some serious need of dental work. I wonder if this is the damage reeked by the heavy metals in my body for so many years. On the heels of Covid, my body drags me to my next initiation … literally by the bones !!! We schedule my second right hip revision surgery for Monday September 27 at Oro Valley hospital.

On this earth plane, I know I am bound by the laws of four-dimensional reality, I both walk in the light and cast a shadow. No matter how hard I try to *'get rid of'* my darkness, or to *'medicate it,'* it does not go away. The decision, in every moment, in every day, whether awake or asleep, is between love or fear. ***And choosing love is always the harder choice.*** My unacknowledged shadows and negative beliefs have quietly and unconsciously wreaked havoc on my body, and my heart struggles to acknowledge the depth of the damage. I know that time is short, there is no enlightened one to lead me to the promised land, no spiritual practice or religion to illuminate my road to salvation, no medicine to *'fix'* me. This is an inside out job. No one but me to heal myself, for I know that I have co-created this mess. Now, I must choose to courageously look at, acknowledge, and stand accountable for my own inner darkness, the current condition of my body, and take a new set of actions.

This means that *'I am fully responsible'* for my condition, and in part, for my contribution to the shadow shit in the world ... as much as anyone else, no more/no less ... **and I do not get to blame.** Not the politicians nor the government, not Putin nor China, not the president(s), not my wife, not some group of differing color, nor Covid, not even the heavy metals ... **I do not get to blame.** Quite simply, the **blaming IS the projection,** making it about someone else, refusing to look at myself, keeping this old unconsciousness in charge, the ego ruling everything. When I look in the fucking mirror, I see where the problem is ... it is me. And it is always up to me to do my own inner work, to do my healing work, to wake the fuck up, to choose love. I know that my body is on an inevitable decline, time and gravity win out, and every life ends in loss, sickness, and death. Still, I feel that deep within my heart and soul there is also *an ascending arc of light.* It is love and gratitude, humility and deep appreciation ... for everything!

In early September, I am having breakfast with a dear friend, who tells me about B, a man in Tucson who grows psychedelic mushrooms and facilitates psilocybin journeys. I meet with B for lunch the next week, and we mutually agree to open the doorway to my next healing journey. He gives me a lengthy set of questions to gather a sense of who I am and what I am seeking from this experience. I write twenty-five pages, tell him all of my *'medicine'* experiences, positive and negative. We meet several times over the next six weeks, and schedule my first journey for the end of October. I imagine that my body would be sufficiently ready a month after hip surgery to handle this experience. Unfortunately, this does not happen. We meet a few days before our session, my hip is still in severe pain.

My drug protocol after surgery includes Oxycodone, an addictive opioid. Remembering the ninety days it took me to kick Percocet, I hold an intention to not use it at all. That intention lasts about two days, the pain is just too severe. Three weeks after surgery, just prior to my scheduled medicine journey, I run out of opioids. I call the doc and tell him that I am still in deep pain. He takes another set of X-rays, structurally the surgery is a success.

He reminds me that my lower lumbar disk is compromised, and that this pain may actually be from the compression of my sciatic nerve. He shares the options: back surgery, injections of cortisone, or neurontin drugs. I see the look in his eyes, I imagine his struggle in not being able to, or not knowing much outside the allopathic model. We make a date in late January for the left hip surgery, we shake hands, and he walks out of the room. I go home and look up this drug, it is essentially a sedative. Side effects are numbling when talking, stumbling when walking, hangovers, forgetfulness, hard to get off of … in essence it is dopey medicine. No thank you, I refuse to take this drug. Instead, I recommit myself to a more organic methodology. I step up my yoga practice, I find a body worker, Ming makes more healing foods, like celery juice and heavy metal detox smoothies. This is the perfect time to take a deeper look at the pain that my body has carried for most of my life, and the body pain in all the men in my lineage.

I arrive at B's house in downtown Tucson at 10 am on Sat Oct 23. A small apartment, well-kept and quiet. Vivid green plants everywhere, his medicine jars and assorted containers colorful and creatively scattered across his two rooms. There is a bare-teeth coyote mounted on the wall. I sit on a mat on the floor, blankets and pillows scattered and available. A large glass of water and box of tissues are on a tray. I honor his meticulousness and order, and his feminine organic grace. At forty, he is a lovely blend of masculine and feminine energies. My body, my soul, and my spirit trust that I am in good hands.

He brings me a cup of tea, three to four grams of freshly harvested psilocybin in a dark brew. He shows me the dried mushrooms, they radiate in beautiful brown, beige and pink colors. They look loving, they also look fierce. I feel like I will be rudely thrust into my own darkness, but deeply cared for, and gradually brought to the light. Within a half hour, I am vividly hallucinating, ordered patterns and bold colors explode like a kaleidoscope in my psyche, all in constant motion. I feel encased inside these structures, they move quickly. I have photographs of my parents, both sets of grandparents, Ming and me, and Dakota and Dylan. Not sure that I had a clear intention in bringing the photos, but I suspected that some conversations would be had with my familial relationships. But now I consciously realize that at least this first part of my journey is about karma. The second intention is more clear: how to make peace with the pain that I carry in my body right now … I imagine there is an overlap. As I focus on a single pattern, a black wooden door opens into a room:

> *I stand at the side of poppy's bed, I see myself as a three-year old snuggling in bed with my back to him. His arm is draped gently over my hip, and his hand rests deeply between my legs. I see a single moment of contentedness on his tortured face, a look that I never saw in him throughout the eleven years we lived together. And I see myself sleeping, quiet and trusting, not yet knowing the impact of this gesture.*

In that very moment, I realize that each person in my immediate lineage has delivered to me exactly what my soul has designed and intended … *both a gift and a wound*. And a second realization … the wound is a gift in and of itself, *its challenge is the gift.* Like the whetstone for a knife, like the barbell for building a strong body, like the resistance each of us encounters in working toward any goal worth achieving. I remember Gurdjieff talking about the musical scale as a metaphor for accomplishing anything ... moving something from a lower octave to a higher one. There are two half tone intervals that need to be consciously engaged in order to ascend to the higher octave. The first interval (mi-fa) is right after the thrill of something new wears off, thoughts like: *"I don't really want this; this is harder than I imagined; etc."* It takes an extra effort, an intentional push to bridge this gap. The energy then travels almost unconsciously until we reach the last interval (the si-do), the finale. Closing the deal, getting to yes, reaching the goal fully, including dotting the I's, crossing the T's, and filing the papers. The resistance says: *"This is good enough, I'll do it tomorrow; etc."*

Each successful ascending octave brings real change, operating at a higher level. Change is hard, conscious change is harder, there is always resistance, fear, the ego's mandate to maintain the status quo. Another example of quantum consciousness, inside time and space and the material world ... is holding the bi-polar shadow energies, the active and the passive poles of each archetypal triangle (from Robert Moore). Holding the tension of opposites, like in yoga, building both strength and flexibility. Holding the either/or in all its binary forms, like holding the masculine and the feminine within. In holding the tension of opposites, for what feels like an interminable amount of time, in not fighting the internal friction, the light of quantum consciousness arises.

Inside my journey, all of this happens in a flash. One by one, as far back as I can see and remember, maybe more ... each lineage member parades before me, each gives me a gift and a wound/challenge. Four great grandfathers, both grandfathers, and finally my father's gift: his loyalty and working-class ethic that drives me to commit to work hard. And his wound: his inability to acknowledge me that drives me to be seen. In that moment, my heart opens, the tears fall, the fight is over … I feel the final shift in my cellular body, binary to quantum.

My inner work is no longer about the need to work hard in order to be seen and acknowledged. It is now, simply, about doing what I love, living my mission, doing what I am called to do in this lifetime, and doing what makes my heart and soul sing.

And then courageously putting all of it into the world. I take a breath, drink some water, my guide checks in with me and asks if I am okay. Marvelous, I tell him, as I take a deep breath, close my eyes, and go back inside. The medicine is still potent, there is more. I say to the medicine: *"Please show me what I need to see."*

It is Halloween, I am seven or eight years old. There is a party at church, my mother is dressing me as a gypsy girl. She offers a round black skirt, the hems tacked with safety pins. She adds a plain white frilly blouse, wraps a scarf around my head and around my neck. She paints my face with her makeup, black liner around the eyes, bright red lipstick, rouge on the cheeks. She affixes big gold clip-on earrings, with round bangly bracelets on both wrists. Before she puts on a little black mask, she has me look in the mirror. I am shocked to see myself as a girl.

On rare occasions does my mother tell me that she loves me. She looks at me in the mirror, smiles, and with tears in her eyes, says: "I love you very much, Den." I feel my heart open to her, she lets me stroke her hair. Somehow, I know that she is afraid of boys and men, especially my grandfather. And she always longed for a girl. Way too much masculine energy for her to contend with, she keeps a hard edge to protect her fragility. Her wooden spoon gave her the power to define her boundary, at least with me. Yet today, in spite of all of that, I feel her love.

To feel my mother's gift of embracing my sensitivity is transformative. No matter how crazy it got within their sexual triangle, no matter how broken she was, she knew that I was a sensitive. She knew I had a tender heart, and never made fun of my tears. Over the years, I had many a woman who welcomed my tenderness. And while I was often manipulative with it, my tenderness was always real. I look at the photo of my mother and my heart grieves. Once I left New York, I kept my mother at a distance. When we moved to Tucson in '90, and had Dakota in '94, we made some peace. Honestly, I never really let her in. And until this day, I have not fully appreciated her acknowledging my feminine side, nor have I truly forgiven her. I kiss her picture, and through tears, I say: *"I love you, mom, I thank you, and I forgive you."* I place my mom's picture right next to the aggregate photos of the men. Her harshness has done great damage, and it has been much hard work with and through Ming to heal. Today my motherwork feels complete.

On the left side of the mat, I pick up the two photos of my grandmothers. In each of their faces, I see love and grace and beauty. While my Persian grandma died when I was in utero, I hold her as one of my guardian angels. Her eyes are soft and tender, her face is gentle and compassionate, there is a radiant glow around her head, like a halo. I grasp her picture and press it to my chest. All I can say is thank you … over and over and over again. She is one of the feminine energies who reside in my architecture. I then see my Sicilian Nona, in my life till she passed in '87. She is still so accessible to me, when we walk in the mornings I see her face in the Catalina mountains that we affectionately call 'Nona.' I can taste her spaghetti and meatballs, I can see her cute wrinkly nose, I can feel her tender love that was always available to me, for in her eyes, I could do no wrong. I clasp both pictures to my chest, I feel both my grandmothers' love alive in my heart, full of gratitude and grace. I have the privilege and good fortune to have danced with some terrific women in my life. No wonder, I now see the feminine side of my lineage so clearly.

At that moment, I see the picture of Ming and me, taken in Mexico, where we were so very happy. Her face is radiant, her eyes sparkle with love. She is the love of my life, the mother of our two wonderful young men, the woman through which I have done my deepest healing. She is my beauty, my muse, my love, my best friend, my teacher, my guide, my whetstone, my great gift and great challenge ... My Soul Mate, My Beloved. My heart is full and quiet, the karma with my lineage is now complete. And right next to this picture, is a photo of Dakota and Dylan. My heart is full of gratitude, as their beauty and good heartedness have arisen from the love and deep work that Ming and I have done together. Indeed, like all parents, we have given them both a gift and a challenge, and Ming and I stand fully in our accountability. In their own way, in their own time, they will work out their own karma. Hopefully, their healing journey will be quicker, so their mission may find them sooner, for the world needs their *'fierce and tender loving'* right now.

I purge frequently during this journey, each time a harbinger of the shadows on the rise. As my body offers up the last wave, I look at the picture of our sons. They stand in front of a waterfall, in the photo it rises right between them as a shaft of light. While none of the other photos offer this illumination, I see this as the next doorway, and it is a mixed blessing. It is entirely possible that this pain in my body will accompany me through this incarnation. And more than likely, I will find true peace only when I no longer reside within my body. But until then, my work is alive in the world. My sacred marriage with Ming is alive in the world. Our sons and their respective missions are alive in the world. And resident, deep within my heart and soul, is this creative energy. Even though my body ultimately descends into dust, this arc of light ascends ... in me, through me, through my work, through our marriage, and through our progeny.

At 3 pm I leave B's apartment. I deeply bow to his spiritual service on my behalf. We have two sessions like this scheduled, with time in between to integrate. I am quiet and deeply content. Ming is home, I share some things, tomorrow is Sunday and wide open. I eat a little, take a nice hot bath, we crawl into bed early. I sleep well, arise at five the next morning, and journal my experience.

Chapter 32: **Eldership**

In the summer of '97, we have settled into our lovely house in Kensington, San Diego. Dakota is three, Dylan is one, Ming and I are in a good place for a change, my work is going well, we are happy with our little family. Our dear friends Kathie and Jim host a 50th birthday party for me, our tribe encircles us. Ming creates an album of photos and memorabilia ... of my MensWork, of our pregnancies and births, of our families, friends, and extended loved ones. Half way to a hundred, I pick up this eldership book as an inquiry into what may lie ahead. I am unable to remember the title or the author, but the singular thread that has stayed alive in me is the writer's theory (stated in my own words, apologies to the author):

"As everyone has embedded within their body a genetic program for puberty, likewise do we have a genetic program for eldership. At about 13, and then again at about 65, a chemical 'switch' gets turned on, initiating a set of physiological and psychological patterns and possibilities that shape the course of a life."

The unfathomable existential inquiry, the one that moves immediately into foreground as the body begins its decline, is death. At fifty, it was theoretical, I was able to push it off into tomorrow. Now at seventy plus, tomorrow is already here, not so easy to deny. While the puberty switch is physically obvious, the development of a teenager is mostly dependent on environmental issues. The elder switch is all too obvious with the body's beginning decline, yet the difference between *'getting old'* and *'becoming an elder'* is more a function of the individual's character, consciousness, and choice. My hip issues present the rude realities of oncoming *'incompetence, incontinence, impotence, and irrelevance.'*

Old age necessitates decay and death, eldership offers the opportunity of learning to die well. My local astro-cartography is about death and transformation. The first is inevitable, the other is optional. While my ego tries to protect and defend and deny what is too painful or too uncomfortable or too terrifying to feel, today my deep self gets to choose how this last stage of my life will go. Choosing love and transformation and a conscious dying and death, my life goes in one direction. Choosing fear, denial, and whining about the pain of getting old, it goes in a completely different direction.

I return to our men in recovery group several weeks after my surgery. I take a seat by the fire. A line of young men stand before me, each bending down to hug me and welcome me back. Among most groups of men, older men hold onto power too long, and younger men crave power too soon. There is so little mentorship, as the *"manbox"* continues to preach competition from that never ending fear of inadequacy. A healthy mentorship for young men, a healthy teaching and sharing of mature masculinity, a healthy aging and respect for eldership ... these are indeed rare. In our extended men's circles, while the old masculine ways are still alive, there are more threads of the new consciousness. Once again, we return to the past to find the healthy path to the future. The ancients venerated the elders and the wisdom they had accrued, having traveled many times around the sun. When the warriors returned home from the hunt, the elders always ate first. Even at the end, the elders knew when they no longer contributed sufficiently to the collective. Often, they would simply walk out into the wild, sit down, and wait to die. What an incredibly courageous act of generosity to do something like that. In our young men's circle, I feel the deep love and respect they have for George and me ... we have mentored them well.

The fear of death is the only real fear, everything else is a subset. As I accept my ultimate finality, and make peace with this inevitable truth, now I get to live the rest of my life as fully as I choose. I acknowledge that at my death, my physical body, my instinctive center will be afraid, as I stand before the portal of my greatest not-knowing. Change is always scary, this change is the scariest. Fearlessness is not about the absence of fear, it is about acknowledging fear's presence and taking courageous action anyway. The *'old warrior'* consciousness from the *"manbox"* tells us that a rea man is never afraid, or at least he never shows it. He lives the motto of *'No Fear.'* This false bravado gets us into all kinds of trouble, for the inflation is dangerous in its inaccurate evaluation of risk and reward. The *'new warrior'* is every bit as fierce as the old, with one added quality: he has cultivated, through his interior labor, an honest vulnerability. And a willingness to pass along what he has learned, what he has suffered through, what he has integrated. His motto is *'Know Fear'*.

My body reminds me every day of my growing fragility. Having done MensWork for many years, I have come to know the beauty and the beast of our masculine nature. Most men come into this work with a quiet desperation, a disturbing place where the ego can no longer effectively manage its affairs. Young men come lost, looking for meaning, looking for a model of masculinity that makes sense in a world gone insane. Middle age men come, frightened by their glimpse of mortality, ashamed at a couple of divorces and their kids or themselves on drugs. But older men are a different story. We come in, knowingly or not, looking for something else.

Back in '92, I staff a training in DC. An eighty-five year old man comes in, carrying two large black trash bags filled with his gear. They are heavy and burdensome, as he struggles to carry them from station to station. I feel an ache in my heart for him, he reminds me of poppy, a part of me wants to help him carry his stuff. Later, on the carpet, I ask him: *"Who are you?"* He tells me that for many years, he held the record for most solo trans-Atlantic sailings. In other words, he sailed by himself across the Atlantic Ocean more than any other human. Talk about being a warrior! I ask him: *"Why are you here?"* He tells me that throughout his whole life, he was an introvert, afraid of other men, and he never knew how to make friends with them. He says: *"I am so lonely, and my time is running out. My wife is dead, my children are long gone, I am here today to learn how to connect with other men."* A couple of tears fall from his eyes, as he looks at me with a longing I see in so many men's eyes. As the tears fall from my own eyes, I wrap my arms around his narrow body, and say: *"I am so glad to meet you, and so grateful that you are here."* Every man on that carpet moves in to place their hands upon this man's body, and we all tell him how welcome he is in this circle.

A couple of years ago, while reading AARP magazine, I see a picture of a white-haired man, naked to the waist, with an upper body muscular and chiseled. The caption says: *"Aging is Not for Sissies."* The physical arc is clear … from crawling to upright to laying back down … ashes to ashes, dust to dust. A muscular body may give me the illusion of youth, but it will not eliminate the fear of that moment when I stand before the portal. In this last segment of my life, the final paradox presents itself:

> *"How do I consciously and fearlessly accept that my body is undeniably descending, while at the same time remember to care for my body, and to serve my interior creative ascending arc of light?"*

Newtonian consciousness has ruled the planet for many centuries, it rules us still. This *'manbox'* thinking is what keeps us stuck in darkness … *it is this thinking that keeps **me** stuck in my darkness.* The rule of the dominant masculine already shows signs of weakening. They know their days are numbered, for the *'feminine'* is unmistakably on the ascent. She is not here to rule over, but to partner with. I believe she is the gateway to our Quantum consciousness, our last gasping call for oneness, and only planetary destruction will prevent this inevitable ascendance. For me personally, this means more than I can yet grasp. I have to stay alert to virtually everything! Covid shows my personal shadows in vivid black and white, these are the very places that call out for transformation. How I think and what I do … across every dimension … will determine the last stage of my life.

Coming back home to Tucson with my Saturn (Death) and Pluto (Transformation), this is a perfect completion. This may indeed be my physical *'end of days.'* Still, I'd rather believe that this is my immaturity's *'end of days.'* I discover a new way of being in the world, a new way of loving, working, serving, a new way of bringing forth my gifts ... a more balanced *'Fierce & Tender'* ... as an Elder Medicine Man. I see my changes over the last two years, I feel myself in the center of more.

Chapter 33: **Thinking & Attitude is Everything**

Gurdjieff tells us that thought is the only dimension that humans are capable of changing. The other ones ... feeling, movement, instinct, sexuality ... are too fast for us to intervene. The idea of oneness is inescapable, the conscious practice of oneness remains a challenge. Currently, identity politics, tribalism, and over-sized egos dominate our self/other perceptions. Each group calls out desperately to be seen and acknowledged, rendering us deaf, dumb, and blind to finding common ground. The individual and collective egos remain in service to salving the wound of separation, the very wound that it instills. My neural pathways are imprinted in binary, bi-lobed, fear-based thinking, and those patterns are not going away anytime soon. Moving from *either/or to both/and,* from *me/you to I/ We,* from *fear to love,* and then to *We Are One* does not come easily. Integration and transformation take energy, awareness, discipline, humility, hard work ... *and a commitment to stay open-hearted.*

An open heart, a deep and humble self-awareness, a vulnerability and willingness to be honest and accountable, a courageous acceptance of life on its terms, a commitment to a mission of service ... the final act of my life begins. Because I have suffered my share of broken-heartedness, I have learned compassion for other people's suffering. I notice that the simple things that are right in front of me are the things worth tending to. I remember an old teaching:

> *"No effort, no matter how small, made in the direction of your sacred intention, ever goes unrewarded."*

These days I make room for the world to be what it is. Covid, oppositional politics, social insanity, the steady decay of the empire, even the planet ... I have no control over any of it. All that I am able to control is what I have direct influence over. Primarily my thoughts, after that, my feelings, attitudes, beliefs, words, and actions.

Chapter 34: **Money**

My history with money is complicated. Both sides of my lineage are immigrant families trying to make it in the new world. Working class mostly, they would cut each other's throats for the almighty buck. My father envies men who have money, and he believes that a man's worth is measured by the size of his pocketbook. At an early age, I hear my father talk about retirement, like it is the holy grail. When he sits down each week to do the math, I know that my brother and I are not a line item. As a kid, I remember one time my mother gave me thirty cents for candy. I felt like the richest kid in the neighborhood, I even bought candy for my two best friends. I never remember my father putting a quarter in my pocket. I have to scrape around the neighborhood to rustle up enough coin for the Saturday matinees. At eleven, I get a job delivering newspapers, and I am a working man ever since.

Somewhere along this road through my parent's endless repetition of depression-era scarcity, I learn to believe that there will never be enough. I learn to covet money, afraid of not having. And ironically, afraid of having it, as I imagine my father loving me because of money rather than because I'm his son. In '58, when we move into a Jewish neighborhood, all my boyfriends' fathers are merchants and business men, lawyers and doctors. They drive nice cars, live in fancy apartments in new buildings, their wives getting their hair and nails done weekly, always dressed to the nines. At sixteen, they buy new cars for their sons. I walk, take the bus, or ride my bike. In comparison, the shame that I feel soon becomes an anger and resentment toward my father. In the first year of college, it is pretty much the same, young smart Jewish boys hitting the books both day and night, struggling to get into medical school. After a year of biology, chemistry, and physics, I know that isn't gonna be me. I move out of the dorms the last half of my sophomore year, withdrawing money from my scholarship fund for room and board. I buy and sell drugs, but I am way too scared to make this a business. And way too busy consuming my own product.

Later on, when I go to work with Larry, and for the next twelve years, I make some serious coin. But the idea of *'saving for retirement,'* long dismissed and buried, never crosses my mind. I spend lavishly on clothes, cars, nice restaurants, drugs, vacations, a condo. When I quit to go to Renaissance in '83, I have a nice stash, but no real equity. After close to a year at the vineyard, then ten months in Europe, the money is depleted. In late '84, I want to go to computer school in LA. I ask my father for a loan, not sure why I even bother. Larry's dad offers, I pay him back every nickel. I get a job working for EDS in '85, arrive in Chicago before Christmas. I am still a working-class kid.

I have a great uncle who lives in Chicago, not far from Wrigley Field. Poppy's younger brother Darius, he is elderly, lives alone. His wife long passed, no kids, living in an apartment owned by his asshole brother-in-law, he is old and needy, and I fear getting drawn into his drama. I remember my childhood, this man came often, always sweet and generous with me and my brother and our family. A far cry from poppy, I kind of wish that he was my grandfather. I am a year in Chicago before I even call him. While he lives not that far away, I make excuses to keep him at a distance. I visit occasionally, once in a while I take him out to eat Chinese, sometimes we sit watching wrestling, or the White Sox. In late '86, when I start shopping for a new car, he offers to contribute. Hard to believe that any of my family members could even consider this. Maybe he is trying to buy me, and even if he is, I try not to think about it. He offers a down payment on a little black Pontiac Fiero with a moon roof. I gratefully accept. Financially, I am doing okay, saving a little money. For the most part, I live within my means. But my champagne taste, cultivated in Europe and Renaissance, stretches my budget and fuels my shadowy relationship to money … attraction and aversion. I see men who live for it, it drives everything. I pray that they worry about money as much as I do.

In early '88, Darius' health takes a turn for the worse. He asks me to take care of him, no way I can do this. He is ninety-six years old, often incontinent, declining rapidly, he needs professional help. I call my father and his two sisters. While all declaring how much they love Darius, no one gets on a plane, they barely even call him. They say that they are all so grateful that I am in Chicago, trusting that I will take care of him. Easy for them to say. I surely do not have the time or energy or resources to care for him. What the fuck do I do now? I ask him where his money is. He shows me his array of bankbooks, he has about a hundred grand all told. We go to his main bank, he gets me authorized to access a single account. There is enough operating money to get him some help. I find a live-in caretaker, a black woman. He makes messes on purpose, resents being attended to by anyone, let alone a black woman. She is just the first in the revolving parade. He wants me to move in, yet I remain clear with my own boundaries. Luckily, I find a Polish woman to take care of him, it is such a relief. She is not in good health either, but at least she gives Darius some stability, and me some space to figure this out.

When I meet Ming, I tell her all about my relationship with Darius. Ming likes him, we take him out to lunch sometimes. On his good days he is a sweet old man. On other days, I see the Latchin in him, just like his brother. Dark, distrusting, possessive, angry. One day he tells me he wants me to have all of his money when he dies, if I will keep taking care of him. Other days he accuses me of stealing his money. Ming and I know that he needs a safe place to go that can care for him. We call and visit a host of nursing homes both in Chicago and up toward Evanston. They are all poorly run, dirty, not up to code, patient care barely acceptable … and way too fucking expensive. Just before July 4, we find a nice little place in Rogers Park, not too far from where we live. It is small and quiet, the Indian people who run it seem to care. It seems clean and safe, and surprisingly reasonable at $3500 a month. Although Darius balks, bitches, and complains, he moves in mid-month. We visit him as often as we can, though never enough for Darius. His first questions are always: *"Where have you been? Why do you never visit me?"*

Slowly, he descends. Some days he is lucid, other days he is in his own terrified inner world. It breaks our hearts, and sadly the more his paranoia increases, the less we visit. In summer '89, Ming and I separate. Shortly after, when I travel to LA to visit Annie, I get a call that Darius has passed away at ninety-nine years old.

I call my folks to tell them the news. They are sad for a moment, then my father asks about his will. Within a few days, I get calls from my aunts asking exactly the same thing. I have held Darius' money in safe keeping, managed it with him in mind. Making sure his needs are promptly attended to, paying all his bills on time, balancing his accounts. I use his money for personal reasons from time to time, but always judiciously. He has generously added me as beneficiary, included with his dear friend Mary, as well as my father, Agnes, and Margaret. I now have possession of the will, as his executor. There is a bit more than fifty grand remaining. Honestly, my first thought is to keep it all. While I know that I cannot do that, still I rationalize that I have been the only one in Darius' attendance for the last couple of years. No one has come to visit, and once inside the nursing home, no one has even called. They are simply interested in his money, even my father. I feel angry, resentful, used, righteous. Of course, I am interested in his money as well. I fantasize that in the absence of any kind of inheritance, this should be it. My ego righteousness reinforces that perspective. Clearly, my father wound is driving this bus, and something in me senses big trouble ahead.

When I mention to my father that I am carefully considering how to distribute Darius' money … all hell breaks loose. I ask many people their thoughts on what I should do, the responses are all over the place. Some say it's illegal to do anything other than follow the will, some say you are a joint tenant, you can keep it all. After seemingly endless weeks of wrestling and wrangling, I finally decide to split the money in half … half for them and half for me. I send each of the four a check for seven thousand dollars, and I keep the balance of twenty-five grand for myself. A month later, my father and his two sisters file a formal lawsuit against me. A lawyer comes to interview me. I turn over all the documentation, he spends several months investigating everything. At the conclusion, he can find no fault, no laws broken, no misappropriation of funds. Maybe guilty of poor judgment and selfishness, but nothing illegal. His recommendation: send some more money to my father and aunts. We agree to another fifteen hundred each, I promptly send each of them the money. What was once a family held together by the slimmest of thread is now threadbare. I do not speak to my parents for a year, even my brother Al is angry with me. I am with Ming, she is my family now. I also take comfort in Ming's family, I talk to her dad about this. He says that the investigator found out the truth, I did what he recommended, nothing else is necessary. He also cautions me about the power of money, and how it can tear at the fabric of everything that we love, especially in families.

Ming and I move to Tucson in '90, we have Dakota in early '94. Only then do I make the effort to visit my mother and father in Sun City. Maybe we can reweave some broken threads. They love the baby, and love being grandparents up close. Becoming a father offers me a new perspective. I am less judgmental of them, as I realize the degree of difficulty in making hard decisions, the challenge of raising children, the complexity of money.

One Saturday morning, Ming and I drive up the pike with the baby to visit Mary and Al. My mother, Ming, and Dakota go out shopping, my father and I sit on the back porch. Like always, we reminisce about the past. And maybe for the first time, I feel my heart opening toward my father, and a willingness to be vulnerable with him like never before. I look over at him and say: *"Dad, I know you always wanted me to be a doctor or a lawyer. But instead, you got an Indian chief. I am sorry that I disappointed you."* I drop my head and begin to weep, my long hair falling in my face. He stands up, walks over to where I am sitting, and gently cradles my head into his belly. He says to me: *"Den, you are a good man, and we all have made big mistakes. You and Al are grown, you both have families now, and here we are together. There is something that I need to say to you, something*

I have thinking about for a very long time. I recall how much we fought about the war in Vietnam, you on the radical left and me on the righteous right. Actually, you were right about it being a bad war. You were right all along and I was wrong. I am so sorry for what I did and said to you, and I am so glad you didn't go." And in that very moment, with that single loving gesture, my father's apology, vulnerability, and accountability help me heal a deep wound in my soul, the archetypal father-son wound of my generation.

In the early years of creating a family of our own, I begin to learn the lesson of generosity. As my heart opens, I become more generous with others, both with money and a willingness to share my heart. There is a Buddhist exercise for when one feels a lack, the invitation is to give something to someone else. I am always moved by simple acts of caring and generosity. Over time, the heartache from the experience with Darius heals. What I initially imagined ... that his money would heal the father wound in me ... only opened that wound further. My grandfather left nothing behind but misery. My father believed that his older sisters would leave something behind for him. They promised him in words, in reality they left him nothing. My father's lineage passed down the wound of miserliness, greed, envy, and selfishness. I am so grateful to now be passing down the gift of generosity.

In '06 in Portland, Al and I make peace on the carpet on a new warrior weekend. Our ongoing conversation and our menswork help us work it through ... in mind & body, in heart & soul. In our healing time together, Al tells me that long ago our father changed his will, leaving everything to him. While it hurts, I know it is the right thing, and I tell Al that. My mother passes in '09, Al and I travel to Sun City to help our father bury our mother. Prior to going to the church service, the three of us sit in the living room. My brother says to our dad: *"Dene and I have been working hard on our relationship, we have healed much, and we are finally good with each other. I want the will to be 50-50 again."* My father quietly acknowledges and supports Al's decision, we all breathe a sigh of relief. This is the character of my brother, the generosity of who he is. His forgiving words awaken me, for now I can forgive myself and all the damage I have done, all the times that I have been selfish with others. Another piece of karma is cleared.

I do not know where generosity comes from. Maybe from our essential nature, maybe from our imprinting. I know that Al never got it from our upbringing, and that is why he is such a miracle. We are many years estranged, and many more to get us here today. Two old men, reflecting on our lives, refusing to be drawn into the drama that brought us all to our knees. We realize that it is an absolute waste of energy to stoke up our ghosts, they are long buried and hopefully have returned to wherever they go. We are here, a bit worn for wear, but we are happy with ourselves, proud of the men we have become … in spite of or even because of the family through which we came. We have forgiven them, our hearts are open, we have laid down our family burden.

These days, I am remembering those who have given me generosity. My dear friend Annie just passed away, I grieve her and celebrate her life. I sharply recall the times when she cut me like a razor, followed by the forgiveness that only a mother is capable of. She saw both the best and the worst in me, and she helped me learn to love myself. In the middle of my separation from my family of origin, I was gifted with love and kindness and acceptance from Ming's family. Her mom and dad were kind and generous, they helped us with a down payment, they forgave us a loan. Ming's sister Cilla has been generous with all her gifts, creativity, and her familial hospitality. Her home in Denver is almost our second home.

When our boys were little, the 90's were exploding with technological wizardry. Ming and I held out from getting them cell phones as long as we could. Alas, we could not stop our children from being the first electronic generation. There is a balance in dealing with the endless asks of children, setting limits is truly an art form. So, when they were a bit older, and could understand the basic mechanics of money and exchange, I said to them:

"There are many things that you would like mom and me to buy for you. However, we have our limits. You have to be willing to contribute to the purchase of whatever it is that you desire. So let us make this agreement: that to the best of our ability, we will cost share with you anything that is not a gift. If you do not have money, then you must contribute something to the cost of your desired item. It could be doing an extra chore, it could be some creative expression of your energy and intention as contribution to the family ... but it must be something. That way, you will have some skin in the game in acquiring what you want, and your choices will mean more."

They agreed, and for the most part it worked. The gift to them is they learned to assess value to things, including their own energy. The gift to me was being generous without spoiling them.

These days I realize how precious my own energy is, and the importance of being disciplined and discriminating in how I spend that energy, at every level. I realize that time and money and effort are just different measures of energy. If I am feeling like *'I can't afford this'* ... it means my input-output energy is out of balance. My body and my emotions always tell me that truth. Long ago, I left the corporate life to follow the path that my spirit and soul were carving for me. Leaving a steady paycheck in exchange for starting a coaching practice was a scary choice, one that changed the entire course of my life. It is a lifelong challenge to find the right balance between the material and the spiritual parts of life, much time and suffering in learning *'to render unto Caesar what is Caesar's, and render unto God what is God's.'*

And now, other than those moments when my body feels old and tired, I do not regret the path that I have walked. I am more than grateful and humbled to have answered this call. I admit to feeling envious of men who have prospered well, and still angry at the greedy men who use and abuse their power with money. This book may sell a dozen copies, it may sell a million. While financial success would be lovely, regardless I continue doing my work and living my mission. I am not a wealthy man, we do not live a luxurious life. I work because I love what I do, and I have no concept of what retirement is.

Writing this book has given me the opportunity to connect the dots along my life's trajectory. I now see how it all fits, how I was destined to be who I have become. This writing has helped heal and integrate the missing pieces along the arc of my life. **Clearly, I have accrued more self-worth, which to me is *'worth its weight in gold.'*** Perhaps this will translate, without any major effort on my part, into more net worth. Years ago, our astrologer friend Ani told us that we will not have a lot of money, but we will always have way more than we need. Linda, my writing coach and dear friend recently said to me: *"Dene, when you take a stand to do what you love, and offer your work into the world from an open-hearted place, they will throw money at you. Just smile, receive, and say thank you."*

It is too late to chase money, it is too late to save up for retirement. I must live the consequences of the choices I have made. Once again, I get to choose how the rest of my life will go. If I choose fear and lack, that is what I will create. If I choose trust and the abundance inherent in the work that I do and the worth that I am, then that is what I will create. Sometimes I get scared, especially when my body is in pain. But most times, I am quiet, grateful, and content with the life that I live.

Chapter 35: Cleaning Up Karma

The Vintage Man

The difference between
a good artist and a great one is:
The novice will often lay down
his tool or brush,

then pick up an invisible club
on the mind's table and
helplessly smash the easels and jade.

Whereas the vintage man
no longer hurts himself or anyone
and keeps on sculpting light.

Hafiz

Early in my marriage with Ming, the conflicts come on us like a rush. I am deeply in it long before I even realize. Been that way for years, every so often it still is. But now I catch it earlier, I notice my reactions more quickly. I choose to not give my anger so much room, I do not spew out my petty annoyances. Instead, I carefully select which battles are worth fighting, and I am increasingly more discerning with my words. Now, I ask myself an important question: *"What about this conflict is actually mine, and what is not?"*

The ego struggles with this type of question. In its binary thinking: **Either** it turns the problem outward, making it about the other, and conveniently taking no responsibility for the conflict: *"It's* **your** *fault, not* **mine."** **Or** it turns the problem inward, making it about the toxic self: *"I'm such a shit, it's* **all** *my fault."*

In both of these choices, the ego is fully in charge. Either best or worst, it matters not, as along as the ego self identifies: **as a unique 'me', something fixed and separate from everyone else.** However, when held from the paradoxical non-binary thinking, where each of us is responsible for our unique part of the problem, there is no blame. Here, the non-ego self identifies as a **'we', something fluid** *and interconnected.* If I meditate for thirty years at the foot of the Dali Llama, I will still emerge with an ego, it cannot be annihilated.

The ego can never be defeated, but it can be trained.

It does many good things, and it regularly needs a pat on the back, an ice cream cone, an acknowledgment like *'good job.'* The little boy in me, someone who never heard it enough from my dad, remains alive in my body, and informs much of my instinctive and emotional reactions. When I am aware of my reactions, I get to make a different set of choices.

This moment of choice … **reacting from** the ego or **responding with** the ego … is indeed an existential **moment of truth**, a choice that I make thousands of times each and every day. A choice that over time and repetition defines who I am in the world. If it arises out of shadow and ego, it is always fear. If it arises out of awareness, it is love. Love is not a feeling, it is an action. Practically speaking, neither choice is right or wrong, for I am no longer in the binary world. **The choice always depends on circumstances and character.** I cannot control my inner reactions, but I can consciously choose my outer responses. This transformational opportunity is where I choose: *'we/love/connected'* or *'me/fear/separate.'* The choice is simple … fear is easy, love is hard. To choose love is a conscious choice, with conscious energy and intention, it is never automatic. Love is when I choose to make someone or something more important than me. In its purity, it is non-egoic, it is selfless, it is humble, it is inclusive. This practice takes great patience and discipline. As I train my ego to stop driving the car from the hood, and invite it to sit in the passenger seat as a navigator, it supports me to accomplish my goals. But it now knows that those goals are set by the deeper self. The ego finally understands how to surrender from being in charge to being an ally for my mission.

Undoubtedly, it is inside my most intimate relationship where this 'I/We' paradox plays out, practicing Confucius' tenet: '… *true to myself **and** kind to others.'* Ming and I have been doing this dance since we met. Our most important contract is the commitment to our inner work and evolution. Reactive emotional energy does not simply evaporate, it has to go somewhere. We either turn it outward as disproportionate reaction, making it about the other. Or we turn it inward as repression, denying, avoiding, judging, self-loathing.

> *Everything that we have turned inward and left unat-*
> *tended is still carried by the body. From conception*
> *to early childhood to adulthood to death and beyond...*
> *this is our karma.*

All that we hide, repress, or deny becomes our shadows ... alive and hungry, waiting for a trigger. To hold the tension between outward reaction and the inward repression is the key. It is a discipline born of a thousand repetitions, learned from a million mistakes.

Astrologically, I am made of fire, Ming is made of water. She is an enneagram six, I am an eight. Within our conflicts, mostly but not always, I am perceived the perpetrator, she the victim. Diametrical elements, sometimes compatible, sometimes conflicting. And like everyone else, we act out our drama triangle, our astrological nature, our enneagram configuration ... all locked in as the personality, the center of gravity, the place of greatest unconscious reactivity.

We are driving to Phoenix awhile back, we usually travel well together. We find the groove in music, in silence, in conversation, in food, in directions, in intimacy. Only since returning to Tucson have we been able to unpack our experiences in Ashland with less reaction. I generally want to talk about it, she generally does not. The entire twelve years on the west coast, the last six in Ashland, were by far the most challenging and painful times in our marriage. Ming lost her mind, I lost my health, we almost lost our marriage, our sons lost their innocence, incurring their deepest wounding. The echoes of that time still haunt us a bit, and the other day my ghosts get poked. Ming says something defensive that hits me unexpectedly in the middle of my chest. I go silent for a long while. She asks me if I am okay, I say no. She asks what, I say I am not ready to speak. She honors my silence.

Inside, I replay so many scenes from our Ashland unraveling. So many times, I wanted to unleash my anger, scream my powerlessness, my righteousness, fear, and hurt. I was afraid to swallow it and say nothing, afraid to say something that comes out as everything, afraid to push her over the edge. Over time, and through relentless practice, I learn to stay silent when I am in the throes of big emotions. Today, I do not bury the pain, I wrestle with it, I feel it from a more conscious place. Neither one of us knew that then, we were way too damaged. I remember Ming's Mars line, the inevitability of conflict. Later that evening, deep into the layered emotions of 'Grey's Anatomy,' my tears spill out. Suddenly I hit the pause button, and say:

> "Ming: I am completely responsible for my experience in Ashland. I no longer blame you, for there is no fault, no right or wrong ... it was simply our karmic drama. We did the best we could under the most trying of circumstances. It was the biggest challenge, and the biggest gift and learning experience of our entire time together. I am grateful for all of it, that we got through it, that we are here now. I love you, I forgive you, and I forgive myself ... for everything."

Surprisingly, she shares all her emotions, and for the first time, offers up her deep vulnerability:

> "Dene: I am so sorry for all that I did to you, all the times I blamed you, all the times I left you, all the ways I hurt you, and hurt our boys. I was so selfish, so blind to the damage I did, unaware of the spell I was in. And you stayed, I do not know how you stayed so long, and that you are still here. I now see all the pain you have endured, and how it has taken a toll on your mind, body, and spirit. I am so sorry, so sorry, please forgive me, please. I promise that I am here now, in the full truth of who I am, and I love you more than words can say. Please let me love you now the way I could not love you then. Please let me love you now."

Tears spill down her face, her body is racked with grief, her sorrow is deep and real. I am shocked, she has never said all this to me before, and I have so long needed to hear it. All along, I know I have carried resentment deep in my body, working hard to keep it well out of view. Now, this huge weight has been lifted from my shoulders, the truth finally revealed. I feel a sense of liberation that I have never felt with her before. Her vulnerability and accountability set us both free. We embrace and weep hard together … it feels like the *'unfinished emotional business'* from our ordeal in Ashland is complete, it has taken us fifteen years. Once again, we affirm that love is a renewable resource. With understanding and patience and the courage to turn toward the pain, we get to tell the hard truths, sincerely make amends, kiss the wounds, and say: *"I am so sorry, please forgive me, I love you."*

I recall my most recent medicine journey, the beauty that Ming is, how far we have come together, the marvelous young men whom we have brought into the world, the healing and richness in our lives, and the creative missions which stand before us. Gratefully, our wanderlust is quiet now, our old gypsy bones comfortably settled in our colorful little Mexican casa. We imagine that much still awaits us. Today, we walk hand in hand, uncertain where we are being led, yet fully trusting.

Chapter 36: **The Feminine**

Since the beginning of Covid, I realize that *'chasing windmills'* is a tiresome, frustrating, and useless endeavor ... and I have been doing this since '65. Whether politics, sports, business, warfare, international affairs, economics, academics ... they are offered through the same *'old masculine'* structures. Today, the internet offers growing pockets of light ... quantum consciousness creatively expressing itself as inclusion, collaboration, scientific breakthroughs, thinking globally and acting locally, and often being led by women and people of color. I trade in the *NY Times* and the *Washington Post* for the *GoodNewsNetwork*. Ming and I celebrate the new thinking with joy, hope, and an open-hearted gratitude.

I see clearly that I control only those things within my immediate sphere of influence. As adamant as I have been about the inclusion of the feminine in MensWork, institutionally it continues to fall on deaf ears, same as the rest. Now I take this stand, in my solitude if necessary, to do what I am here to do. I trust myself, I trust my intuition and instincts, I trust my heart, and I especially trust my deep communion with the sacred feminine. She/they speak to me through my open heart, and they are grateful for my opening this door even wider. Within the circles I frequent, I speak both from the fierceness of the masculine, and the tenderness of the feminine, both alive within me. My tears come easily, I do not hide them. These days they are tears of gratitude and overflowing. And my voice is sharp and clear.

Today, I see clearly our growth trajectory as men, especially in relation to women and the feminine. Having been told as boys that almost anything feminine is bad, having no conscious memory of our mother imprint from conception through early childhood, having this unrelenting physiological urge and need to connect with her without any instruction as to what sex is or how to effectively navigate its tricky pathways ... is it any wonder that she is frightening? We know in our bodies that she has much power, yet we still refuse to acknowledge it. We keep our fear, weakness, and not knowing well hidden. In our testosterone-driven obsession to possess her, in our *'little boy'* need to be nurtured by her, in our fear of the real power that she has over us, we act out in a whole variety of dysfunctional ways.

Years ago, my uncle says that poppy may have raped my mother. I remember her being hospitalized after my brother was born. Her body always carried a constant anger, fear, and tension. Given my father's job at the factory, where he worked the swing shifts, she was home alone with the old man during the dark hours every two out of three weeks. If the assault happened, she never told my father. She knew that he would kill him, go to prison, leaving her alone with two young sons. My father did his best to love her, but there was just no opening. No amount of love or medicine could ever fill that deep hole inside her. She endured this for eleven years before we finally left that house.

Only in hindsight do I understand the horror that ate at her. I imagine that rape is a wound that never truly heals. When I think about the raw number of women across the millennia of history who have been raped, my heart breaks. Maybe it breaks for my own mother as well. When the *#metoo* movement gives voice to the true global horror, my unexpressed anger, grief, and shame flow from my quivering body. I have imagined for many years that this dark truth lies underground, a toxic shadow held by Mother Earth. And it is only a matter of time before the heat and light of truth is revealed, for neither Mother Earth, abused women, nor my mother's ghost can carry it for long.

In '17, *#metoo* goes viral following the story of Harvey Weinstein. I recall bringing to my men's circles the notion that all men have some degree of culpability, if not active then passive. I am disturbed but not surprised at the large number of defensive responses. Blind to our own feeling function, how can we possibly allow ourselves to actually *'feel'* the horror that the women of this world have had to endure forever. We are all a part of this rape culture, even the ones who turn a blind eye to all the evidence. It isn't masculinity that is toxic. Rather, the instinctive, unconscious imprint of the harsh, shaming mother, and the imprint of the tough, hard, unemotional, disconnected father ... **this is what is toxic.** I receive the imprint from my mother, from my father, from my grandfather, from the boys in the neighborhood, from the culture at large. Immature men teach boys how to be immature. Mature men teach boys how to become mature men.

As long as a man's ego remains in charge of his actions, he will fumble and stumble his way in intimate relationships with women. When he finally comes into some kind of inner work, when he acknowledges that he is in pain, lost and confused, stuck, lonely or broken hearted, that he does not know who he really is ... that is when he steps onto the beginning path of the deep masculine. He discovers what his real feelings are and why they are there. He heals his father wounds, cleans up his karma, learns how to acknowledge and care for the little boy that lives inside him. Here, he places his stake in the ground, knowing his own power and his weakness, celebrating his light and owning his shadows. Then he may be ready to engage the feminine in a conscious way, respecting both her beauty and her terrifying power. Here, he finds his way to the mother work. Until then, he will struggle mightily. And even after that, he will struggle, for she is the great mystery. But he will have tools ... communication skills, body-centered self-awareness, vulnerability, true power, and real humility. Women, children, the earth, and the feminine within us are waiting for us to meet them in this place.

The Blood of Eden
"I caught sight of my reflection
I caught it in the window
I saw the darkness in my heart
I saw the signs of my undoing
They had been there from the start
And the darkness still has work to do
The knotted chord's untying

FIERCE & TENDER: *Healing the Deep Masculine*

The heated and the holy
Oh, they're sitting there on high
So secure with everything they're buying
My grip is surely slipping
I think I've lost my hold
Yes, I think I've lost my hold
I cannot get insurance anymore
They don't take credit, only gold
Is that a dagger or a crucifix I see
You hold so tightly in your hand
And all the while the distance grows
between you and me, I do not understand
At my request you take me in
In that tenderness I am floating away
No certainty, nothing to rely on
Holding still for a moment
What a moment this is
Oh for a moment of forgetting
A moment of bliss ... Oh
I can hear the distant thunder
Of a million unheard souls
Of a million unheard souls
Watch each one reach for creature comfort
For the filling of their holes
In the blood of Eden lie the woman and the man
I feel the man in the woman and
the woman in the man
In the blood of Eden lie the woman and the man
I feel the man in the woman and
the woman in the man

Peter Gabriel

Chapter 37: **Moving The Work Forward**

In Oct '19, George and I offer our first Desert Wisdom workshop, out at G's ranch in Mescal. As veterans of MensWork, we both see the necessity of bringing more awareness of the feminine into men's circles. While he is more connected to MKP institutionally, we both agree that having this conversation with them is useless. I have been holding this theme for many years, and now, finally, we do a workshop offering men the deep dive into the feminine … it is a huge success.

In March '20, MKP shuts down all the NWTA's, our singular initiatory experience in sacred masculine space is closed indefinitely. Through all of '20 and '21, men are void of this sacred rite of passage. We keep our men's circles open, initially on zoom, as soon as possible in person again. Men are hungry, the waiting lists for the NWTA are long across the country. Locally, we feed them the soul food that we are able, the deep need is both disturbing and encouraging.

In April '21, G and I hire a film crew, gather twenty-five men and film a men's carpet training at Dee's ranch in Prescott. The video we create … *"Raw Men Alive"* … speaks to the pain of men, invites an opportunity for men to do their inner work, and clearly calls forth the necessity for men across the globe to do whatever is necessary to heal their broken hearts. We are trusting that the right venue will present itself. With the success of DWI, we consider doing another in the fall.

Over the summer, G and I talk about another Desert Wisdom workshop. Dee offers his site, we solidify the date, find a fourth facilitator. When I present my history with the feminine, and describe the success of DW1, we are all excitedly on board. As the four of us are married, we know all too well how long overdue this workshop is. To our knowledge, this is the first of its kind within our greater men's network. As we design the flyer, the outline, the intentions, we are all clear that the section on the feminine needs to be expanded beyond what we did in DW1. In Nov '21, we present our second Desert Wisdom workshop (DW2). Twenty-four men attend a four-day workshop, the responses from participants are overwhelmingly positive, the surveys and comments clearly state both the appreciation of and the deep need for work in the area of the feminine. G and I are encouraged and inspired to continue this theme.

This past week I get a call from an old friend in Texas, he and his beloved want to know if I would resurrect the *'Leaving My Father's House'* workshop, and bring it to Austin. I call G and ask if he is ready and willing to do this. He reminds me that we now offer a men's workshop on mother issues, and a women's workshop on father issues. With this book and a second one in planning, with our video as a calling card, and with two unique gender workshops to offer, as we look into '22, we are loaded and ready. They say a man's work is never done … how true.

I am in a most terrific place,
deeply into the mystery,
and firmly trusting the Spirit Guides in my life.
The incessant small voices of fear are everywhere,
like flies on a horse's ass.

I allow the discerning aspect of my Masculine
to function as the gatekeeper to my psychic house.
I allow only those thoughts
that nurture and sustain my well being
to pass into my emotional center,
and editing out those that steal energy.

This gift I give to my
deep loving Feminine consciousness.
It is of utmost importance
to be vigilant and connected.

Biography

Dene Maria Sebastiana is a native New Yorker, a teacher, master coach, and medicine man. He is a current Leader Emeritus and the former Executive Director of The ManKind Project, an international men's educational and training organization and network. Dene has initiated open men's circles in many communities throughout the US and Mexico for more than thirty-five years.

Dene's work teaches men, women, and couples how to break through their unconscious patterns, emerging more authentic, self-aware, and open-hearted. He brings a compassionate fierceness, and a multi-leveled capacity to get to the heart of the matter, through his workshops, trainings, and writing.

Dene is passionate about gender balance and equality: in himself and in all his relationships. His commitment is to change the world through changing himself. He and his beloved Ming celebrate a sacred marriage of over thirty years. They live in Tucson, AZ.

Contact Dene Maria Sebastiana:

> Dene@DeneMariaSebastiana.com
>
> www.DeneMariaSebastiana.com

Future Books:

> *Celebrating Heartbreak: Tools for Men*
>
> *A Sacred Marriage: A Journey Across Time*